BUYING OPTIONS
Wall Street On a Shoestring

BUYING OPTIONS

Wall Street on a Shoestring

ANTONY RODOLAKIS
NICHOLAS TETRICK

Reston Publishing Company, Inc.
Reston, Virginia

A PRENTICE-HALL COMPANY

Library of Congress Cataloging in Publication Data

Rodolakis, Antony
Buying options.

Includes index.
1. Stocks. 2. Put and call transactions.
I. Tetrick, Nicholas joint author.
II. Title. III. Title: Options.
HG6041.R63 332.6′45 76–993
ISBN 0–87909–109–6

Reston Publishing Company, Inc.
A Prentice-Hall Company
Reston, Virginia 22090

The information in Appendix D has been compiled by Moody's Investors Service, Inc. of New York, from sources believed to be accurate and reliable. However, Moody's and the publisher do not guarantee its accuracy or completeness. The reports are drawn from Moody's Handbook of Common Stocks, Winter 1976 Edition, with updated material through November 1975, subject to revision quarterly.

10 9 8 7 6 5 4 3 2 1

Printed in the United States of America

To Heidi and Amalia

Contents

Preface

There was a time not so many years ago when it was possible to make a living trading stocks. There were a group of people who were known variously as traders or day traders or speculators. These people inhabited the board rooms of brokerage offices, watched the ticker tapes, and actually made profits on short-term trades.

You occasionally see traders even now in brokerage houses—old men who will tell you stories about what it was really like in the good old days when a man with a limited amount of capital *could* make a living in the market if he was careful and knew what he was doing. These men thought of themselves as professionals running their own businesses. They were a proud group, and the ultimate defeat for them was to be forced to take a job and "work."

The traders are gone from the stock market now. They were driven out by the very people they supported—the stockbrokers. Brokerage firms reacted to rising costs to handle small transactions by increasing commissions. The ever rising commissions made it more and more difficult for traders to take small profits. As more traders quit, the market was increasingly dominated by institutions and characterized by a lack of liquidity and increased volatility.

But now we have the new options markets. The Chicago Board, the American Exchange, and the PBW Exchange all offer call options on stocks. The commissions are much lower than those on stocks, and short-term trading is popular again. It can also be profitable.

Since these are new markets we need to develop novel approaches and innovative methods of trading; however, at the same time, we should also investigate how the traders operated in the old days before they were driven out. This book was written with the hope that modern options markets will encourage a new generation of traders.

The book is divided into two parts. Part One assumes that the reader has no knowledge of options, and is designed to present to the novice *in simple English* an explanation of the options markets and a philosophy for trading in them. Part Two assumes that the reader has some knowledge of options or has read Part One, and that he or she wishes to study the subject in much greater detail.

Both parts deal only with the *buying* and *trading* of options. We feel that many books are available which cover the subject of option writing; however, it should be noted that option writing requires large sums of capital, more capital than the average person has. This book is about buying options —Wall Street on a shoestring.

The information set forth herein was obtained from sources which we believe reliable, but we do not guarantee its accuracy. Neither the information, nor any opinion expressed, constitutes a solicitation or recommendation by us of the purchase or sale of securities.

This book constitutes opinions entirely of the authors and is not to be construed as a set of infallible rules by which the investor cannot lose.

ANTONY RODOLAKIS
NICHOLAS TETRICK

PART ONE

1 | The Dream Versus . . .

Most people, at one time or another in their lives, dream about making it big in the stock market. For the majority it is only a dream, but a sizable number of people actually try to do it. A very few of them have a vague idea of what they're getting into, but most of them are almost totally naive. They have no clear understanding of the odds against them. And the odds are against them.

IMPROVING THE ODDS

This book is about odds: the odds on the stock exchange and the odds in the options markets, and how you can improve *your* chances of doing well. There have been hundreds of books written about the stock market, and a lot of them are very good, but the good ones tend to be about very specialized subjects and techniques (we shall review some of these in a later chapter), while what is needed is a book that strives to teach a rational approach to markets.

The options markets are similar to any other markets where buyers and sellers come together to trade something, be it stocks and bonds on an organized exchange in New York or London or Zurich, or vegetables and fruit in a village square in Asia. All markets have a lot in common, and before we take on the options market it may be wise to learn how to handle ourselves in any market. Although this book will be mainly concerned with options, the approaches can be useful in a study of other markets.

Your All-Important Attitude

Probably the most important determining factor in a person's success in a market is the psychological attitude that he carries with him. Knowledge and experience are, of course, very necessary, but a lot of people who are veterans of many years of market activity still manage to lose money consistently. There does not seem to be any proven correlation between age and success or experience and success. However, it is likely that a very strong correlation could be shown between rational attitudes and success. If you are psychologically prepared with reasonable expectations about the probabilities of making money in volatile markets, it is more than likely that you will do well.

What do you expect to accomplish in the market? Obviously you have the dream of doing something substantial or you wouldn't be reading this book. It is important to examine your dream, because if you don't have a clear idea of where you're going, it is very unlikely that you're going to get there. Also, by examining your dream you can probably develop a better one and in the process begin to see some of the things you will have to learn in order to make the dream a reality.

A WAY TO PROBABLY LOSE

Let's look for a moment at the dream that most beginners start with. It could be called the *one-shot dream,* and it is the root cause of most of the disillusionment in the stock market today. The one-shot dream is that you, with little or no prior experience, are going to pick the next Syntex, Polaroid, or Xerox, the stock that will go from 5 to 300 with several splits along the way. This dream is fostered by the brilliant clarity of hindsight. If you had bought, or if someone had bought for you, just one share of IBM at the end of World War II, look where you would be today!

Well, let's look at the one-shot dream and do some simple calculations. What do you figure the odds are against your picking an IBM or a Syntex or a Xerox in its infancy? Would you agree with 100 to 1? It's much higher, but just for the sake of this example, we'll use that figure. Now, of those who saw the potential of birth control pills and bought Syntex in the beginning, how many do you think held on until it reached its all-time high? There weren't very many, because most people tend to chicken out and take their profits after a stock has doubled or tripled. Let's say that one in ten actually held. That means that the odds are 100 times 10, or 1000 to 1, against your *both* picking the right stock and then picking the right time to sell it—at least 1000 to 1.

So you say that you're going to buy more than one stock and that that will lower the odds against you. O.K., somehow you come up with enough money to try 100 different "great ideas." That means $1000 \div 100 = 10$. The odds are still 10 to 1 against you, but it costs you 100 times as much money. Any stockbroker will be glad to get you in on the ground floor in solar energy, some new cancer research, lasers, cable TV or a recycling franchise. The list of great new ideas that are bound to succeed is endless, but your capital isn't.

ON BECOMING A PROFESSIONAL

Let's face it. In any market you are up against competition. If you're a tourist in the Middle East, for instance, and go to a market to buy a piece of jewelry, you may think that you can wheel and deal and talk that old man on the sidewalk down to a price that is considerably below his cost, but the smart money will bet on the old man. He's a professional. You're not. And until you become a professional you're going to lose.

So why don't we substitute the dream of becoming a professional trader for the one-shot dream? It will greatly improve your chances of success, and it's a better dream anyway. What you're really after is money, so why not go after it in the manner most likely to result in success?

Erich Remarque, the author of *All Quiet on the Western Front*, once wrote: "A true idealist strives for money. Money is coined freedom and freedom is life." Most people who want to make money in the market are really hoping that somehow that money will take them out of the life situation in which they find themselves. Most people aren't happy with their jobs. They would like to live in a better climate. They would generally like to change themselves, but they can't, because they're trapped in an existence characterized by lack of money and the necessity to eke out an economic subsistence in the most practical manner, which almost always means working eight hours a day, five days a week, for the rest of their lives for a corporation. The state of mankind really hasn't changed much over the centuries. We're obviously better off than we were as serfs in the Middle Ages. In a material sense the differences are overwhelming, but the essential situation of the individual is that he is still dependent upon someone higher up the socioeconomic ladder for his daily subsistence. How long could *you* get along without your pay check?

THE GOOD LIFE

Consider, for a moment, the advantages of being a professional trader. First of all, the professional trader is his own boss. He works for himself; he doesn't have someone always telling him what to do. He doesn't have to worry about being fired. He does things the way he wants to. This is called independence.

Independence offers a lot of peripheral benefits. You don't like the eight-hour day? The market is open only about six hours, but that shouldn't bother you. You should be able to handle your business in less than an hour a day. You don't like the five-day week? Who's going to tell you to come to work every day—your stockbroker?

And consider the choice of locations available to the professional trader. There is a brokerage office in every major city and in most minor cities in the non-Communist world, and there are telephones to everywhere else. You decide where you want to be, and it's likely that you can find a stockbroker there to handle your account.

Now if you add to this picture of independent living a considerably increased income, you can begin to see that the possibilities for a custom-made life style are endless. As a professional trader you ought to be able to take care of your business in a very small percentage of your time, leaving the rest of your time for the more important business of living. "Money is coined freedom, and freedom is life."

THE IMPORTANCE OF TRAINING

At this point you are probably saying that the dream of being a professional independent trader is no more realistic than the one-shot dream of picking the next IBM or Syntex. But you're wrong. You can train yourself to be a professional trader, but there is no way to train yourself to pick the next really long-shot winner. It would take just blind luck.

Suppose that you wanted to become an Olympic long-distance runner. The chances of your running a four-minute mile right now are not any better than becoming independently wealthy through the market, but you wouldn't expect to run a four-minute mile your first time out. You would expect to train up to it, right? For example, you'd probably go out and run every day. You'd study every aspect of physical conditioning. You would have to change your life style and give up things like drinking and smoking. And you would have mentally to prepare yourself for some severe competition. In short, you would almost become a different person. But if you did all this for several years, your chances of running a four-minute mile would be much greater than they are today.

In the same way, you can begin now to train yourself to be a market professional. It will take daily practice, and it will mean changing a lot of your present methods of thinking and acting. It will take years of work and study, but it will be worth it.

The rest of this book is designed to present an idea of how you might go about this important training process. We shall look at why people fail in markets and why the options markets are almost ideal for what we want to accomplish. Then we'll learn the basics about trading options and go from there to consider the methods and the skills we need to develop to make money in any market. What we're trying to do in this book is to present you with a guide that will start you in the right direction, but no book can do it all. A book like this can suggest how to pick the right option to buy, but ultimately you have to do the picking, which means that you have to work at it. However, if you spend a half hour to an hour a day working at the suggestions that this book will offer, you will have a good chance of becoming that independent professional trader we've been talking about—in several years. Don't kid yourself. From where you're starting now it will probably take several years, and that is a tremendous commitment of time and energy. On the other hand, if you don't make the commitment, you're likely to be doing about the same things in the future that you're doing now.

If you agree that only professionals are likely to succeed, that you're unlikely to make a killing overnight, and that it takes years to become a professional, you're probably already years ahead of other beginners. Having the wrong kind of dream almost assures that your dream won't come true.

2 | . . . The Reality

So now we're agreed that in order to beat the professionals you need to become a professional and that becoming a professional in the market will take some time. But you probably already want to go out and try your luck at the market. The purpose of this chapter is to tell you about some of the things you will be going up against.

ASSUMING YOU'RE NOT RICH ALREADY

Unless you are already an experienced trader *and* unless you have several thousand dollars of pure risk capital, it can be predicted with a high probability of certainty that when you start trading in the stock market you are going to lose money. Your lack of experience and lack of capital almost certainly doom you to failure. To try to illustrate this point, let's imagine a typical beginner who gets excited about buying a stock.

The typical beginner gets an idea about a good stock to buy. Maybe he reads a newspaper or a magazine article; maybe he "hears" that the company's earnings are going to be up; maybe a friend at a cocktail party tells him about a winner he just bought; maybe he sees a need for a new product or service and does some research on the companies in that field. Then he builds a logical case in his mind for why this particular stock should go up. He probably can find some very good reasons why it *should* go up.

Next, the beginner decides to *watch* the stock, and for several days, maybe even for a couple of weeks, he keeps an eye on the price. It may go sideways for awhile and then begin to move up, so he decides that he should buy now before it gets away from him and he loses his chance. Or the stock begins to move down, and he decides that he should buy now before he misses the bottom.

Having picked his stock and decided that now is the time to buy, he calls up a brokerage firm. The switchboard operator connects him with a broker, who listens to his idea and agrees that it is probably a good buy and that now is probably as good a time to buy as any. The broker opens an account, and the beginner puts in an order to buy ten shares, since the stock is selling at 40 and he does not have very much money to put in the market.

On the face of it, it appears that this person has done everything that a reasonable person can be expected to do and, therefore, he should be entitled to look forward to a reasonable probability of success. After getting the idea, he thought about it for awhile, he watched the stock for awhile, he got a broker's opinion before he put in the order, and he did not risk any more money than he could afford to lose. From his point of view he did everything right, and that is probably the source of his undoing. From the point of view of the market professional, he did everything wrong. Let's go back and look at his actions one by one, take them apart, and see if we can do better by changing your point of view.

WHICH STOCK TO BUY?

Let's start by considering the selection of the stock to buy. How did the beginner get his idea? He got it from a newspaper or a magazine or on a tip. In other words, he got it from some outside source, some source outside of himself. It's true that he was smart enough to recognize the potential in a good thing, but still the fact remains that he did not generate it himself. Now, if the best happens and the stock goes up and this person makes a profit, he will be in real trouble—first, because he may not always be able to draw on this source of ideas in the future, and second, because having seen that it is *possible* to make money in the market on other people's ideas, he will undoubtedly risk too much money on the next idea that comes along.

It is far, far better for you to develop your own system for picking the potential winners. You want a system that will consistently deliver ideas to you so that you can depend upon a steady flow of profitable trades, and you want a system that will allow you to be independent of everyone else. It is an old adage on Wall Street that *everyone* is usually wrong. Later in this book we shall devote an entire chapter to how you can build your own information system.

Stockbrokers get a great many calls about stocks that start with the letter "A." People decide that they want to get in the market, and the first thing that they do is read down the list of stocks in the newspaper. They look at the yearly high and low columns, and soon they find one with a big difference between the high and the low. They think they've found a hot one, and they call their broker. This is not a good way to pick winners. There are about 2000 stocks on the New York Stock Exchange, and that means that there are many that may suit your purposes, but there are better, more logical, and more systematic ways of choosing them than to read through the newspaper price listings.

Another popular method of choosing stocks is by their price. Because beginners don't have very much capital, they limit themselves to buying cheap stocks, of which they can buy a larger number of shares. Brokers also get many questions about stocks selling under $10 that start with the letter "A." It is generally true that low-priced stocks are selling for a low price for a good reason. That reason is that the market, in indicating supply and demand, has assigned a low price to the less than favorable prospects for the company's future. Better prospects demand higher prices. Consequently, this is not a good method for selecting stocks, because you are limiting yourself to stocks with a poor future. Leave the cheap stocks for the bargain hunters.

WHEN TO BUY?

Our imaginary beginner watched his stock for several days or a few weeks before deciding that the time had come to buy, and he thought that he was doing the reasonable thing. But let's look at his *timing* decision from a much broader perspective. He made the specific decision to buy on a specific day by watching the price action of the stock, but what about the general timing decision? What about the month and the year? Most people buy when they get the money together, and that is generally not the right time to buy. Other people decide that the time to buy is just after they finish reading a new stock market book or an article in a magazine. These are truly random events, and their correlation to the movement of the market is a very tenuous affair.

If you look at a chart of a stock's price movement you will see that the prices move in big tides, smaller waves, and little ripples. Our beginner who watched the price of his stock for a few days might have been seeing a little ripple. If he had bought on the basis of his little ripple back in 1929, he would have shortly been swept under by a great big tide.

We said in the first chapter that you should study the market for several years. One of the reasons is that you can't expect to watch a stock for a few days or even a few weeks and expect to trade profitably. You need several months of price history on a chart to be able to make an intelligent decision about in which direction a stock is going to go.

WHO TO BUY FROM?

After unwisely picking his stock and his time, our imaginary beginner really made a mistake in choosing a broker. When you call a brokerage firm, the switchboard operator gives your call to one of the brokers—either the one she likes the most or the one who just got out of training school. Either way he just may not be the right broker for you. We shall talk more about finding the right broker in a later chapter, but in general you shouldn't telephone. Rather, go visit *several* brokers. In that way you will learn some elementary information, such as how old they are, how they act, how well organized their desks are, and dozens of little things that will not come through on a telephone. A good broker will try to find out all he can about you, but you want to find out all you can about him. Since you are going to learn to make your own market decisions, you really want a broker that you can work with, not one that you can use as a crutch. Here the important thing is that your personalities don't clash, so go meet your prospective broker in person.

Another word may be in order here. Our beginner asked the broker if he thought XYZ was a good stock and if now was a good time to buy. If you went to see an automobile salesman, would you expect him to say that his automobile was not a good one, or that now was not the time to buy? If you don't rely on other people for advice, you won't be getting any bad advice.

And You're Not Going To Get Better

This imaginary example of a beginning speculator may or may not be totally or even partially relevant to your condition, but if it is, it shows that you are up against some real problems that only time, experience and persistent effort are going to solve. But you have another, more immediate problem in the stock market, and this is lack of capital. You may already have thought of some of the obvious and not so obvious disadvantages that a speculator faces in the stock market if he doesn't have adequate capital. He generally has to buy lower-priced stocks. He has to buy odd lots and pays an extra differential to the odd lot dealer. He has to pay a higher percentage of commission on his small trades, and therefore his breakeven point (the point to which a stock has to move up before he starts to make money after commissions) is higher than for those more fortunate speculators who can afford to deal in bigger amounts. Also, his broker may not give him much service, because the broker probably does more work for his bigger customers. Clearly, the smaller trader is at a disadvantage in the stock market, but the main disadvantage escapes the attention of most people. Because the small speculator lacks capital, he is unlikely to get *better*.

The army teaches recruits how to shoot rifles by letting them shoot at targets. You fire a shot, and if it's high, you adjust your aim; if that one's low, you fire another shot until you begin to get the knack of how to fire a rifle. The army doesn't worry about all that ammunition. It has plenty of rifle cartridges to teach its recruits how to fire rifles.

It would be ideal if you could approach learning about the market in the same way that army recruits learn how to fire rifles, that is, by taking a lot of chances, buying different stocks and seeing how it works out. If you had unlimited capital you could do so, but if you had unlimited capital you could do a lot of things.

Since you are bound by a small amount of capital, you can only afford an occasional trade. This means that you get less experience and it takes you longer to learn. Of course, you could make your trades on paper, i.e., buy and sell stocks on actual dates and with actual prices, but don't actually make the trade through the broker—just write it down on paper. However, few people are able to do this. It seems to call for a superior form of discipline, and it's not much fun. It's a bit like kissing a girl's picture instead of the girl herself. The emotional detachment keeps you from getting in trouble. There is no way that paper trading can really be real. If you're not risking your money, you will take chances that you would not otherwise take. You will not have the involvement that will affect your reasoning processes. So we are back to the original dilemma. We can't learn unless we practice, and we can't practice enough because we don't have enough money to practice with. We believe one answer is to buy options—*carefully*.

However, you're not ready yet. It is going to be a long time before you're ready, so slow down and prepare for a long war.

3 | Buying Options as the Answer

The purpose of this chapter is to convince you that the options markets are better places to speculate than the stock exchanges or the commodities markets or the racetracks. The options markets have some unique advantages that make them better markets for speculation.

INVESTMENT VERSUS SPECULATION

An option is not an investment. It is probably worthwhile to elaborate on this point to clear up an area of confusion that most stock market beginners have. Fuzzy thinking here about investment and speculation leads inevitably to a lot of problems later on.

Investment is what you do with money that you are saving for a purpose in the future. It is money that you want to keep safe from undue risk of loss. You invest it for the purpose of getting a return on your money and for the purpose of making the money grow (hopefully at a faster rate than inflation is eroding the future buying power of the money).

Speculation is what you do with money that you can afford to lose. You are not looking for a steady return on your money or for a steady appreciation of your capital. You want big capital gains.

Of course, it is often difficult to draw a clear line between investment and speculation. Most financial endeavors contain elements of both, that is, some return and some chance for significant capital gains. Buying options is a pure speculation.

Everyone should invest. It is only common sense to provide for your financial future, and it's all right for most people to speculate *if* they are also investing. If you try to speculate with all your money, you must have nerves of steel, or you will be so uptight that you will not make a good speculator. So put most of your money in good, safe investments like savings accounts and mutual funds and then set aside the rest for the speculative program outlined in this book.

This book is about *planned* speculation. There are hundreds of ways to speculate, but you want to pick a method where the odds against you are reasonable. It might, therefore, be wise to think for a moment about what the ideal market for speculating would look like. We think it would have some of the following attributes.

THE IDEAL SPECULATIVE MARKET

First, the unit of trading should be standard. Only the price should be variable. Many people speculate, for instance, in gold coins. The dealer who sells you the coin will undoubtedly think a given specimen is more nearly perfect than the dealer who buys it back from you. The second dealer will notice all sorts of minute imperfections. This puts the speculator at a disadvantage, because he not only must have expertise in the market for gold, he must also be an expert in grading coins.

Another attribute of an ideal speculative market is that the unit of trading should be small. A small unit of trading allows a larger number of people to play the market (including yourself), and this means a better market. When a market is thin, i.e., has few buyers and sellers, prices tend to fluctuate erratically. The round lot of 100 shares on the major exchanges limits trading. The average man on the street can't participate on a regular basis except at the disadvantage of higher per share commissions. Much has been written in recent years about the problem of the lack of liquidity in the stock market. This is what it's all about. Not enough people are involved, and the markets become thin. The small investor sits on the sidelines and watches. Smaller units of trading would help.

A third characteristic of an ideal speculative situation is the probability that the winners will be those who are most skillful, not just lucky. A lottery, for instance, does not require skill. Therefore, you can't improve; you can't get better at it; you can only hope for better luck. Trusting to luck is the antithesis of this book.

Another desirable characteristic would be a low cost of doing business. Commissions on the stock market are so high as to discourage speculations. If it costs too much to play, you should look for a different game.

Finally, your speculative situation should be fun. If it's fun, you'll become more involved and you will learn more. If it's not fun, it will be just another job, another drudgery. You might as well have fun while you're making money.

OPTION EXCHANGES MEET THE REQUIREMENTS

The new options markets meet all of the requirements for a great speculative market. Let's see what this means to you.

To start with, buying options can be done with far less capital than you need for speculating on the stock market. One hundred shares of a $20 stock would cost you $2000, but you may be able to buy an option on 100 shares for between $50 and $200. If you have only $2000 of risk capital, that 100 shares of stock will take all of your capital. If it turns out to be a loser, you will have nothing else going for you. But if you buy options instead, your $2000 will allow you to purchase a nice portfolio of several options and still keep some money back in cash for special opportunities. The first principle of portfolio management is diversification. With diversification you are able to spread your risk. If some of your stocks go down, the chances are some others may be going up. But if you have only one or two thousand dollars capital, you cannot get meaningful diversification in the stock market. You can in the options market.

However, many of you don't have even that much money to risk. Most investment advisors will tell you to stay out of the markets entirely, and they are probably right, because almost everyone who takes on the stock market with only a few hundred dollars will end up losing it. However, you're probably going to try it anyway. So instead of buying 10 shares of a $20 stock, buy an option. You are severely limited either way, but with the option, you at least have a chance for a meaningful profit. In Chapter 5 we shall talk about strategy and look at some very stringent rules to follow if you are starting out with only a few hundred dollars of capital. If you follow these rules, you will be surprised at how much you can do in the options market with limited capital.

LIMITED RISK

The second important advantage of options is that your risk is limited. The amount of money that you can lose is fixed the day you buy an option. You can't lose any more money than you paid for the option plus commission. Going back to our example of a $20 stock, if you had 100 shares and the stock dropped three points, you would be out $300. If it dropped two more points, you would be out $500. It could keep on going down. If you bought an option on the same stock, however, and that option cost you $100, that plus commission is all you could lose, even if the stock goes to zero. You are not liable for more than the cost of your option.

It could be argued that all you have to do to limit your risk in the stock market is to use sell stop orders (a sell order that will automatically be executed when the stock declines to a certain price). But stop orders will not protect you in cases where stocks are suspended and then open ten or twenty or thirty points below the previous day's close, which has happened all too often in recent years.

Options can be said to have automatic stops. If the stock underlying the option plummets, you lose only the amount you paid for the option. However, the option still may be "resurrected" if the stock rebounds during the lifetime of the option. Consequently, options are better than stops. They will effectively stop your loss, but you can't be "stopped out."

Options can be purchased on a *cash* basis only. This means that you do not have the problem of a margin account with margin calls from your broker when your stocks go down. Further, options are absolutely not like commodities, in that you are not liable for more than the cost of the option.

Being able to fix the limit to your risk enables you to plan more effectively and to make decisions on the basis of risk–reward ratios. If the chances for profits greatly exceed the cost of the option, you have a favorable risk–reward ratio.

Of course, you don't have to lose *all* the money you put into an option. Using the rules we shall discuss later, we shall attempt to salvage a good percentage of the money we place in any option that goes against us.

LOWER COMMISSIONS

Lower commissions are the next great advantage of buying options over buying stock. This works in two ways. You pay a lower dollar amount in commissions to control the same number of shares of stock, and your break-even point after commissions is lower.

A typical commission on 100 shares of a $20 stock would be $44. If the option were selling at $100, the commission would be $25 for the first option, which is a considerable savings. But the dramatic savings appear when you buy more than one option. The commission on two, for example, at that price might be $26.60. You could buy several options, each controlling 100 shares of the stock, for the $44 stock commission.

LOWER BREAKEVEN POINT

For a trader, the important consideration is the breakeven point. This is the level to which the stock must move up in order for you to start making a profit after the commissions. Figuring a buy and sell commission on 100 shares of a $20 stock, your breakeven point is seven-eighths. The stock has to move up seven-eighths of a point just for you to break even after commissions. Remember, one point is equivalent to $100. On *one* option selling between one and ten dollars per share your breakeven point is one-half point ($25 to buy and $25 to sell, figured for an option of 100 shares). On two options the breakeven point will be just over a quarter point.

Table 3–1 Breakeven Points on Trades

If you trade:	*And the one-way commission is:*	*The breakeven point will be:*
50 shares	$50	2 points
100 shares	$50	1 point
1 option	$25	½ point

This lower breakeven point means that many trades that wouldn't be profitable in the stock market will be profitable in the options market. The odds are tilted just a little less against you. Years ago, when commissions were considerably less on the stock market, there was a breed of people known as *day traders.* These people would buy in the morning and sell in the afternoon, always trading the more volatile stocks, and they could make a living on the daily fluctuations. As commissions increased, it became impossible to do this profitably, and an important source of market liquidity was lost. Now with the new options markets it is possible that we shall see the return of the day trader.

OPTIONS ARE MORE FUN

Another advantage is that you will have more fun watching and trading the options. A $20 stock may fluctuate a point or two or three over a period of a few weeks. But that same movement, which is a small percentage move in the stock price, is a dramatic move in the price of the option. The time element from the point when you buy the option to the point when you have

Table 3–2 Comparative Percent Changes in Stocks and Options

	If the stock price is 20	*And the option price is 1*
A 1-point move is an increase of:	5%	100%
A 2-point move is an increase of:	10%	200%
A 3-point move is an increase of:	15%	300%

a decisive profit or loss is much shorter. You will not have time to get bored with your options. This means you will have greater interest, and it will be easier to sustain it; therefore you are more likely to learn more.

A side advantage to buying options is that your broker will be much more likely to take an interest in what you are doing. This is because option business turns over a lot faster than stock business, and although he will get smaller commissions, he will get many more of them. When he sees that you are giving him a steady flow of commissions, he will suddenly find time to talk to you and will work harder at getting good executions. If you go in and buy ten shares of stock at a time, don't expect to find a red carpet.

YOU WILL LEARN MORE

By far the greatest advantage of the options market to you is that it is a better learning vehicle. You will have a *little* money in each option, so you will be interested, but not uptight. You will be able to spread your money over a few options, so you will have several learning experiences going on all the time. You will learn faster, because it will not take the options market as long to teach you a lesson.

The lessons you learn *speculating* in the options market can carry over to *investments* you make in the stock market or in real estate or whatever.

You can see that the principal advantages of the options exchanges, such as lower capital requirements, lower commissions, limited risk, etc., all combine to lower the odds against you. Since you are going to speculate, you may as well do your speculating where the odds are the best.

It is popular opinion that the options are among the wildest speculations available. It is true that they can be if they are improperly used, and in some of the later chapters we shall see just how overwhelming the odds can be on some options. But we are not looking for the long shots. We want to play the percentages over a long period of time.

THE DISADVANTAGE

It can also be argued that there is one great disadvantage to buying options. They expire after a period of time (at most, nine months), and if the stock stands still between the time you buy the option and the time the option expires, you cannot possibly make any money and you are almost certain to lose money, whereas if you had bought the stock and it stood still, you would only lose your commission. This is true. If the stock stays the same over a period of time you will lose money on the option. But don't worry about it staying the same. Worry about it going down.

Table 3–3 Advantages and Disadvantages of Options

Advantages	*Disadvantages*
Less capital required	You will lose if stock stands still or drops
Limited risk	
Lower commissions	
Lower breakeven point	
Better learning vehicle	
Faster price movement	

So far in this book we have been developing an approach to the market. Now we must take that approach or philosophy and apply it to the nitty-gritty of the options markets. First let's review the important points that you should have picked up so far.

We have decided that to beat the pros we have to become professional traders. This should be our overriding goal, and it will take years to attain. We should also agree on the absolute need to do one's own work and not to rely on others for advice. Finally, we should keep the distinction between investment and speculation clearly in mind, and realize that one of the best ways to speculate is to buy options. Now we can begin to build our expertise in options. One of the best sources of information on the options market is the prospectus issued by the OCC which can be obtained from most brokers.

4 | First You Need to Know the Basics

The lack of fundamental knowledge about the operations of a market is one of the prime reasons that people lose money in markets. You have two alternatives, really. You can either do some research and reading before you begin to trade, or you can pay your tuition to the school of hard knocks and learn the hard way. Before we go on to strategies, we should first get some basic background knowledge.

DEFINITIONS

An *option* is a business contract. It allows the buyer to buy or sell 100 shares of a stock at a certain price (the *striking price*) for a certain period of time, no matter how high the stock goes or how low it falls during that time.

A *call* is an option that you buy if you think that the stock is going to go up. Calls are the only type of options currently traded on the Chicago Board (CBOE), the Amex, and the PBW Exchanges.

A *put* is an option that you buy if you think that the stock is going down. The exchanges plan to begin trading puts in a limited number of stocks sometime in the near future.

The *premium* is what you have to pay when you buy an option. It is the price of the option. The premium fluctuates from minute to minute as the options are traded on the floor of the exchange.

The *writer* is the person or bank or company that sells the option. In the options business, sellers are referred to as writers. Later in this chapter we shall examine who they are and why they do it.

The *buyer* is you—the person who is hoping that the option is going to go up in value, thereby allowing you to make a profit.

The *expiration date* is the day on which the contract between the writer and the buyer expires. It is the last day that the option can be exercised.

The *striking price* is the price that the buyer pays the writer for the stock if he decides to exercise his option.

These definitions probably do not mean much to you yet, so don't be discouraged if they raise more questions in your mind than they answer. Let's now go through the basics in greater detail, starting first with the easier concepts.

TIME

The length of time for which an option contract is good is set by the Options Clearing Corporation. The expiration dates are all standardized. They are the Saturday following the third Friday of the expiration month, and they are three months apart. At any point in time only three expiration dates are traded on a particular stock. For example, when the January options expire, the exchange will begin trading in October options, and there will be three months for the trader to choose from—April, July, and October. When the April option expires, the exchange will begin trading January options, and a trader can choose among the July, October, and January options. In a later chapter we shall discuss how to make this choice.

The standardization of the expiration dates is one of the things that makes the options exchanges possible. Without standardized expiration dates, there would be no way to maintain a continuing market where the buyer can sell back his option.

STRIKING PRICE

The striking prices are also standardized by the options exchanges. At the beginning of trading in an option the striking price is set at a convenient number close to the actual market price of the stock. These numbers are multiples of five—for example, 20, 25, 30, 35, etc. Once the striking price is set, trading continues in options at that striking price until the expiration date. But other striking prices of the option can be introduced by the exchange if the stock moves up or down. For example, when trading begins in October options, XYZ stock may be at 24. The Chicago Board would most likely start trading in options with a striking price of 25. If the stock falls to 20, trading could start in October options with a striking price of 20. If the stock falls further to 15, trading would start on October 15's, but it would continue trading in the October 25's and 20's.

A specific striking price *and* date is called a *series* of the option. The proliferation of series due to the passing of time and the fluctuation of stock price presents the trader with both opportunities and pitfalls, the opportunity being that some very good speculations will very likely develop, and the pitfall being that it is very easy to buy one series of options when another would have been much better for your purposes.

The striking price is an important determinant of the price of the option. If the striking price of an XYZ October option is 40 and the market price of the stock is hovering around 20, and if it is already the middle of October, the premium is likely to be very low—probably 1/16. The reason is that with two weeks to go until the expiration date the stock has to double just to get back up to the striking price. Therefore, the option is not worth very much, because it is an extremely rare occurrence when a stock moves from 20 to 40 in two weeks.

Conversely, if the market price of the same stock were 50, then the same option would be selling for something over 10, because the market price is already 10 points over the striking price.

How To Read The Option Quotes On The Financial Page

A glance at option prices published in *The Wall Street Journal* and many daily newspapers illustrates some of the definitions discussed.

For example, take Burroughs in Table 4–1. Options were available in expiration months of January, April, and July. Four striking prices of 70, 80, 90 and 100 were also offered. As indicated by footnote b, no Burroughs July 100 option was offered. The Burroughs options expire on the Saturday after the third Friday of the expiration month. Let's look at the Burrough's 80 option. The Burroughs Jan 80 option traded 111 contracts on that particular day. This appears under the "Vol." (volume) column. The last transaction took place at a price or premium of 6¼. The buyer paid the seller $625 for the right to purchase 100 shares of Burroughs at a price of $80 a share any time on or before the expiration date in January. Burroughs itself closed at 81⅜ on the New York Stock Exchange.

THE AUCTION MARKET

The exact price of the option will always depend on many factors. The striking price and the length of time left until expiration are, of course, very

Table 4–1 Selected Option Quotes

AMERICAN EXCHANGE
OPTIONS QUOTATIONS

Thursday, November 20, 1975

Closing prices of all options. Sales unit is 100 shares. Security description includes exercise price.

		— *Nov* —		— *Feb* —		— *May* —		*Stock*
Option & price		*Vol.*	*Last*	*Vol.*	*Last*	*Vol.*	*Last*	*Close*
A M F	15	2	5	2	5½	1	5⅝	20¼
A M F	20	107	⅛	38	1½	11	2 1/16	20¼
A S A	. . 30	120	⅝	66	3⅝	94	5⅛	30½
A S A	. . 35	59	1/16	82	1⅝	131	3	30½
A S A	. . 40	a	a	66	⅝	336	1¾	30½
A S A	. . 50	a	a	5	¼	b	b	30½
		— *Jan* —		— *Apr* —		— *Jul* —		
Aetna	. . 20	32	4½	11	4⅞	16	5½	24¼
Aetna	. . 25	29	1⅛	14	1¾	13	2⅝	24¼
Am Cya	20	12	5⅞	5	6½	a	a	25¾
Am Cya	25	97	1⅜	43	2⅛	5	2⅝	25¾
Am Cya	30	27	¼	b	b	b	b	25¾
Am Hom	30	15	5⅞	2	6⅝	b	b	35¾
Am Hom	35	141	1 13/16	21	2⅞	23	4	35¾
Am Hom	40	69	⅜	29	1⅛	39	2 1/16	35¾
Am Hom	45	2	⅛	b	b	b	b	35¾
Beat F	20	18	4	8	4⅜	a	a	23⅞
Beat F	25	43	¾	12	1 9/16	25	2¼	23⅞
Burrgh	70	40	13⅜	19	16½	3	18½	81⅜
Burrgh	80	111	6¼	14	9⅞	2	12⅜	81⅜
Burrgh	90	256	2⅛	88	5⅝	33	7⅞	81⅜
Burrgh	100	130	11/16	58	2⅜	b	b	81⅜

Total volume 16,139. Open interest 418,112.
a—Not traded. b—No option offered.

important. Naturally, an April option will always sell for more than a January option, and a July option will sell for still more, because there is more time remaining until expiration. (See Table 4–1.) The price of the stock as it moves up and down also affects the price of the option, but don't expect to find an exact correlation between the price of the stock and the price of the option. First of all, the stock is traded in one location, and the option is traded in another. Likewise, the stock and option are traded by two groups of people, and these two groups may not always agree on future prospects. These are two entirely different markets tied together only tenuously by the price of the stock. Second, the further away the market price moves from the striking price, the less the market price affects the option price. For example, if the striking price of an XYZ option is 25 and the market price is 25½, a small move up or down would probably be reflected quickly and almost exactly in the price of the option. But if the striking price is 25 and the market price is only 15, then a move in the market price for the stock will probably not move the option price, because there would be little hope for that option unless there were many months to expiration.

The options exchanges work like other auction markets, with trades taking place between the highest bid (buyer) and the lowest asking price (seller). Prices are expressed in eighths of a point (dollar) above the price of 3, and sixteenths of a point below 3. The quoted price of the option multiplied by 100 (the number of shares covered by the option) is the cost of the option. For instance, an option quoted at 5½ sells for $550 plus commission costs.

WHY YOU NEVER WANT TO EXERCISE AN OPTION

Since the options exchanges are continuous auction markets, it is possible to sell back an option that you have purchased. This is exactly what you will do *all* the time. You will never want to exercise an option, because to exercise an option you have to come up with the purchase price of the stock and you have to pay extra commissions.

Let's say that you have an option in October XYZ at a striking price of 20. The market price is 24. You could exercise your option and buy the stock at 20, but you would have to tie up $2000 of your capital, and you would have to pay a buy commission of approximately $44 on the stock. Then you could take your profit by selling your stock on the market at 24, but you would have to pay a selling commission of approximately $50. It is far simpler just to sell the option and take your profit on the option and pay commission of only $25. Furthermore, no extra capital for purchasing the stock is required to realize the profit. It is important that you understand this point, because the entire book is based on the assumption that you will take your profits by selling options and not by exercising them.

Just as we take profits by selling back the options, we shall also reduce our losses by selling our options and salvaging as much of our capital as possible when a trade goes against us. In all cases we shall sell our options whether they go up or down and not exercise them or let them expire.

The Over-The-Counter System

Before the Chicago Board Options Exchange was formed, options were traded on the over-the-counter network. There was no standardization of expiration dates and striking prices, and therefore there could be no auction market where the options could be resold. This meant that the only way to take a profit was actually to exercise the option—and to pay the resulting commissions. There was really no good way to salvage a portion of your capital when a trade went against you.

The over-the-counter market for options is still in existence, but the options exchanges will take over more and more of the business as they enlarge the number of options that they trade and as they move to begin trading puts as well as calls.

The strategies in this book are designed only for marketable options traded on a market where the options can be resold.

What Happens To Dividends?

On the options exchanges, the owner of the stock, who writes the option, gets the dividend. This is unlike the over-the-counter system, where the buyer gets the dividend. It is handled this way to simplify bookkeeping, but it also simplifies our decision-making processes.

As a buyer of options, you are interested only in capital gains, because you are not entitled to any dividends. Therefore, you will pick your options on the basis of which are most likely to increase in value without any regard to the percentage dividend that the stock pays.

How Your Trade Takes Place

When you give your broker an order, it is transmitted by teletype to the trader on the floor of the exchange who represents your broker. He then executes the order at the market or at a limit, according to how the order has been written. There are no specialists on the Chicago Board, so trades are held by the floor brokers or are placed on the Board Brokers' books. The AMEX, however, still utilizes the specialist.

When your order has been executed, the Options Clearing Corporation assumes a position as guarantor for both sides of the contract. When you sell back your option, you are closing out your position with the OCC and not with whoever sold you the option. Therefore, you do not have to worry about a situation where the writer of the option that you bought fails to make good on the contract.

The Writers

At this point you are probably wondering just who is selling the option in the first place and why they want to do it. Most writers are people who own the stocks underlying the options. They are also trust departments of banks, insurance companies, mutual funds, etc. These people generally are not playing the market, but are attempting to increase their rate of return on the stocks by writing options. They believe that the percentages are with them, in that the majority of the time the stocks will not move enough one way or the other and they will be able to collect their premiums on a regular basis.

Of course, some sellers of options are people who bought them earlier. When you sell your option, it is sold to a buyer. That buyer might be a new buyer, or he might be a previous seller who is buying back his option to close out his position. You will probably have to think about this for a minute to let it sink in (like a Chinese puzzle).

Writers of options are analogous to the "house" in a gambling casino. The odds are in their favor, because in those cases where the stock stays the same the options will decrease in value over time. The buyer will lose in those cases, and the seller will gain. Writers (like casino owners) tend to be wealthy, and they have many transactions going at once. Their gains and losses even out to a nice percentage gain. (Most writers hope for 15 to 20 percent yearly on their money.)

Once you understand that the odds are against you (the buyer), you have already made great progress. Now you can go on to develop a plan to improve the odds.

5 | You Have to Have a Plan

Most people in the stock market today do not have plans, and most people lose money in the market. These observations are probably related. By *plan*, we mean something more than a vague general strategy that one carries in one's head and which tends to vary with changing market conditions. We mean detailed written rules for your market behavior—a list of rules that you refer to constantly and follow precisely.

IF YOU DON'T HAVE A PLAN

People who don't have plans are likely to run into several problems when they start trading in the market. First of all, they are much more likely to take other people's advice, and the quality of advice floating around these days is about as poor as it has ever been. They are subject to all the whims and fancies of which the human mind is capable.

People who don't have plans and who make mistakes in the market will probably continue to make them. If you don't know what you're doing wrong, you will probably do it again. But if you have a comprehensive plan, you can see, for example, that one of your rules is causing you to lose money. Therefore, you change the rule. At the same time, if you did something right and weren't following a plan, you may not be able to understand what you did, and so you won't be able to do it again. If you have a plan, you can see which of your rules are making money for you, and so should be retained.

Finally, if you don't have a plan, you are apt to feel very insecure, because you don't really know why you are doing what you're doing. When you feel insecure, you are more likely to panic and make very bad mistakes.

IF YOU DO HAVE A PLAN

People who have plans are more disciplined, because they are following a set procedure. They are much more consistent. What they are doing is likely to make sense. It may not make money, but at least it is likely to make sense. Therefore, you will have the security of knowing why you are doing what you are doing.

But It Has To Be Written

If you don't write your plan down on paper, you can forget some of the details. Anything you keep in your head is likely to be very vague and lacking in the necessary detail. If your rules are not written down, it is very easy to bend them or change them or forget them altogether as soon as some "great opportunity" or crisis comes along.

This need not be a major literary undertaking, but your plan should contain several rules. It should take into account how much money you have to risk, what your situation in life is, what your goals are, etc. It should be a personal document that you write by yourself.

HOW TO START

After making adequate allowance for basic necessities, you may be able to put together a certain amount of money that you can speculate with—money that you can afford to lose, meaning that your life style would not be affected in any way by its loss. How much you start with—how much you can safely speculate with—will greatly affect the kinds of risks you can take and therefore the kinds of rules that you will incorporate into your plan. So, the first thing you should do is take a long hard look at your financial situation. Then start your plan by writing at the top of the first page: "Plan for Speculating in the Options Market with $xxxx." And kiss the money goodbye. By deciding how much you're going to fund this project with, you will be taking an important first step towards psychological detachment in the market. You will be setting yourself up as a trader. In other words, you will be starting a little business of your own. Every new business has to have some form of capitalization. Your capitalization will be that amount of money that you can afford to risk.

Some of you may find that you don't have any money that you can risk, but you're still interested in getting into the market. We suggest that you radically change your spending patterns for a few months until you save the $500 to $1000 that is probably the bare minimum for starting to buy options. Another possibility is going together with a friend or relative. But make sure that they realize that they can lose all the money that they contribute, or you may lose a friend.

Since you're running a business, you will want to keep good records. You should keep a record of all purchases and sales and the resulting profits and losses. Periodically you should add them up to see exactly how you're doing. Do this every three months or so—you can call it your quarterly report. As your records accumulate over time, it will be possible for you to see how well you're doing and whether or not you're improving. Keeping good records will give your whole enterprise an added dimension of professionalism, and they will come in very handy when you have to fill out your income tax forms.

RULES TO CONSERVE CAPITAL

Before you can make money you have to guard against losing it. You can hope to avoid losing money by knowing what and when to buy and when to sell—these subjects will be covered in later chapters. However, there are even more fundamental things to consider first that will help you conserve your capital.

You should continue writing your plan by writing down a series of rules to follow *all* the time. Your rules should be like a constitution. You never break the rules, but if you find as time goes by that one is unworkable, you should amend it. Here is an example of a rule.

RULE / Never buy more than x options on one stock.

If your capital is less than $1000, then $x = 1$. If your capital is greater than $2000, then $x = 2$ or more (because of the break in commissions), but the idea is to spread your money around. If you have $20 and go to the horse races, you wouldn't put $20 on a horse in the first race, because that horse might lose and then you wouldn't be able to bet the rest of the afternoon. Instead, you would probably put two dollars on a different horse in each race. You would have more fun betting all the races.

The principle is the same in the options market. Right from the beginning you want to strive for diversification. It could mean that you'll get a little winner right away that could have been a big winner if you had only put all your money on it, but by following this rule you will be sure that you will not be wiped out in one trade. You will have several chances, and therefore you will have several opportunities to learn and improve.

RULE / Never make more than one purchase on one day.

In other words, do not buy four ABC October 20's and three XYZ January 30's. Buy one or the other option, but not both. It may be the wrong day. You may have the market timed perfectly, but if you spend all your money at once, someone could be assassinated ten minutes later and you would crash with the market.

Once again, what we are trying to do is spread the money around. You don't want to spend it all on one thing, and you don't want to spend it all at one time. You may think that you are safe enough by just having a diverse portfolio, but if the market moves against you it will probably move against *all* your options.

RULES TO IMPROVE THE ODDS

By buying at different times you lessen the impact of bad timing decisions. Timing, of course, is the most important skill to learn, and we shall go into great detail studying the problems of correct timing when we look at charts in later chapters. But if you have never been in the market, here are two common-sense rules.

RULE / Buy only after the Dow Jones Industrial Average has been down for three straight days except under extraordinary circumstances.

RULE / Sell only after the Dow Jones Industrial Average has been up for three straight days except under extraordinary circumstances.

These rules won't assure you of buying low and selling high, but they will save you from buying high and selling low. Most stocks move with the market, and most options move with their underlying stocks. The market generally moves for a few days in one direction and then turns around for several days in the opposite direction. These moves are called waves, and a move of several days can make a big difference in the price of an option. Most waves last at least three days. By following these two rules you will undoubtedly miss some markets. Don't worry about it. The market will be there tomorrow, and there will always be more chances. It is better to miss a chance by following your rules than to lose money by not following your rules.

What we are trying to do with all these rules is to begin to tilt the odds in your favor. If you follow the rules about waiting three days, you will avoid buying at all-time highs and selling at all-time lows, and you should consistently get slightly better prices. Also, by waiting three days you will be going against the opinion of the majority, and that is exactly the way you want to go.

"Extraordinary circumstances" in these rules refers to situations when the price action of the stock is running strongly contrary to the movement of the market or when there are specific chart formations that develop in the stock which indicate the advisability of following other rules than the simplistic three-day up or three-day down rule.

RULE / Use limit orders on *all* buys.

There is a bid price and an asked price on the floor of the exchange. If you put in a market order, you will usually get the asked price. The asked price is generally an eighth or sixteenth above the last trade, and the bid price is generally slightly below the last trade. Sometimes the last trade will have taken place at the bid or asked price. Your broker has all this information on a television screen at his desk. It is up to the minute most of the time.

Put your order in at or slightly below the bid. During the normal fluctuation of a day's business your order will be filled. Use day orders only on buys. If the market moves away from you, say goodbye to it. If you really want the option, put your limit in at the price of the last trade, but do not always pay the asked price.

In heavily traded issues brokers prefer to use market orders. This is because market orders are always filled while limit orders are often not filled and cost the brokerage firm money. Most stockbrokers, however, consider it a challenge to try to get limit orders filled. If your broker objects to your use of limits, explain that you're trying to learn. If he still objects, find yourself another broker. You want a broker to fill your orders, not give you static or advice. If your broker understands what his relationship to you is to be, he will probably be very glad to take your orders. But if you allow him to bully you because in the beginning he knows more than you do, you deserve to pay the asked price.

RULE / Use limit orders on sells if the market is stagnant. If the market is moving down at all, put in a market order.

This rule is mainly to protect profits, but once you have decided to sell you don't want to waste much time. If your limit doesn't fill immediately, it is probably a bad sign. Change it to a market order and get out. This is because bear markets fall faster than bull markets go up. Profits are hard to come by, and when you get one, don't quibble for that extra fraction.

The time to use limit orders on sells is when you think it is about, but not quite, time to sell. Then put your limit above the market at just a fraction below where you think the option can climb. If the market moves against you, get out.

RULES SHOULD CHANGE

As you gain experience and capital, you will want to change your rules. Undoubtedly, some of these rules will not work for you because they will be contrary to your basic nature. The idea is to remain flexible and open to change, but to continue to have a basic plan to govern your behavior. As you gain experience, your plan should evolve to become more and more valuable as your method of playing the market, and it should grow and change to be able to handle the increasing amount of money that you will have as your trading capital in the future.

6 | You Need an Information System

You should not try to trade the options market in a vacuum. You should have a continuous flow of information about what is happening in the market and in the world in general. This flow of information can be called an "information system," because it systematically provides you with all the relevant information you need to *attempt* to predict the price movement of options. You should begin now to set up the information system you will need to become a professional market trader over the next few years.

TOO MUCH OR TOO LITTLE

The quality and quantity of your information will, of course, affect the quality of your trading. Most people run into one of three problems in their search for information. The most obvious is too little information. If all you have to make decisions with are the stock prices in your local newspaper, you will have difficulty in spotting the market trends, let alone in understanding them. Conversely, too much information will take too much of your time and confuse you with unnecessary details. Too much information may result in decisions based on "great ideas" that you read about and not based on your own systematic plan.

Perhaps the most insidious problem is that experienced when you try to trade with the wrong information. Knowing what the sales and earnings of a company were for the last twenty years may be nice and it may help in buying the stock, but it is unlikely to affect the price of the option over the next few days unless there is an announcement of a major gain or drop in the earnings. Knowledge of a company's products is unlikely to be helpful in predicting what an option will do in the period of the few days or weeks that you hold the option.

HOW TO SET UP YOUR INFORMATION SYSTEM

The best traders concentrate on a very few stocks. They don't try to follow dozens of stocks, but rather they limit their attention to a small number of very volatile issues. They don't need to keep up with what is happening in the stocks that they don't follow, but they do need to be alert to anything that could possibly affect the stocks that they do follow.

A good trader may watch a particular stock for months or even a year or two before he makes a trade, but when the time is right—wham!

In the next chapter we shall talk about how to pick the options and stocks that we shall want to watch, but for now remember that there will only be a few and that you will be an expert in those few.

What kind of information do we need about the underlying stocks for our options? First of all, it might be nice to know the history of the stock. If you go to the horse races, you want to know how fast a horse has run in the past, on different kinds of tracks, before you bet on him today. The way we follow a stock's history is to keep a price and volume chart.

STOCK CHARTS

A chart simply records each day's action in the trading of a stock. A vertical line is drawn for each day from the high price to the low price. A short horizontal line is drawn to indicate the closing price. A line is drawn at the bottom of the page to show the volume.

Over a period of time the stock will form recognizable patterns on the chart. The charts tell us many things. Among them are the likely levels of support (the price at which buying interest will come in and hold up the price of the stock) and resistance (the price at which people are likely to take profits and thus hold back an advance in the stock's price). Charts can indicate how a stock performed in similar markets in the past and therefore how it is likely to perform in the future. Charts should show potentially good buying areas and give you an idea of how far the stock should run before you want to sell your option.

The charts have many uses, but the most important for us to consider is the help that they give in the timing of purchases and sales. You have, no doubt, heard of the age-old controversy between fundamental and technical research. Fundamental research deals with sales and earnings and tries to predict what the stock will do on the basis of what the company's prospects are for the future. Technical research deals with charts of the stock's price history and tries to predict what the stock will do based on what the charts show it has done in the past.

A long discussion of the merits of fundamental research versus technical research would serve no useful purpose, but it is important to know that the fundamentalists are generally long-term investors and the technicians are generally short-term traders. Options are short term by their very nature, since they expire on a given date a few months in the future. Because of this you can't trade options on the fundamentals. You should be aware of the fundamentals but rely on your charts for trading.

There is a whole science that has developed around stock market charts, and you will have to learn it. This book will present a few of the basics, but you should get two other books to give you more detailed information. The first of these is *How Charts Can Help You in the Stock Market*, by William L. Jiler.[1] This is an introduction to the subject that will get you started with a few hours of study. The second is *Technical Analysis of Stock Trends*, by Edwards and McGee.[2] It is a much more detailed book that you will need for reference. It is considered to be the Bible of technical analysis. No chartist is without a copy.

After you have read these books, you will have a better understanding of the rationale behind this book. They are the beginning of your apprenticeship as a trader.

Charting Paper

Don't go out and buy common graph paper for charting stocks. It won't work well. Your charts will either be hard to read, or your stocks will run off the page. Special charting paper has been designed by John McGee, Inc., 360 Worthington Street, Springfield, Massachusetts, 01103. Drop them a postcard, and they will send you a sample and their price lists. Their paper is semi-logarithmic, which means that the same *percentage* move will look the same at the bottom of the page as it does at the top. The paper is easy on the eyes and can withstand the constant use to which you will subject it. Each page

[1]William L. Jiler, *How Charts Can Help You in the Stock Market* (New York: Trendline, 1962).

[2]Robert D. Edwards and John McGee, *Technical Analysis of Stock Trends* (Springfield, Mass: John McGee, Inc., 1966).

covers a year's stock history. (Get the kind with the dates already printed in.) They also offer a nice binder for your charts and a percentage calculator that you will need.

WHY YOU SHOULD DO YOUR OWN CHARTING

Of course, it is possible to buy charts that are printed each week and airmailed to you each Monday morning. There are several firms that offer this service. The problem is that they are usually very expensive. You get hundreds of charts to look at, but we think that it is better to do your own charts. Then you will be intimately familiar with a small number of stocks. You will see the charts develop and learn more about charting, and you will save the substantial fees of a charting service. The time involved in charting stocks is only a few minutes a day, but it will force you to look at each chart every day. This discipline will pay off with an intuitive "feel" for your stocks within a few months.

CHART THE STOCK, NOT THE OPTION

You may be wondering why you shouldn't chart the price of the option instead of the stock. The main reason is that the stock is permanent, and it is possible to develop many years of stock price history. The option can run for only nine months at the most.

Second, the price of the option will tend to follow the price of the stock anyway, so by charting the stock you are developing the data for predicting the price movement of the option.

Finally, for any one stock there will be at least three and probably many more options being traded (different expiration months and striking prices), so you would have many more charts to keep. And they would be rather boring, since they would all be going up and down together.

DAILY INFORMATION

To get the daily high, low, and closing prices and volumes for your charts you will need to subscribe to a good newspaper. The best business paper is *The Wall Street Journal.* It can be delivered to your door every morning, and in addition to the prices, it contains other useful statistical information and articles that will help keep you abreast of what is going on in the market and the business world.

With *The Wall Street Journal* you may have difficulty finding the prices for the options, since not all local papers print this information. Since almost everyone else who is operating in the market reads the *Journal,* if you don't you may find out too late that one of your stocks was panned in a *Journal* article. You will be at a disadvantage without it. The *Journal* will provide you with a liberal education over the years if you take the trouble to read it thoroughly. We think that it is well worth the subscription price.

If you read the *Journal,* you probably won't need any other subscriptions to market-oriented publications. News stories have a tendency to be repeated and paraphrased from one magazine to the next. They all talk about the same subjects. No other field of endeavor except sex has such a proliferation of publications as does the stock market. There are hundreds of investment advisory services that you can subscribe to. You should avoid all of these and develop your own expertise, so that you can make your own decisions without the advice of the "experts." If any of these services really picked the winners consistently, everyone would find out about it. If everyone found out about it, it would negate the value of the information.

BOOKS

Besides the two books on charting already mentioned, you might consider buying *A Strategy of Daily Stock Market Timing for Maximum Profit,* by Joseph E. Granville.[3] This book will suggest other useful technical indicators that will give you a feel for the movement of the market as a whole.

Granville also has a system called "On Balance Volume" that can be used as an adjunct to charting. This is described in *Granville's New Key to Stock Market Profits.*[4]

Over the years you will probably collect many books on the market. However, you should go slowly at the beginning. The two books on charting will keep you occupied for several months until you assimilate all the finer points of charting.

[3]Joseph E. Granville, *A Strategy of Daily Stock Market Timing for Maximum Profit* (Englewood Cliffs, N.J.: Prentice-Hall, 1960).

[4]*Granville's New Key to Stock Market Profits* (Englewood Cliffs, N.J.: Prentice-Hall, 1963).

A GOOD SYSTEM

Your information system should provide you with both all the information you need to trade options and a continuing education, but it should do this within a reasonable cost and without requiring an unrealistic amount of time.

All the supplies, a subscription to *The Wall Street Journal*, and the charting books can be purchased for considerably less than $100. This is less than one point on one trade, so the cost of this information system is really quite reasonable. If, however, you go overboard on subscriptions and books, the additional costs will not provide you with cost-justifiable additional information.

Reading the *Journal* and charting your stocks should not take more than an hour per day, five days per week. Your weekends should be free. Remember that you are embarking on a long-range program and don't try to do too much in the beginning. Otherwise, it won't be fun, and if it's not fun, it will turn into a job just like the one you already have.

7 | How to Decide Which Option to Buy

In the last chapter, we decided that it would be useful to chart the stocks underlying the options. We shall buy options on these stocks, but first it is necessary to pick the stocks that we are going to follow and chart. How do we go about picking the stocks?

THE LIMITATIONS OF TIME

To begin with, you must recognize that you alone can not chart all the stocks underlying the options that are traded on the options exchanges. You won't have time. A good estimate of the time needed for charting is one minute per day per stock. Don't think that you can do thirty in half an hour or so, however, because you will want to study the ones that are forming interesting patterns.

You will, of course, want to keep your charts up to date each day, but inevitably something will happen occasionally to put you behind—you'll catch the flu or have to go on a business trip, etc. Furthermore, once you start charting, you will begin to think of each chart as a work of art, so you won't let anyone else do them for you.

We suggest that you pick about twelve stocks to start with. You should be able to get a feel or understanding for twelve. You will become bored with a few and delete them, and become interested in others as time goes by.

THE BEST STOCKS TO CHART

The higher-priced stocks have higher-priced options. This is only natural, because the possible moves in dollars in a high-priced issue are usually greater than in a low-priced stock. This means that if your capital is limited to only one or two thousand dollars, it would be better for you to concentrate on the lower-priced stocks, which will have lower-priced options. By buying lower-priced options you can spread your money around and get more diversification. You will probably want to have most of your charts on stocks that sell for under $50.

There is another, more important reason for charting the lower-priced stocks. Lower-priced stocks are more volatile. Studies have shown that the *percentage moves* made by lower-priced stocks are greater than the percentage moves made by higher-priced stocks. You naturally want to follow the stocks that will have the greatest percentage moves, because these offer you the greatest profits.

Another way to pick stocks to chart is to pick the ones with the highest variability estimates. How you can use variability estimates to your advantage is a subject covered in a later chapter.

Your Portfolio Of Possibilities

Once you have started to chart, you have a portfolio of possibilities. You will trade options on some of the stocks that you chart. You will grow to know them rather intimately over time. Don't take flyers on tips about other options or stocks. You have no expertise in the ones you don't chart.

From your charts you will begin to get ideas about which stocks are about to make moves. These ideas will come naturally and easily *if* you have taken the trouble to read *How Charts Can Help You in the Stock Market* and *Technical Analysis of Stock Trends.* If you haven't you may still get a lot of ideas from your charts, but you shouldn't trust them. In the next chapter we shall go further into this question, which is really a question of when to buy.

WHICH MONTH TO BUY

Now let's suppose that one of your charts shows great promise and you think it's time to buy an option on that stock. But which option? There may be three expiration months, each with four striking prices, giving twelve options that you could purchase. Which is the best?

First, let's decide on the expiration month. At any given time there are going to be three traded. The closest month will be the cheapest. The second will cost more, because that option has three more months to run. The third or longest option will have six more months to run than the first, and it will be the most expensive of the three because it has the most "time value." Time value is merely that amount of money that people are willing to pay for the privilege of holding the option until the expiration date. The more time left, the more time value.

Now you will be risking less money on the closest month, more money on the second, and the most on the third, because the amount you risk is what you have to pay for the option. At the same time your *level of risk* will be greatest on the nearest month and least on the last month, because there is less time for your option to make its move before the expiration of the nearest month.

You have a trade-off. The nearest month will cost the least and have the highest level of risk. The farthest month will cost the most but have the lowest level of risk. Therefore, a rule of thumb obviously presents itself: buy the middle month. The middle month gives you enough time for your stock to make its move and for you to get out, which reduces the risk of buying the nearest month and having the option approach expiration just as your stock starts to move. The middle month costs less than the farthest month, which also limits risk. If you are very sure of yourself and there are still a couple of months to expiration in the nearest month, then buy it. If you are unsure, then buy the farthest month (but if you're very unsure, it may be better not to buy anything).

Don't waste your money by buying the nearest month when there are only a few weeks to expiration. The time value of an option tends to decline on a straight line until near the end, and then it falls off sharply.

Another consideration is that you should not concentrate all your options in the same expiration month. Remember to always strive for diversification.

To expand on our trading rules you should add this one, especially if you are just beginning to buy options:

RULE / Always buy the middle month unless you have a very good reason to buy the near or far month.

WHICH STRIKING PRICE TO BUY

The next question is which striking price do we want to pick. There may be several for the stock in which you are interested.

To start with, you will probably want to buy options that are out of the money. Remember that "in the money" means that the market price of the stock is above the striking price of the option and "out of the money" means that the market price of the stock is below the striking price of the option.

The reason that you want to buy out-of-the-money options is that you want to limit your risk. If the market price of a stock is 40 dollars per share and the striking price is 35 dollars, the option may be selling for 6 dollars. But 5 of those 6 dollars are made up of the market price of the stock over the option price (40 − 35 = 5). It would be better to buy the option with a striking price of 40 and selling for 1. The reason is that if the stock suddenly falls, you could lose $600 on the 35 striking price, but only $100 on the 40 striking price. The 35 striking price also ties up more of your capital—capital that you could put to better use in buying other options.

There may be two or three or more out-of-the-money options. Which one should you buy? Your charts will help you with this question.

Since you have already decided which month to buy, you can make a mark on your chart for that expiration date at the various striking prices. Take a large protractor and use as your center point today's closing price. Then figure the angle of incidence to the striking price/expiration date. If that angle is greater than previous rises in the stock, forget it. The odds are overwhelming that your stock cannot sustain such a rise. This means that the option with that striking price can only hope for a small move on rallies. There will be very little speculative interest in that option, because there will be very little hope. Go to the next lower striking price and figure the angle until you have one that is possible.

Another way to do this is to use the percentage calculator that you can purchase from John McGee, Inc., along with your charting paper. Measure from today's closing price to the striking price to see what percentage move up is necessary. Check that against similar moves in the stock in the past to see if the stock has ever made such a move before. Any move more than 25 percent in three months is very unlikely.

It doesn't matter if the stock has moved down from a certain striking price in a matter of days. It almost certainly can't move back up so fast. In the stock market, as in life, things can be destroyed much faster than they can be built.

The use of the protractor and percentage calculator can be supplemented by the following rule, which you should use at least until you gain considerable experience in trading options.

RULE / Always buy the nearest out-of-the-money option unless there is an in-the-money option with the market price less than a point above the striking price.

For example, if the market price is 17, buy the option with a striking price of 20, but if the market price is 15½, you probably want to buy the option with a striking price of 15 because it's a long way back to 20.

By buying the nearest out-of-the-money option, you will probably be buying the option with the most speculative interest. It will also be most responsive to movements in the price of the stock.

Options that are far out of the money won't move significantly until the stock has moved several points back up towards the striking price and it once again becomes a good possibility that the stock can go above the striking price before the expiration date.

You should always adhere to this rule unless (1) you foresee a tremendous move in the stock, (2) you have plenty of time before the expiration date for that move, and (3) you are buying the option when the stock is on a firmly established support line. You should have all three to buy an option far out of the money, but even if you do, you should consider the fact that the nearest out-of-the-money option would *also* make a good move under these circumstances.

Now that we know which month and expiration date to buy, we can go on in the next chapter to consider that all-important element of the timing of our purchase.

8 | How to Decide When to Buy

If you're not already convinced that you need charts to trade options, this chapter should convince you. By taking a look at how the average investor buys stocks, you will see that the traditional methods, which work very poorly in the stock market, won't work at all with options.

DON'T BUY THEM WHEN THEY'RE DOWN

The most popular way of deciding when to buy stocks is to "buy them when they're down." The idea is to buy a "good" company after its stock has fallen considerably and then to hold it until it eventually comes back. The stock has fallen so far that it must be near the bottom.

The first difficulty with this method is that when a stock is moving in a certain direction it generally continues to move in that direction until something happens to turn it around. In other words, the stock is likely to continue going down after you buy it before it makes its move upward. And this means that you could have gotten the stock a lot cheaper and that your capital is tied up during the rest of the downward move and the process of reversal.

The second difficulty with this method is that a lot of stocks never come back. Ever hear of Levitz, National Homes, or Winnebago? Many people bought these stocks after they had fallen considerably, only to see them fall much more and never return.

If you have charts you can avoid these difficulties. After a stock falls sharply, it rarely turns around in a V formation and goes back up. Usually a stock goes into a recognizable reversal or consolidation pattern before starting an advance.

Once you are able to recognize reversal and consolidation patterns, you will be able to buy with much more sophistication instead of using the simplistic "buy them when they're down" approach.

DON'T BUY THEM WHEN THEY'RE HOT

The second most popular method of buying stocks is the "buy them when they're hot" approach. This is really just getting on the bandwagon. It has considerably more merit than buying stocks when they're down, because, once again, stocks tend to continue moving in the same direction until something happens to turn them around.

However, if this method worked everyone would do it. (At times everyone does—this phenomenon is called a bull market.) The difficulty here is that as the stock moves up, more and more people chicken out and take their profits, and it takes an increasing number of suckers like you to continue buying and running the prices up. As the stock climbs higher and higher, it becomes more and more vulnerable—rather like the house of cards that was quite stable with only two stories.

If you were lucky enough to get in near the beginning of the stock's move, you may do all right (assuming, of course, that you're smart enough to know when to get out). But if you don't have a chart that shows similar moves by the stock in the past, how do you know if you're buying in at the beginning or middle or end of the move? Think about that for a minute. And if you don't know, what kind of rational basis do you have for deciding when to sell?

DON'T BUY ON THE RUMOR AND SELL ON THE NEWS

There are many platitudes that pass for stock market wisdom, but "Buy on the rumor, sell on the news" is one of the most asinine. The idea is to buy when you hear about a new development that should make the stock go up, but that hasn't been made public yet. You should then be buying with the insiders. When it hits the papers, you sell, because the insiders are also going to sell and force the price down. The only reason that this ever works is because so many people believe it. The fallacy in the whole system is that the insiders have already done what they're going to do before *you* ever hear about anything. There may be a small move left in the stock before the news gets to the public, but we don't recommend this as a good consistent trading method.

If you really want to know what the insiders are doing, watch the charts and watch the tape. Insiders leave more tracks than bears walking in mud.

However, the insiders are not always right. Unless they control a high percentage of the outstanding stock, they are subject to the same market circumstances that plague the rest of us.

DON'T LOOK FOR A REBOUND

Quite frequently you will see that a stock has fallen several points in one day because of some announcement such as slightly lower earnings or the discontinuance of a product line. You may rightly believe that it is only panic selling that has caused the drop and that there will very likely be a rebound during the next day or at least within a few days.

You go in and buy, and the stock continues to fall. Why? Because every chartist in the country who has a chart of that stock has gone back and found the next support level for the stock, and they won't buy until the stock reaches that support level. They have considerable clout in the market, and their lack of buying just encourages more people to sell.

If you don't have charts you don't know where the support levels are. You are just flying blind.

Stocks And Options Go Together

By now you should be getting the picture. There are countless simple one-sentence systems for playing the market. None of them works well enough to keep bread on the table.

Chart reading is a complex art. It doesn't always work, but it does work better than any other method we have seen. It works especially well in predicting what will happen near term—that is, in the next few days and weeks. Always remember that when you buy an option you accept a deadline. That deadline sets the amount of time that the underlying stock has to make its move. If it does not, then you will lose on the option. This makes charting and options inseparable, because the charts are especially good at predicting the short-term moves that you need to know about to trade the options.

The time to buy the option is the exact same time that the chart tells you to buy the stock. Don't watch the price of the option; watch the price of the stock. The option market will mirror the stock market, with minor adjustments reflecting the more speculative environment of the options market.

What can the charts tell you that you can't learn elsewhere? The charts show trading ranges where the stock fluctuates back and forth between logical buying and selling points. The charts show trend lines with channels and logical buying points along the trend lines. Further, the charts show a variety of bottoming formations that are clear buying signals, such as reverse head and shoulders formations, double bottoms, triple bottoms, and saucers.

STAY WITH THE MARKET TREND

In addition to your chart of individual stocks, you should keep charts of the Dow Jones Industrial and Transportation Averages. The same formations that appear on individual charts appear on charts of the averages.

It is always important to check the trend of the market before buying an option. The chart of the stock may look beautiful, but it is a rare stock that can buck the trend of the market. It is important for you to learn to coordinate your option purchases with the general market trends.

Sometimes a chart of a stock will show no pattern other than a long-term downward trend line with no indication as to where the next support will lie, because it has already gone below all previous support levels. This is a time when your charts of averages will be especially helpful. When the averages reach a support level, the renewed firmness of the market in general will tend to support the price of your stock. By constantly referring back and forth between individual charts and charts of the averages, you will be able to learn more than just by looking at individual charts.

9 | How to Decide When to Sell

Most people make their decisions to sell a few seconds before entering the sell order. These decisions tend to be spur-of-the-moment affairs made in frustration after their stock or option goes down or in panic as their profit begins to erode.

Most people spend a lot of time deciding what to buy, a little time deciding when to buy, and almost no time deciding when to sell. But all three decisions are of equal importance in determining your profit or loss, and therefore all three decisions should be given equal time and thought. Furthermore, all three decisions should be made together at the same point in time. In other words, you should tentatively decide *when* to sell at the same time you decide what and when to buy.

You may say that this is impossible or at least foolish, because you don't know at the time you buy what the market will have done by the time you get ready to sell. It is true that you don't *know*, but you can try to *predict*. In fact, everyone who buys a stock or an option is predicting that his particular stock or option is about to go up. The problem is that most people stop there. They do not go on to take the next logical step—that is, to predict how far the stock is going to go up.

In defense of the people who don't try to decide how far the stock is likely to go, it can be argued that such a prediction is a very difficult prediction to make. It is analogous to determining how high is high. Without charts, the question of how high is high is very subjective. You are likely to have thoughts like, "This seems high now and maybe I should sell, but maybe it will go higher." Such thoughts lead to ulcers, not to profits.

CHARTS CAN HELP

If you have charts, you are more likely to have thoughts like, "This stock ran into resistance at 38½ five months ago. If I buy the option now while the stock is on support at 33, I should probably think about selling the option when the stock runs back up to the 38½ area." This is more objective, because you have past history instead of a hunch on which to base decisions, and you are headed in the right direction, because you have already begun rationally to approach the decision of when to sell.

RULE / At the time you buy, figure how far the stock is likely to move up and determine probably to sell your option at that point.

Basically, you should decide when you buy the option that when the stock moves up to a certain level, you will sell your option and be content with that profit. You should also decide that, if the stock moves down instead of going up as you had predicted, there is a certain price level at which you must admit that you were wrong and therefore you must sell the option to salvage as much of your capital as possible. Really, you have the stock bracketed. If it goes up so far, you sell your option, and if it goes down so far, you sell your option.

RULE / At the time you buy, pick a point at which you will admit that you were wrong if the stock falls, and determine probably to sell your option at that point.

However, your decision-making process has to go further than this. What happens, for instance, if the stock just sits there and hardly moves—week after week? Because you have bought the option and not the stock, you face an expiration date that is moving inexorably closer. You can't just sit there as you would if you held the stock; you have to *do something.*

What you should do is make a rule that you will try to get out of all option positions well in advance of their expiration dates. How far in advance? If you chart the options themselves, you will note a tendency for them to fluctuate very closely with the price of the stock until the last two to three weeks before expiration date. Then the prices of the options begin to fall off, slowly at first and then more and more sharply. This "drop-off effect" occurs because everyone is trying to close his position and salvage what he can. If you make it a rule to get out by at least a month before expiration, you will avoid the rush and the drop in price. Also, you will be holding options while the stock price action, not the impending expiration date, is the main determinant of the option price action.

RULE / Generally try to sell options by at least a month before their expiration dates.

Of course, this rule should not be applied too strictly. For example, if there is exactly a month to go to expiration date and the stock is in a sharp uptrend, let the option go until the stock begins to show signs of faltering.

BRACKETING THE STOCK

Now we have three general parameters of when to sell the option. We know that we want to get out well ahead of the expiration date, and we have decided how much profit we will be happy with and also how much loss we are willing to sustain. However, this still leaves (see Fig. 9–1) a large area of discretion. How do we go about deciding when to sell in this "grey area?"

The average trader will want to at least get out even. This is a very common and understandable desire. No one wants to lose money, so if your option goes down you will have a very natural tendency to hold it, hoping that it will go back up so that you can get out without a loss. You should recognize this tendency and try not to be stubborn. Ask yourself what the stock's real chances are, what the market is about to do, etc., and try to make an objective decision based on facts and charts. The price at which you bought the option has absolutely nothing to do with what the option is going to do in the future.

Two people could probably trade the market better than one. Under such a system, one person would have the responsibility of selling the option but would not know at what price the option had been bought. He could then decide to sell on the basis of the available objective data and not be emotionally involved. There is no place for your pride in the stock market.

Another related problem arises when a person's option goes way up in value and he doesn't sell because he thinks it will go higher and then it comes back down. There is a natural tendency to want to wait until the option goes back up to its previous high before selling. Sometimes, of course, it doesn't go back up there, and the person loses what would have been a nice profit by trying for a great profit.

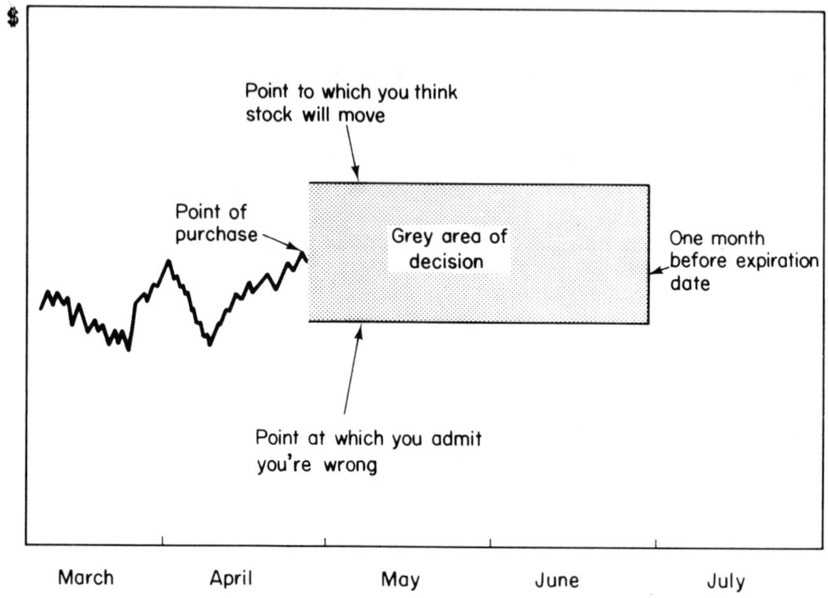

Figure 9–1. ***Bracketing the stock.***

Trying to wait until the stock goes back to a given price at which one could have had a profit or bought the stock in the first place is the basis of what chartists call *resistance levels.* You will learn about these and about support levels in the books that we have recommended on charting. The point is to be aware that your own psychological tendencies are the basis for making the charts so useful for people who know how to read them properly. Therefore, try to be aware of why you do what you do in the market and why other people do what they do. Then use this knowledge to make money instead of being a victim like the rest of the herd.

Remember that it isn't necessary to make a profit on every trade to make money in the market. People lose money just because they try to make money on every trade. Once a trade begins to run against you, the logical thing to do is to try to determine what will be the best price at which you can reasonably hope to get out, irrespective of the price at which you bought the option. This is just another way of limiting losses, but the point is that over dozens of trades this kind of reasoning will result in greater overall profits, and it is this overall figure at the end of each year that will ultimately determine your success or failure as a professional trader.

TRACKING THE STOCK

Now let's go back to the earlier question of what we can do in the "grey area" in making the decision of when to sell. Once you have bought the option, *track the stock.* The option will follow the stock. Chart the stock day by day; know exactly what it is doing and whether it is gaining or losing strength.

If you bought the stock on the basis of what the chart indicated, you probably bought on a long-term support area or on an uptrend line, or on a breakout or a clearly defined reversal pattern. Fine, you did your homework and you had a logical basis for your buy decision. But your work isn't finished yet. You have to continue charting the stock after your purchase. A lot of money is lost in the market because people get lazy and don't follow their stocks with the same intensity after the purchase as they did before the purchase. This is especially true if the stock goes down. When the stock starts to go down many people don't want to be reminded that they own the option. This is stupid. Remember that it is just as important to limit losses as it is to increase profits. A dollar saved equals a dollar earned when the final reckoning is arrived at at the end of the year.

RULE / Once you have purchased an option, track the stock daily.

What do you look for when you track the stock on a chart? First, there is probably some kind of trend line that you want to follow. As long as the stock stays on the left side of an uptrend line, you are probably all right. The line has not been broken, and therefore the trend should continue in effect.

However, all trend lines will eventually run into resistance of some sort, and you should be aware of where these resistance areas lie. When your stock approaches such a resistance area, you should pay particular attention to its price action and volume. It may falter, or it may go through to establish a new breakout. Whatever happens you should be aware of it.

The head and shoulders formation is the best-known chart formation there is, and it can form in only a few days from an otherwise perfect uptrend line. If you don't track your stock, you may suddenly find yourself with a big loss and wonder why you didn't pay attention to business.

The same is true with a double top. Everything can look perfect, and if you neglect your charts for a week you may find yourself with a very sick stock. Of course, none of these formations are always sure to predict the future course, but if you don't track the stock the odds are that you will be at least a few days late in making the moves that the market previously indicated.

It takes so little time to track a stock once you have bought the option that it seems almost a crime not to make the effort. The effort expended will pay huge dividends in terms of your own feelings of confidence in knowing and "feeling" that *now* is really the time to sell. If you spend enough time on this aspect of your trading apprenticeship, it will, more than anything else, assure you of future success in the market.

TRACKING THE AVERAGES

Tracking the stock alone, however, is not enough. It is also necessary to track the Dow Jones Averages to know at all times what the market is about to do. No matter how strong your stock is, it will be affected by an impending downtrend in the market. Only by coordinating your trading with the general behavior of the market can you hope for consistent success in the market. Your most important chart will always be your chart of the Dow Jones Industrial Average.

Finally, remember that once you have made the decision to sell your option, do it quickly. Don't quibble about an eighth of a point. If you see something negative in your chart, there are thousands of other chartists in the country who see the same thing. If you hesitate, it could be costly.

10 | Getting Started

You now know enough theory about buying options to get started in the market, but before you do, here are a few random thoughts that you might consider.

The first is the need for psychological detachment from the market. This means not being affected by what other people think and feel about the market and not being emotionally affected by your own profits and losses. It is self-explanatory that if you are detached you are more likely to be rational and objective in your decisions and you therefore have a greater chance for success.

GO IT ALONE

With the information system that you have set up, or are about to set up, you really have all the data necessary to successfully trade in the market. You don't need to ask other people what they think. What they think isn't important. This includes what your broker thinks. If you don't believe this, the next time someone volunteers advice to you ask him what his sources of information are, and why he believes what he believes. These questions will probably show up some very shaky reasoning processes. Most people who talk to you about what they are doing in the market are really only trying to get your concurrence to reinforce their own feelings of insecurity about what they are doing.

Unfortunately, playing the market is a status symbol in America, and we all seem to feel a need to tell others about the money we have won or lost. The newest super-status symbol in the cocktail circuit is the options market, so you will face the temptation to tell people about what you're starting to do. The problem is that they will remember about it later and ask you how your options project is coming along. If it's not going well and you're truthful, their derision is likely to undermine your confidence. If it is going well, your stories are likely to affect your judgment on future decisions. All in all, it's probably better to keep your operations to yourself for the first few years. If you do well, word about your prowess in the market will spread quickly. In a brokerage office everybody knows who the good traders are. The brokers treat them like gods.

PROVIDE FOR THE FUTURE

One way to improve your psychological detachment is to have a long-range program that will assure your financial future regardless of how you do in the options market. If you set up a long-term savings program, saving a reasonable amount each month, you should be able to look forward to a future of financial security.

Most corporations have some sort of employee stock purchase program where an employee can contribute up to 10 percent of his gross income and the company puts in 15 to 50 percent of what the employee contributes. If there isn't a stock purchase plan, there is usually a savings program or credit union plan. It is important that the money be set aside permanently as your financial independence fund and not be used to buy cars and boats and vacations in Hawaii.

Most people should be able to save 10 percent of their gross incomes. If you really look at your budget, there are very few things that are absolute necessities. You just think they are necessities. A lot of expenditures are pseudonecessities—a nickel here and a dime there.

One way really to cut back on expenses and dramatically improve your financial situation is to start paying cash for everything. If you can't pay cash for it, don't buy it. Burn those credit cards. Most people dream at one time or another about how great life would be with nothing but a lover and a grass shack on an island somewhere, and then they go out and buy a lot of *things* that just clutter up their lives with bills. Look around your home for a few minutes and count up all the *things* you'd rather return for cash, and then think about that the next time you whip out the credit cards.

If you have your personal finances under tight control, the money you are using in the options market will be pure risk capital—like money in a Monopoly game—and your decisions will not reflect worries about paying the bills.

Many people in the market today are affected by the "ultimate doom syndrome." They think that the present skyrocketing inflation may eventually cause the collapse of the world monetary system and with it the stock market. They worry that they should have all their money in gold and silver and Swiss francs. They have a lot of good arguments. On the other hand, even in depressions the world seems to muddle through.

If this really worries you, keep a chart of the gold price that's listed daily in *The Wall Street Journal.* Then, whenever the price is right, buy an ounce or two. Buy from a local dealer so that you see what you're getting, but make sure that you don't pay more than the prices listed in the advertisements in *The Wall Street Journal.* Then, once you have taken precautions against a great crash, your mind should be free to concentrate on making profits in the options market.

When you are ready to begin, go to visit several brokerage houses and talk to some of the brokers. Ask them a lot of questions. See how they think. See if they agree with some of your ideas, and see how well you get along together.

What you really want in a broker is someone who will do a good job in executing your orders, and someone who will take the time to give you up-to-the-minute quotes. The responsibility for determining the relationship rests with you. If you let it be known that you want to give orders and are not interested in hot tips, your broker will probably be satisfied with that relationship. It's really less work for him.

If for any reason you're unhappy with your broker, just open an account with someone else and stop buying from the first one. People change brokers quite frequently, and many people have more than one broker.

Final Comments

You're now ready to begin. Remember to keep good records and continually review how your rules are working, to determine if they should be changed as you go along. The idea in the beginning is to learn as much as possible. The money should come naturally after you have the knowledge.

The rules in this book should keep your money spread around so that you won't get uptight about any one trade. You want to have fun, and we are sure that it will be fun for you when you begin to become really proficient at tracking your stocks. When they start doing what you thought they were going to do, you will know that you're making progress.

The second part of this book is devoted to a deeper look at the options markets. The chapters that follow should widen your understanding and help you to improve your performance.

PART TWO

11 | Buying Options: Feast and Famine

How would you like a 3400 percent profit in three weeks? It happened in April 1975 with the remarkable Monsanto April 60 option. During the week of April 7, 1975 that option touched 1/4 ($25), while the stock traded as low as 54 3/4. With only three weeks left until expiration on Monday, April 28, there was little hope that Monsanto could rise more than 5 1/4 points, or 9.6 percent, to close above 60 to make the option profitable.

Out To Lunch

However, Monsanto made the spectacular move in that three-week time period, rising 25 percent to 68 5/8—a nice move for the common stock trader. But in reality, the stock trader was out to lunch while the option speculator was having a feast! The option which sold for 1/4 three weeks prior rose to 8 3/4 during the week of April 21. An option speculator with 40 options at 1/4 (a $1000 investment) could have possibly sold at 8 3/4 for a delicious profit of $34,000, or 3400 percent. Not bad for three weeks work.

More Feast

From October 1974 to April 1975 the Dow Jones Industrial Average rose 200 points, or 35 percent. The CBOE (Chicago Board Options Exchange) was trading 312 marketable call options on 32 underlying securities with expirations in October 1974, January 1975, and April 1975. The July 1975 options had not yet started trading. In that six-month time period 31 of the 32 underlying stocks advanced in value. There were 84 April 1975 options available. Fifty-nine of those options (70 percent) rose substantially in value. Three options rose over 1000 percent. Twelve rose over 500 percent, and 46, or more than one-half, rose over 100 percent. Another thirteen options rose up to 100 percent, while 24 declined in value and one remained unchanged.

If one were able to purchase equal dollar amounts of each of the 84 April options at the October 4, 1974 closing prices and sold these options at the April 11, 1975 closing prices, he would have done well indeed! If he had invested $10,000 equally among all 84 April options, his holdings would have tripled to $30,000 for a 200 percent return on his original $10,000 speculation. We certainly do not mean to advise anyone to speculate in this manner. Methodical and logical methods for purchasing options are developed in later chapters. If one were to purchase blindly as indicated above, one would almost certainly lose all his money over a period of time.

Famine

The feast referred to above came only after a great famine. In the first year and a half of operation of the Chicago Board Options Exchange, April 1973 to October 1974, the stock market was in a general decline. The Dow Jones Industrial Average dropped 30 percent from about 925 to 650. In this time period, 38 percent of the options purchased expired worthless. In addition, about 57 percent of the options bought were sold before the expiration date. Many of these were sold at losses to the buyer. Only three percent of the options purchased in this time period were exercised.

LOSE YOUR TOTAL INVESTMENT QUICKLY

Remember what we said in an earlier chapter about trying to buck a market trend. In a general market decline, stay out of the market. What happened to those poor souls who tried to beat a down market? Take the bull (with some bucks) on McDonalds (MCD), for example. He had plenty of "good" reasons to buy. He and his kids loved "Big Macs" and their vanilla shakes. And, "People," he would proudly proclaim, "will always have a dollar to buy a meal at McDonalds (and get some change back)—even in a recession." But the old Big Mac went from 61¼ on June 14, 1974 to 47⅞ on June 28, 1974—a disastrous two-week slide certain to give the option buyers indigestion. The Big Mac stock decline was 22 percent, but this drop was miniscule in comparison to the drubbing the MCD July 60 option took. It lost all but 3 percent of its value, dropping from 3⅞ to a paltry ⅛. Don't

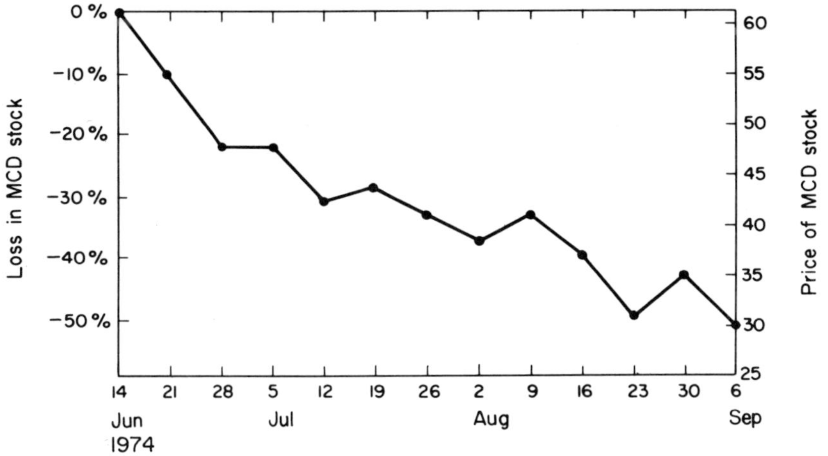

Figure 11–1. ***Percentage loss in McDonalds stock from June 14, 1974 to September 6, 1974.***

despair completely, though. The MCD October 60 option did considerably better than the July 60. It retained seven times the value that the July 60 retained. It retained 21 percent of its original value, dropping only 79 percent in two weeks! It dropped from 7 to 1½. Those were stout-hearted men with cast iron stomachs who played that disastrous market.

Figure 11–1 shows the weekly price fluctuation in McDonalds Corporation common stock in the twelve-week period from June 14, 1974 to September 6, 1974. On September 6, 1974 MCD closed at 30¼, a drop of nearly 51 percent from its twelve-week earlier level of 61¼. Figure 11–2 shows how the July and October 60 options behaved in the same time period. The July 60 option had expired worthless, but again the October 60 option outperformed the July option substantially. The $700 our bull paid for that option back on June 14 could now be sold in a closing transaction. With the proceeds he received from that transaction, he could go out and celebrate. He would have to be frugal, though, because he would have only enough money to buy a case of cheap beer. But that's better than having bought the July 60 option. In that instance he would need a case of whiskey but couldn't afford a drop.

MULTIPLY YOUR MONEY JUST AS FAST

If you were not the fainthearted type and had more dollars (than sense), you might have been fortunate enough to buy options on McDonalds on

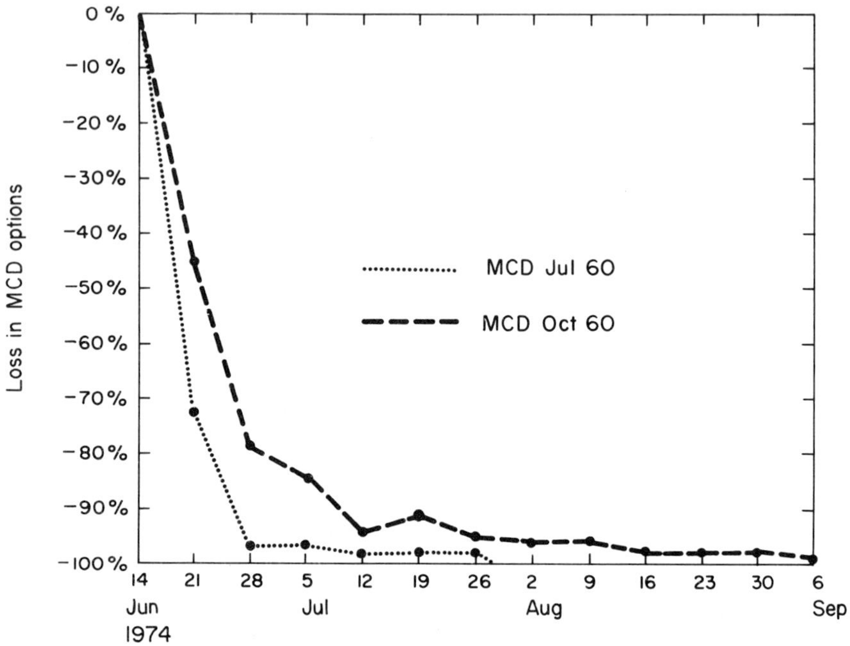

Figure 11–2. ***Percentage loss in McDonalds options from June 14, 1974 to September 6, 1974.***

January 31, 1975 when MCD closed at 34¼. The April options on MCD, with only 12 weeks left until expiration, rose dramatically as the stock increased 16 percent over the next two weeks. The July 35 option rose by nearly a factor of two. The April 35 option went up by a factor of 2.4. The speculator who purchased the April 40 option was happiest. His stake tripled in two weeks' time.

Figure 11–3 shows the weekly price fluctuations in McDonalds Corporation common stock for a twelve-week period starting with closing prices on January 31, 1975 to April 25, 1975, the Friday prior to the Monday expiration date of the April options. On April 25 MCD closed at 53⅛, an increase of 55 percent over its twelve-week earlier price of 34¼. Figure 11–4 shows how the April 35, April 40, and July 35 options behaved in the same time period.

Over this longer time frame the person who purchased the July 35 option was very pleased. His investment had gone up by a factor of 4.24 from 4½ to 18. The person who purchased the April 35 option watched his stake increase by a factor of 6.17 from 2⅞ to 17¾. But the person who bought the April 40 option, because of his good fortune, ceased to call himself a speculator and began to consider himself a brilliant investor. (He also began to refer to his original *stake* as an *investment*.) His "investment" went up nearly a factor of 10. He had bought 10 of the April 40 options for 1⅜ and sold them all for 13¼. He bought a case of whiskey for the other two unfortunate investors and almost had enough left over to buy himself a Mercedes 450 SL.

A HALF-BLIND STRATEGY

In the first example previously presented we showed that you could lose all your money very quickly if you happened to buy options at an inopportune time. We next showed that you could make an incredible gain if you purchased at a better time. Proper timing is often a matter of chance. It is interesting to investigate what the results would be if we employed an option buying strategy through a market cycle on McDonalds Corporation.

McDonalds went from 54½ in May 1974 to 21¼ in October 1974. By May 1975 it had rebounded to 54. The fact that the stock price went

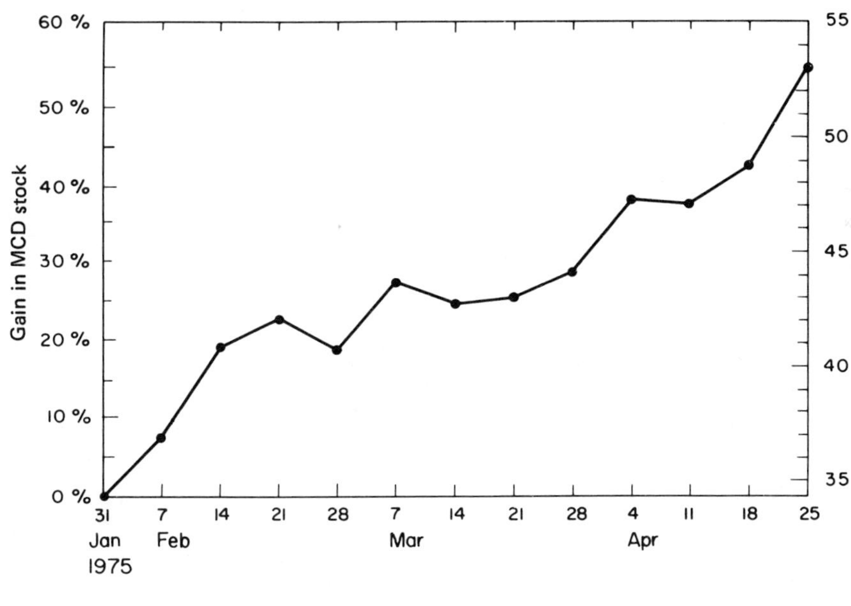

Figure 11–3. ***Percentage gain in McDonalds stock from January 31, 1975 to April 25, 1975.***

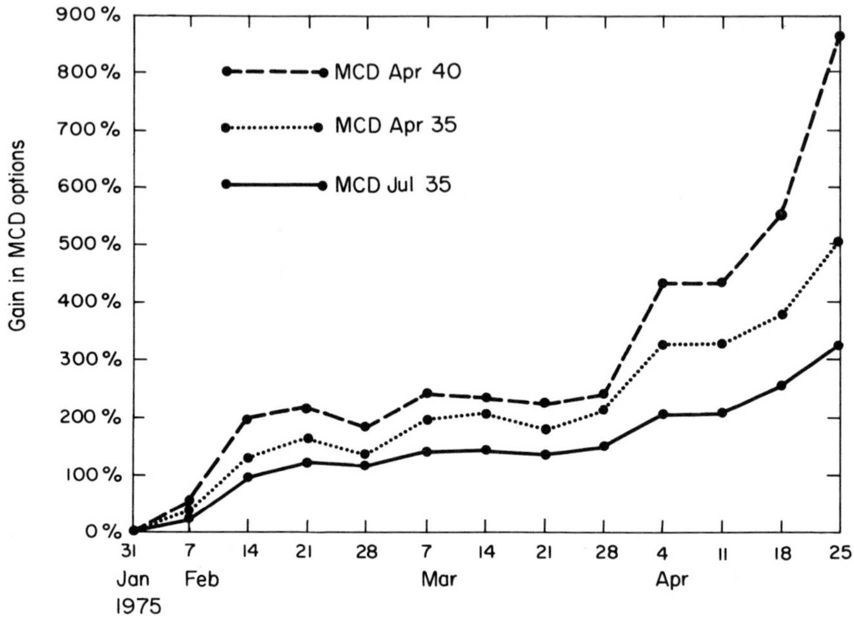

Figure 11–4. ***Percentage gain in McDonalds options from January 31, 1975 to April 25, 1975.***

through a complete cycle in exactly one year's time lends itself to an interesting analysis.

Let's assume that at that time you had about $5000 that you were willing to speculate with for a year's time. Since you didn't want to take the risk of losing all that money on your first transaction, you planned to invest about $1250 at three-month intervals. If you happened to lose most of your $1250 on your first transaction, you would then take another $1250 from your pot in order to play round two for the next three months.

We shall call this strategy the "half-blind strategy," because we are not using any meaningful criteria to select when to buy and sell the option and at what price. The half-blind strategy has two steps:

1 / *Buy the option that expires in the middle month. For example, if July, October, and January options are being traded, buy the October option.*

2 / *Buy the option whose striking price is just above the price of the stock. If there is no such option, buy the option whose striking price is just below the price of the stock.*

These steps are made to apply only to this example. Do not confuse them with the rules previously given.

We shall begin the game on May 31, 1974, when July, October, and January options were being traded on McDonalds. We start by purchasing the middle expiration month (October) option. Table 11–1 outlines the strategy to be employed for the market cycle. At the end of three months, we sell the October option and purchase the January option, whose striking price is just above the price of the stock. The result of employing this strategy with MCD is a gain of $514 after commissions. We lose money on the first two transactions (−$1235) and profit on the last two ($1749). The return on the average outlay of money for the year is about 26 percent. The detailed results of this strategy are given in Appendix A. We are not recommending this type of strategy. In a sustained stock decline lasting for more than one year the investor utilizing the half-blind strategy would lose most of his money. Unfortunately, most new option speculators use some type of half-blind approach.

IMPROVING YOUR ODDS TO WIN BIG

The trouble with the half-blind strategy is that we did not use any meaningful criteria in evaluating the option prices. We just purchased and sold options on a fixed day, paying no attention to whether or not the option was priced to our advantage. The crux of Part Two of this book is to show how you can determine whether or not an option is underpriced. If it is underpriced, it is more likely to be profitable to you, the buyer. By following the plan which is slowly developed, you will learn when to buy an option and at what price.

If the techniques to be developed in this book had been applied to McDonalds options from June 14, 1974 to June 13, 1975, a $4000 investment

Table 11–1 Half-blind Option Strategy

	Option Expiration Months			
Date	*Oct*	*Jan*	*Apr*	*Jul*
May 31, 1974	Buy			
Aug. 30, 1974	Sell	Buy		
Nov. 29, 1974		Sell	Buy	
Feb. 28, 1975			Sell	Buy
May 30, 1975				Sell

could have grown to an excess of $110,000 after commissions. That is a 2650 percent gain on a stock which on June 13, 1975 ended 16 percent below its closing price on June 14, 1974!

If you are filled with desire to learn the techniques involved in improving your odds to win big, you must prepare yourself to struggle through the remaining chapters. One reading will not be sufficient. You will have to study if you wish to become a professional. Remember, "Money is coined freedom and freedom is life."

12 | Factors Affecting Option Prices

This chapter is intended to give you something more than an intuitive feeling for determining the factors that affect option prices. The least it should do is to provide you with some concepts to consider in arriving at any conclusions. It lays the groundwork for identifying options that should be purchased, while leaving open for further consideration options which might be purchased.

DETERMINANT FACTORS OF OPTION PRICE

The primary intangible factor that determines option prices is the trading environment of a competitive marketplace. It is the classical fulfillment of the forces of supply and demand for options involving the underlying stock. During periods of *expected* rising stock market prices, there is increased interest in purchasing options because of the investment leverage they give the buyer. On the other hand, the owners of the underlying securities demand higher premiums so as not severely to limit their potential gains. The option prices are bid up until the period of rising expectations passes. At this point the premiums tend to decline.

There are four particular factors which are instrumental in restricting option prices within the bounds of a competitive trading environment. These are stock price, time left until expiration, stock volatility and dividend rate or yield of the underlying stock.

Stock Price

The relationship between the current market price of the stock and the striking price is the most important factor affecting option premiums. Let us assume that an investor pays a premium of $3 for an option whose striking price is 50 and whose market price is 50. If the stock rises ten points to 60, an investor wishing to buy the option at this point will pay a greater price for the option than the original investor who had only a hope that the stock would appreciate in value. The investor buying the option at the higher price may be another speculator or the writer of the option who wishes to nullify his obligation to sell his 100 shares at 50 by repurchasing an option of the same description that he originally sold.

Time

Normally, the more time remaining until expiration, the higher the premium will be, all else being equal. This is so simply because the more time that remains before the option expires represents additional time for the underlying stock to rise in price. An option can be thought of as having a time value that is a wasting asset in addition to any tangible value. The tangible value of an option is just the amount the stock price exceeds the striking price at any time. Options whose striking prices are above the price of the stock have no tangible value. They have only time value. As the expiration date approaches, time value declines and eventually becomes zero. The time value usually declines rapidly in the last few weeks prior to expiration.

Volatility

The volatility of the underlying stock affects the premium of the option. If the underlying stock is volatile and fluctuates a great deal, the option commands a higher premium. This is dictated by the demands of both the writer and buyer of the option. The writer of an option who owns the underlying stock wishes to obtain greater protection in the event of eroding stock prices and also wishes to participate more fully in the case of rising stock prices to compensate for his risk of holding a volatile stock. He accomplishes this by demanding a higher premium. On the other hand, the buyer is willing to pay the higher premium because the prospect of the underlying stock rising substantially within the expiration period is greater for a highly volatile stock.

Yield

The investor who wishes to realize a specified total return on his portfolio must write options that take into account not only the volatility of the stock but also the yield. The owner of stock who writes options in the listed markets receives all dividends as long as the option is outstanding. To assure himself of a specified return, he is willing to receive a smaller premium, since he receives the dividends. To realize the same return on stock whose yield is lower, but where all other factors are equal, the writer must demand a higher premium. If he is unable to get the higher premium, his total return is reduced.

In some option pricing theories the prevailing short-term interest rate is considered to be a factor in determining option prices. In reality, a very small change in the apparent volatility or yield of the stock weighs much more heavily in option price determination than a large change in short-term interest rates.

Figures 12–1 and 12–2 compare the option price determination factors discussed above. These are typical option premium curves. You can plot your own curves from the quotes in the newspaper. Tables 12–1 and 12–2 list the option prices from which Figs. 12–1 and 12–2 were derived. The distinguishing fact to note about the option premiums is the relationship between the striking price and stock price. If the striking price (Pst) is 45 and the stock is at 50, the premium will always be greater than 5 (the difference between

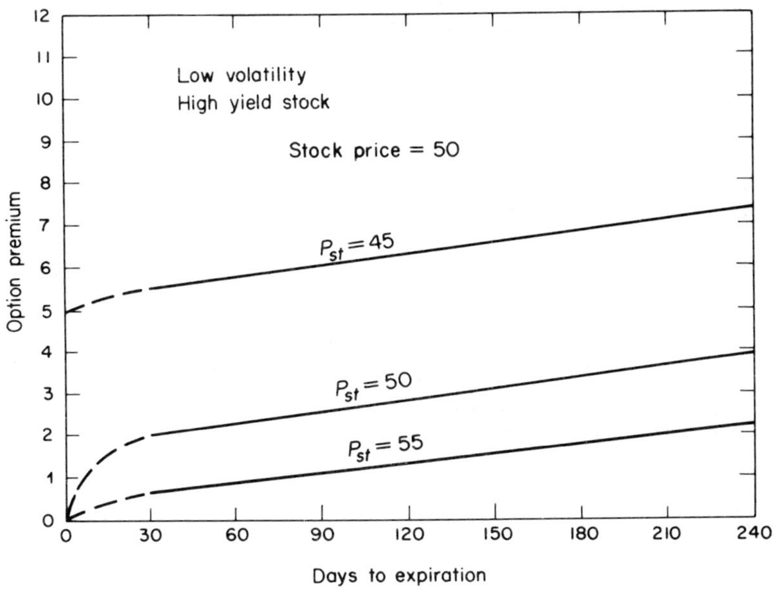

Figure 12–1. ***Typical option premiums on low-volatility, high-yield stock. Pst = striking price.***

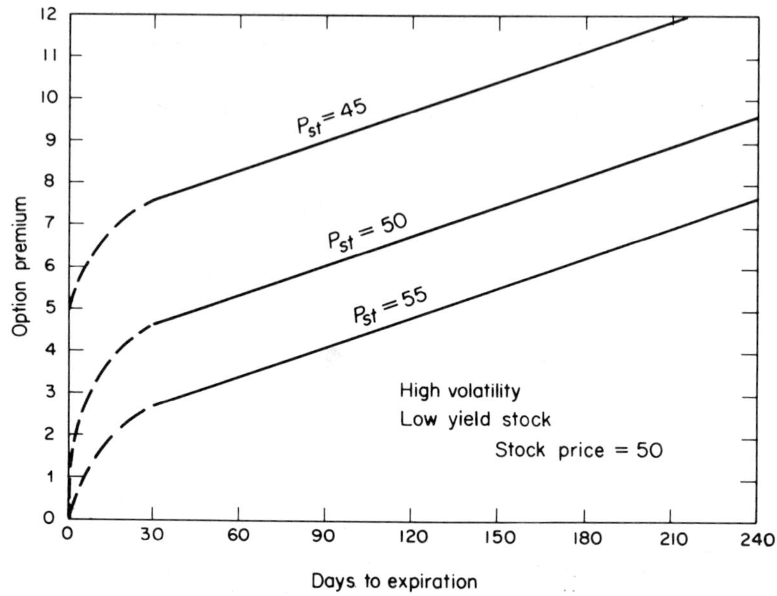

Figure 12–2. ***Typical option premiums on high-volatility, low-yield stock. Pst = striking price.***

50 and 45). Five is the tangible value of the option. Also note how the option prices increase with time left until expiration—the more time left to an option, the greater the time value portion of the premium. The option premiums on a low-volatility, high-yield stock are much lower than those on a high-volatility, low-yield stock.

The slopes of the option price lines of the high-volatility stocks are always greater than those of low-volatility stocks. This is so because in any

Table 12–1 Option Premiums for Low-volatility, High-yield Stock

Striking Price	*Expiration Month* Jan	Apr	Jul	*Stock Price*
45	5⅞	6½	7⅜	50
50	2¼	3	3⅞	50
55	⅞	1½	2⅛	50
Days to expiration	60	150	240	

Table 12–2 Option Premiums for High-volatility, Low-yield Stock

Striking	*Expiration Month*			*Stock*
Price	*Jan*	*Apr*	*Jul*	*Price*
45	8¼	10½	12⅝	50
50	5⅜	7½	9⅝	50
55	3⅜	5½	7¾	50
Days to expiration	60	150	240	

given time period a high-volatility stock can advance more than a low-volatility stock.

Which Month To Buy

Normally, in the last few weeks in the life of an option there is a rapid drop off in its price. (See Figs. 12–1 and 12–2.) This is true if the price of the underlying stock does not move appreciably. If you do not wish to lose money rapidly, then do not buy options that have one or two months left until expiration. A general rule to follow is to buy options with three or more months left until expiration. Of course, there are exceptions to this general rule. There are times when it is desirable to buy options with only a month or two left until expiration. Remember the Monsanto option that rose 3400 percent in its last three weeks? Until you become more knowledgeable and sophisticated, it is best not to purchase options of short duration.

In Part One a rule was stated concerning which month option to buy.

RULE / Always buy the middle month option unless you have a good reason to buy the near or far month.

BREAKEVEN PREMIUM

The breakeven premium, or intrinsic premium, is an interesting concept to explore before we get into which striking price option to buy. This premium is defined as the striking price minus the stock price plus the option price. The breakeven premium is the amount (excluding commissions) that a stock has to go up by expiration for the buyer of the option to break even. Suppose that we purchased an option for 3 when the stock price was 45 and the striking price was 50. If the stock were at 53 at expiration, the option would be worth 3, exactly what we paid for it. The stock had to rise 8 points, the intrinsic premium, for us to break even.

Figures 12–3 and 12–4 show typical option *intrinsic* premiums of the option premiums shown in Figs. 12–1 and 12–2. Tables 12–3 and 12–4 list the option *intrinsic* premiums of the option premiums listed in Tables 12–1 and 12–2. Comparison between the tables shows that a particular option with a high premium has a low breakeven premium. An option with a low premium has a high breakeven premium.

An "in-the-money" option whose striking price is below the stock price has a high premium and a low breakeven premium. It represents an option that requires more capital (high premium) but has less risk (low breakeven premium). It has less risk, because the stock needs only to rise an amount equal to the intrinsic premium to recoup the initial investment by expiration. An "out-of-the-money" option whose striking price is above the stock price has a low premium and a high breakeven premium. In order for one to break even on the investment, the stock has to rise an amount equal to the intrinsic premium by expiration. Purchasing this option requires less capital but has greater risk.

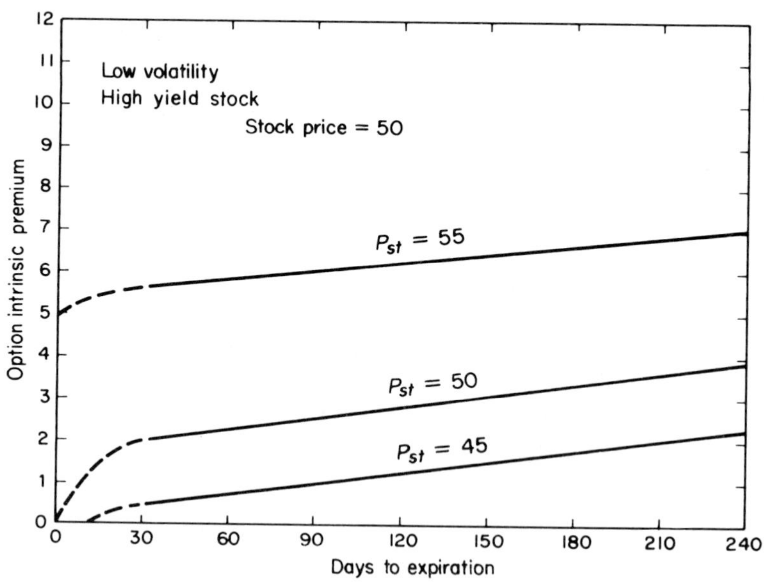

Figure 12–3. ***Typical option intrinsic premiums on low-volatility, high-yield stock. Pst = striking price.***

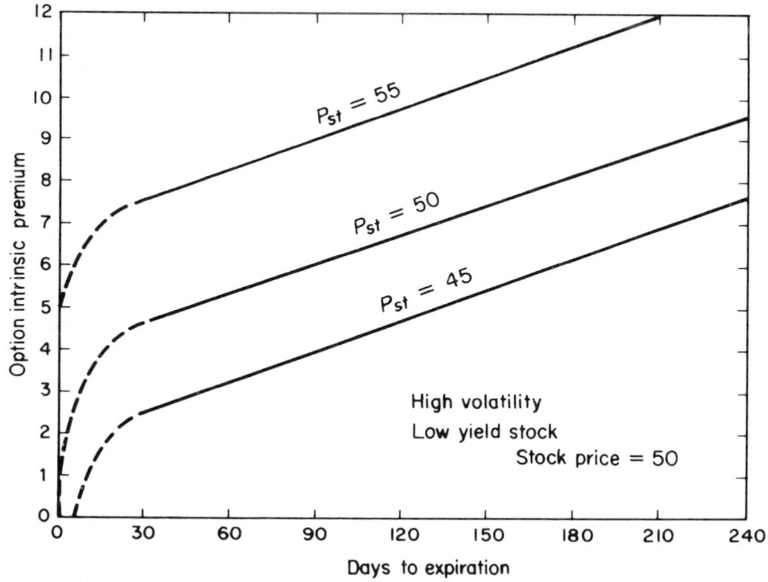

Figure 12–4. ***Typical option* intrinsic *premiums on high-volatility, low-yield stock. Pst = striking price.***

WHICH STRIKING PRICE TO BUY

If an option is trading deep in the money with the price of the stock substantially above the striking price, the premium one pays for the option is just a little bit more than the difference between the stock price and the striking price. There is practically a point-for-point correlation between the stock price and the option price. If the stock goes up or down one point, the option will also go up or down one point.

Table 12–3 Option *Intrinsic* Premiums for Low-volatility, High-yield Stock

Striking Price	*Expiration Month* *Jan*	*Apr*	*Jul*	*Stock Price*
45	⅞	1½	2⅜	50
50	2¼	3	3⅞	50
55	5⅞	6½	7⅛	50
Days to expiration	60	150	240	

Table 12–4 Option *Intrinsic* Premiums for High-volatility, Low-yield Stock

Striking Price	*Expiration Month*			*Stock*
	Jan	*Apr*	*Jul*	*Price*
45	3¼	5½	7⅝	50
50	5⅜	7½	9⅝	50
55	8⅜	10½	12¾	50
Days to expiration	60	150	240	

If an option is trading out of the money with the striking price substantially above the price of the stock, one pays a small premium. The correlation between the stock price and the option price is not point-for-point. The stock can advance or decline by five points and the option may advance or decline by one-half point or less.

These aspects of option prices as a function of underlying stock prices are illustrated in Fig. 12–5 for various striking prices. The figure shows how a particular option would change in price if the underlying stock moved from one price to another much prior to expiration. Table 12–5 is structured from data in Fig. 12–5.

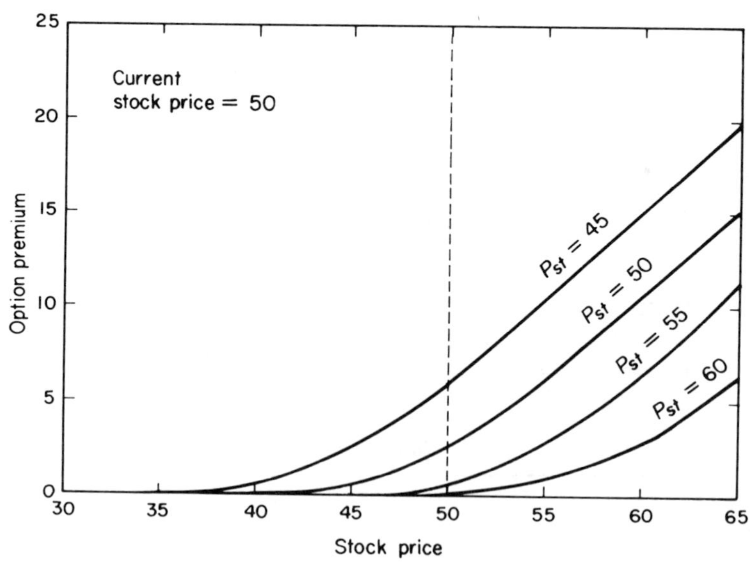

Figure 12–5. ***Option premiums as function of stock prices for various striking prices, Pst.***

In order to demonstrate which striking price option represents the best buy, let us look at what happens if the stock suddenly advances or declines by 5 points from 50. We assume that we bought each of the four options when the stock was at 50. Table 12–5 lists the option prices for each striking price at stock prices of 45, 50, and 55. Table 12–6 shows the profits and losses sustained. The best performance was experienced by the option whose striking price was 55. It gained 200 percent on the advance and lost 57 percent on the decline, for a 48 percent average gain.

Table 12–5 Option Prices at Various Stock and Striking Prices Much Prior to Expiration

Stock Price	*Striking Price*			
	45	*50*	*55*	*60*
45	2⅛	¾	⅜	3/16
50	6	2⅜	⅞	½
55	10⅝	6¼	2⅝	1

In this case the best option to buy was the option whose striking price was just above the price of the stock. It is generally true that options with striking prices just above the stock price can provide the greatest expected return to the buyer if they are purchased when they are undervalued. However, these options are usually the ones that are overvalued. We estimate that, on the average, a smaller percentage of the options with striking prices just above the price of the stock are undervalued during a normal market. Care must be taken in selecting an option that is underpriced. Chapter 16 tells you how to determine when an option is priced right for purchase.

Table 12–6 Option Profit and Losses for a Sudden Advance or Decline in Stock Price

Stock Price	*Striking Price*			
	45	*50*	*55*	*60*
45	−65%	−68%	−57%	−63%
50	0	0	0	0
55	+77	+163	+200	+50
Average gain	4%	32%	48%	−4%

This information leads to a reaffirmation of the rule which was previously stated in Part One:

RULE / Always buy an undervalued option whose striking price is just above the price of the stock unless you have good reason to purchase an option with a lower or higher striking price.

In general, avoid purchasing options that are deep in the money, i.e., options whose striking prices are 15 or 20 percent below the stock price. These options cost more than higher striking price options, and you are tying up a lot of capital for smaller expected returns. This is not a strict rule. There are times when these are also undervalued in relationship to the volatility of the underlying stock and represent a good purchase.

Another generality is to avoid purchasing options whose striking prices are 20 percent or more above the price of the stock. These options have low premiums and are attractive to the buyer because they are so cheap. It takes a large upward move in the price of the underlying stock to move these options up slightly. For example, look at the option whose striking price is 60 in Table 12–5. When the stock price is 50, the option is priced at ½. The stock has to go up five points to 55 for the option to go up one-half point to 1. This does not seem bad, but the 55 striking price option tripled from ⅞ to 2⅝.

RULE / Do not purchase an option whose striking price is 15 to 20 percent (or more) above the price of the stock unless you have good reason to do so.

Part of the basis for formulating the rules mentioned above for purchasing options has to do with the consideration of leverage, which is discussed in the following chapter.

13 | Leverage: "Five Will Get You Twenty-Five or Lose You Five"

Options have leverage, and this is one of the main reasons for buying them. Leverage is the multiplier of your investment. Leverage is when you speculate with one dollar and get back either $10.00 or a dime. If a stock goes up 1 percent and the option goes up 10 percent, the leverage is 10. Leverage is defined as the percentage change in option price for each percentage change in stock price. You invest $5 in an option and the leverage is 10. If the stock advances 40 percent, your option will go up 400 percent to 25. If the leverage works against you and the stock declines 40 percent, your loss is limited to the $5 you invested. Thus, "Five will get you twenty-five or lose you five."

The sporting folks who purchase options and plan to hold these until expiration (something we don't recommend) want the largest level of leverage compatible with the least risk. Leverage is the multiplier by which their investment will grow for each percent that the stock closes above the striking price. The risk they take is the amount that the stock has to move in order to recapture their breakeven investment. With this, as with most things, "You don't get something for nothing." Normally the higher leverage you want, the greater risk you must take.

LEVERAGE AT EXPIRATION

Options have leverage that changes continuously while they are trading. At expiration of the option the leverage is fixed. At expiration, the leverage is zero for all stock prices up to the striking price. This means that if a stock closes at or below its striking price at expiration, you lose your investment.

If the stock closes above the striking price, the leverage is a fixed positive value. We shall see that *leverage at expiration* is equal to the *stock price divided by the option price.*

In order to determine the leverage at expiration, we must learn how to calculate our profits and losses over a wide price fluctuation of the common stock. We shall consider three cases: (1) striking price equals stock price, (2) striking price below stock price, and (3) striking price above stock price.

Striking Price Equals Stock Price

Let's consider an option with a striking price of 50 selling at 2½. The stock is also selling at 50. If the stock closes at 50 or below at expiration, the option is worthless, and we lose 100 percent of our investment. In order for us to break even, the stock has to close at 52½, a 5 percent gain, making the option worth what we paid for it, 2½. If the stock closes at 55, a 10 percent gain in stock price, the option will be worth 5, the difference between the stock price of 55 and striking price of 50. This is a 100 percent gain in the option price. Figure 13–1 shows the value of the option at expiration as a function of the stock price. Figure 13–2 shows the percentage profit and loss

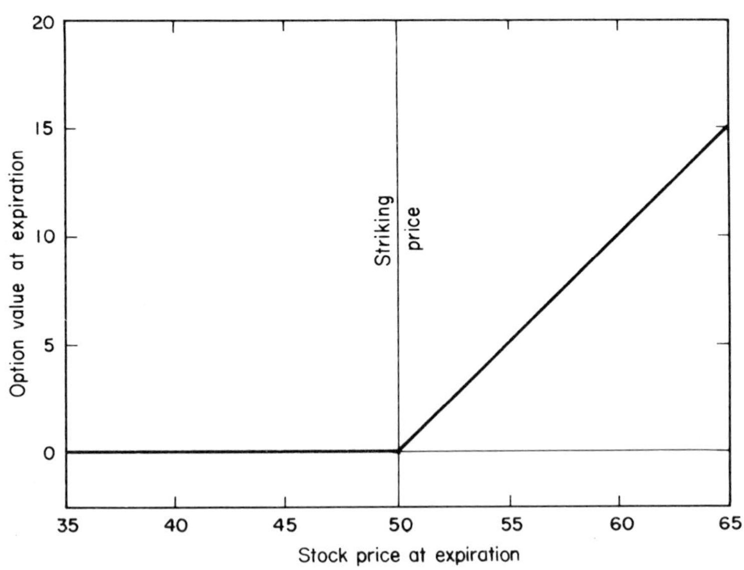

Figure 13–1. ***Option value at expiration as function of stock price at expiration. Striking price equals 50.***

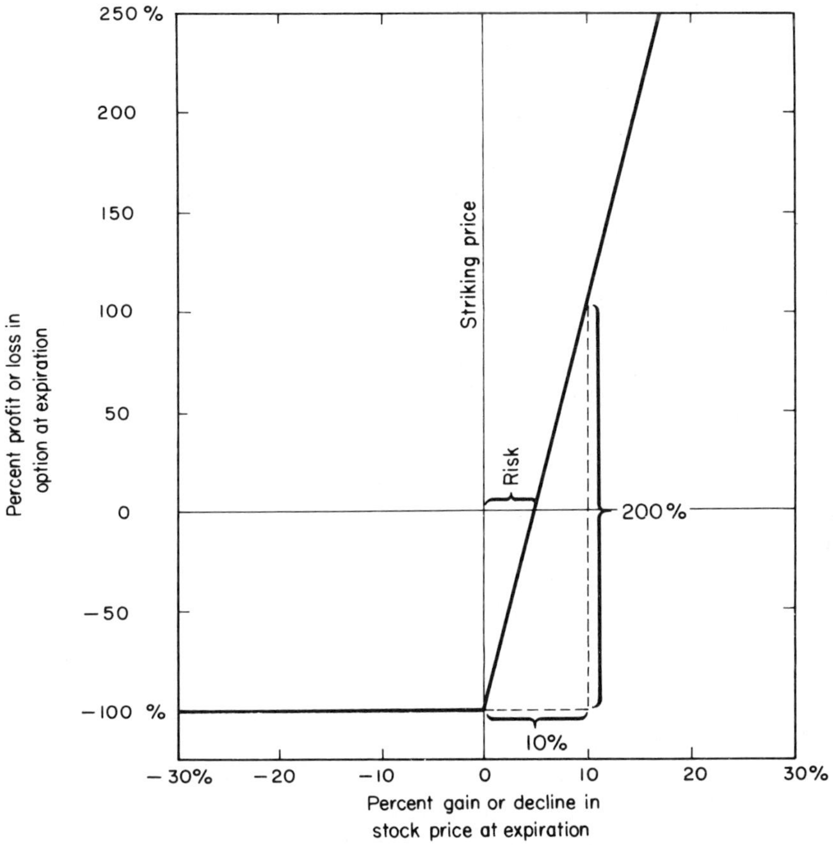

Figure 13–2. ***Profit and loss in option as function of gain or decline in stock. Original price: option, 2½; stock, 50.***

in the option as a function of the percentage gain or decline in stock price. If the stock goes up 10 percent in value, the option value changes by 200 percent. It went from −100 percent to +100 percent. The leverage is 20 (200 percent divided by 10 percent). We shall consider two more examples in order to demonstrate how leverage is related to risk.

Striking Price Below Stock Price

An option with a striking price of 45 has a premium of 6 while the stock is trading at 50. If the stock closes at 45 or below at expiration, the option expires worthless for a 100 percent loss. If the stock closes at 50 at expiration, the option will have a value of 5, a one-point, or a 16⅔ percent loss. If the stock closes at 55, the option will be worth 10, a 66⅔ percent gain. In order to calculate the leverage, we compare how much the option changes in value to how much the stock changes in value.

When the stock price changes from 50 to 55, an increase of 10 percent, the option value changes from a 16⅔ percent loss to a 66⅔ percent gain. This was a net change of 83⅓ percent in the price of the option, which took place on a 10 percent change in the price of the stock. The leverage in this case is 8⅓. The leverage is smaller than in the case where the striking price equaled the stock price; however, the risk was also less. In order for one to break even the stock had to rise only an amount equal to the breakeven premium. The breakeven premium is the striking price (45) minus the stock price (50) plus the option premium (6), which equals 1. The stock had to advance only one point or 2 percent in order for one to break even on the 8⅓ leveraged option. In the previous case, with the option leveraged at 20, the stock had to advance 5 percent in order to break even.

Striking Price Above Stock Price

An option with a striking price of 55 is selling with a premium of 1 while the stock is trading at 50 prior to expiration. If the stock closes at 55 or below at expiration, the option is worthless. In order for us to break even, the stock must close at 56, making the option worth its original value of 1. At 55 we had a 100 percent loss. A one-point move to 56 allows us to pick up that 100 percent loss. For each one-point move of the stock above 55, we make an additional 100 percent on the option. A one-point move is equivalent to a 2 percent change in the stock price at 50. For each 2 percent increase in stock price we experience a 100 percent gain in option price. The leverage in this case is 50. As we said earlier, you don't get high leverage without giving up something in return. In order for us to break even, the stock must rise from 50 to 56, a 12 percent increase.

Figure 13–3 shows the option profits and losses as a function of the percentage change in stock price from its original value of 50. For the low striking price option the leverage was 8⅓, while the stock had to advance only 2 percent for us to break even. When the striking price equaled the original price of the stock we had a leverage of 20, but the stock had to go 5 percent for us to break even. When the striking price exceeded the original price of the stock, the leverage was 50. However, the stock had to advance 12 percent for us just to break even.

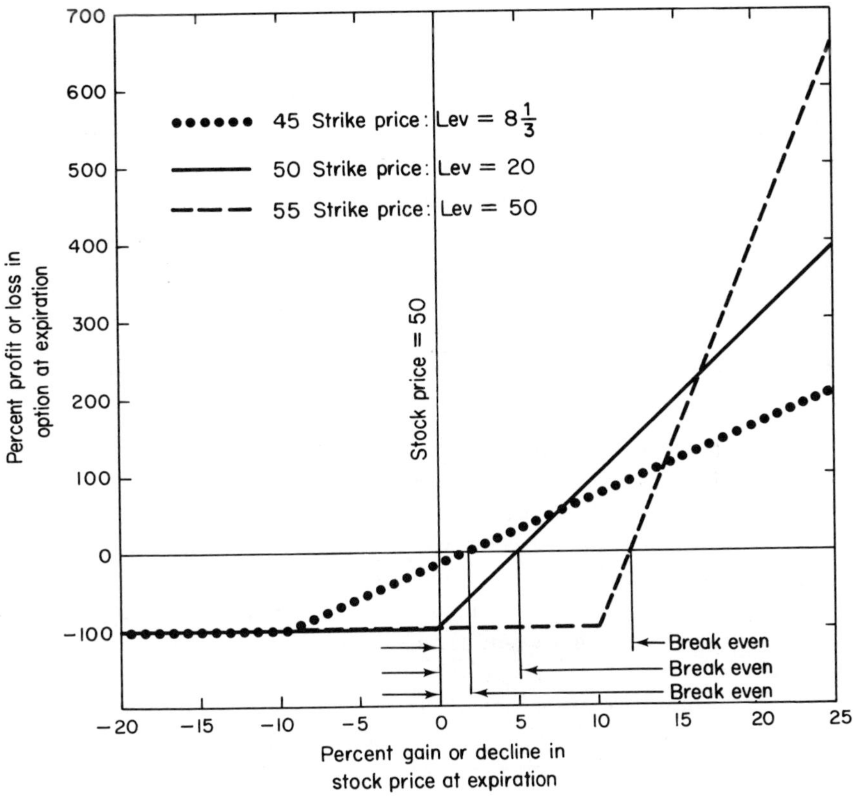

Figure 13–3. ***Profits and losses for various striking price options as function of stock price at expiration.***

The pattern is clear: the higher leverage you seek, the greater risk you must take. It is difficult to say which is the best option to buy. You will have to decide this for yourself. You have to find the fine balance between reward and the risk you are willing to take, which lies within yourself.

Leverage Factor Calculation

To simplify your work, it turns out that the leverage factor can be obtained by dividing the stock price by the option price. For the 45, 50, and 55 striking price options the premiums were 6, 2½, and 1, respectively. Divide the stock price of 50 by the option premiums and you get 8⅓, 20, and 50—the three leverage factors.

Risk Factor Calculation

In order to get the risk factor, we must first determine the breakeven premium. Remember, this is just the striking price minus the stock price plus the option premium. The breakeven premiums for the 45, 50, and 55 striking price options were 1, 2½, and 6, respectively. Divide the breakeven premium by the stock price at 50, and you get 2, 5, and 12 percent—the three risk factors.

Risk/Leverage Factor Calculation

Now, simply divide the risk factor by the leverage factor for each respective option to get the risk/leverage factor. In Table 13–1 all three options were essentially equal buys, since they all had comparable risk/leverage factors. In this case the selection would be simplified by how much money you had to invest to buy these options. The 45 striking price option cost $600, while the 50 striking price option cost $250, and the 55 striking price option cost $100. The last option would tie up the least capital and might be chosen for this reason.

If you purchase an option whose striking price is much lower than the stock price, your risk to break even is lower. If you purchase an option whose striking price is much higher than the stock price, your risk for breaking even is very high, but your leverage at expiration is also higher.

RULE / Buy options with a low risk/leverage factor.

Table 13–1 Leverage, Risk and Risk/Leverage Factors

Striking Price	*Leverage*	*Risk*	*Risk/Leverage*
45	8⅓	2% = 0.02	0.0024
50	20	5% = 0.05	0.0025
55	50	12% = 0.12	0.0024

Appendix B gives a mathematically simple way for determining the risk/leverage (R/L) factor. It presents a formula that enables you to calculate the R/L factor for an option in just a few moments.

Normally the R/L factor is less for options with less time to expiration. This might lead some people to think that they should purchase options with the shortest periods to expiration. This should not be done. Be reminded of how the time value of an option rapidly decreases just prior to expiration. (See Figs. 12–1 and 12–2.)

The R/L factor is just another tool, which is constructed to help you see what is involved when one is selecting an option for purchase, namely, risk and leverage. It is a calculation that is based on holding the option until expiration. As stated earlier, we do not want to hold options until expiration unless we have good reason to do so. Do not purchase options using the R/L factor unless you carefully read and understand Appendix B and Chapter 16.

LEVERAGE PRIOR TO EXPIRATION

The leverage prior to expiration is a more difficult concept to grasp. Leverage still is the percentage change in option price for each percentage change in stock price. The leverage was calculated for low-, medium-, and high-volatility stocks; the results are shown in Fig. 13–4. The main feature to note in this figure is that low-volatility stocks have a higher leverage than high-volatility stocks! This may come as a surprise to most of us, but it will be explained in an example given later.

The other feature to note is that the maxima of the curves occur at stock prices below the striking prices. This reconfirms the rule concerning which striking price options to buy. If you want maximum leverage, purchase the option whose striking price is just above the price of the stock. By obeying this rule we find that leverage works for us in a positive way. Let us illustrate with an example. Suppose that we purchase an option with a striking price of 50 on medium-volatility stock when the price of the stock is 45. The leverage is about 7 (see Fig. 13–4). If the stock declines in price, the leverage is reduced. This means that a lower leverage is working against us. As the stock increases in value, the leverage also increases up to a certain point, and a higher leverage is working for us.

RULE / Purchase options whose striking price is just above the price of the stock unless you have good reason to do otherwise.

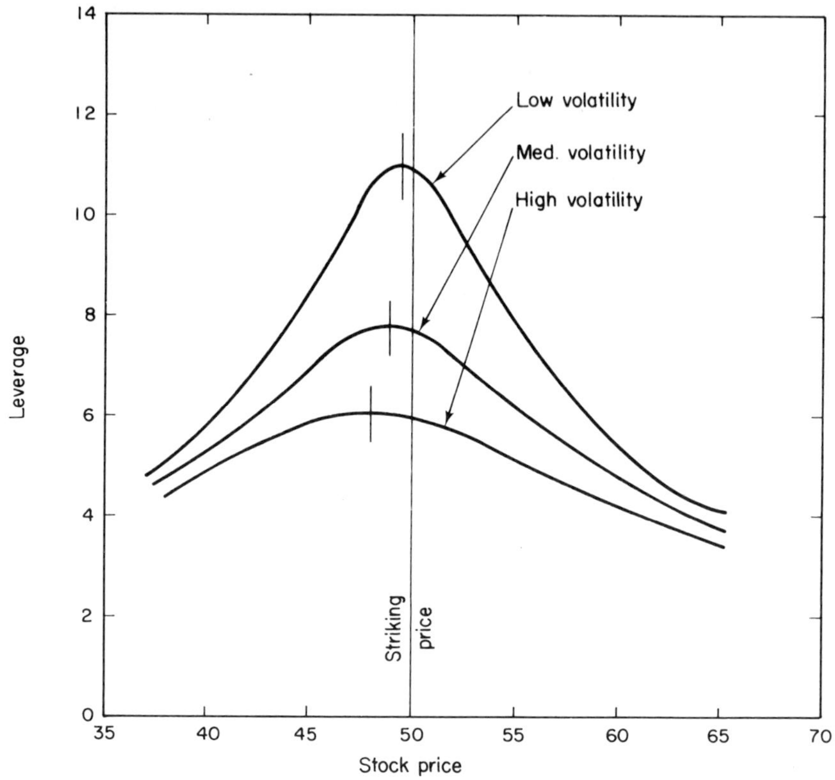

Figure 13–4. ***Leverage as a function of stock price for various volatilities.***

LEVERAGE AND VOLATILITY

Let us now present an example which illustrates why low-volatility stocks have a higher leverage than high-volatility stocks. Let us compare options of a high- and a low-volatility stock.

XYZ Corporation, a nonvolatile common stock, is trading at 50. The October option is selling at 2. XYZ makes a move to 55, and the October 50 option goes to 6. XYZ advances 10 percent, but the option advances 200 percent. That is a leverage of 20.

ABC Corporation, a volatile common stock, is also trading at 50. Its October 50 option is selling at 4. The option premium is higher for a volatile stock, because it has a better chance of advancing substantially in price. ABC makes a 10 percent move to 55, and the October 50 option goes to 8. This option advances 100 percent for a leverage of 10.

Why is it that the nonvolatile stock option had leverage of 20 while the volatile stock had a smaller leverage of 10? The answer is simply that XYZ has a much smaller chance of advancing 10 percent than ABC has.

The next chapter deals with volatility and variability, which are synonymous. It explains how to measure them and how to use them to produce greater profits.

14 | Variability: A Price Seesaw

Variability and volatility are words that are often used interchangeably when one is referring to fluctuations in stock prices. They are simply a measure of the degree to which a stock has advanced or declined over fixed time intervals in the past. A highly variable stock is one that has taken sharp advances or declines in previous time periods. Stocks that have a particular variability tend to maintain a similar level of variability in the future. This assumption is basic to enabling us to predict the probabilistic future price of a stock.

HOW HIGH OR LOW? YOU CAN ONLY ALMOST KNOW!

The science of statistics is used in a very profound way in arriving at valuations for options. Common stocks have a historical record of advances and declines. Chartists rely heavily on this information in an attempt to predict whether a stock or the market will advance or decline in the future. Statisticians are less bold in their predictions. They are inclined to answer as did J. P. Morgan, the great financier of the nineteenth century, when asked what the stock market would do: "It will fluctuate." To that degree the statisticians are in agreement with the great J. P. Using statistics and probability theory, they calculate how much a stock or the market is expected to fluctuate.* They will not say in which direction it will fluctuate, since the probabilities are equal that it will move either way. They can give you probabilities of how high or low a stock will go. But in which direction?—you can only almost know!

*Probability is used as the best estimate of what may happen in the future if past price fluctuations are maintained. A plan based on probabilities assumes that stock market prices are random variables and therefore disregards the fundamental approach.

THE BELL-SHAPED CURVE

The bell-shaped curve, Fig. 14–1, is used to describe many random statistical phenomena. The one most familiar to readers is the description of IQ, or intelligence quotient. The area under the curve represents all people tested. Since the curve is symmetric around 100, half the people in the population have IQ's less than 100 and half have IQ's over 100.

If we selected a person at random out of a crowd, there would be a 50–50 chance that he would have an IQ above or below 100. If we randomly tested 10,000 people, approximately 5000 would have IQ's below 100. What fraction of people have an IQ over 130? It is proportional to the relative area under the curve beyond 130. As you can see, it is very small.

Stock prices are another random phenomenon that can be described by the bell-shaped curve (Fig. 14–1). In a random market a stock which closed at 100 has a 50–50 chance of advancing or declining from its closing price of 100. The probability that a stock will close above a certain price at the end of a specified time period is proportional to the area under the curve beyond that price. Figure 14–2 shows the probability that a stock will end at a particular price, having started at 100. The shaded area, representing 25 percent of the total area under the curve, is beyond the price of 110. Thus, there is a 25 percent chance that the stock will close above 110. The probability that it will close below 110 is 75 percent.

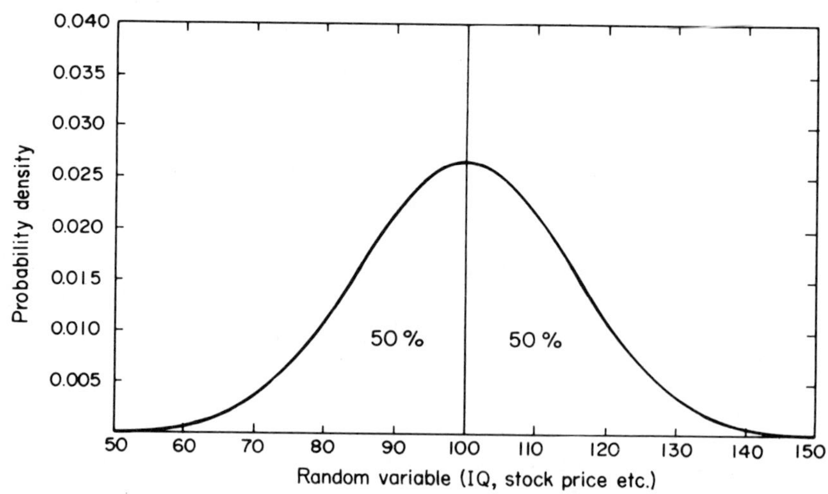

Figure 14–1. ***The bell-shaped curve.***

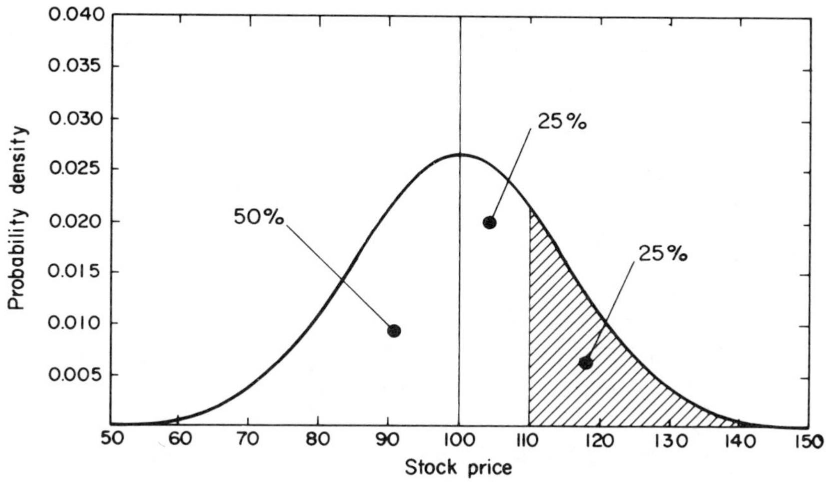

Figure 14–2. ***Probability of stock's ending at a particular price, starting from 100.***

*Probability Of Advance**

Figure 14–3, which resembles a reversed, stretched-out "S," gives the probability that a stock will close above a particular price. It measures the area under the curve of Fig. 14–2 beyond the particular price listed on the horizontal axis. It gives the probability that a stock will end up beyond that price. For example, there is a 75 percent chance that the stock will end up beyond 90; a 50 percent chance that it will end up beyond 100, and a 25 percent chance that it will end up beyond 110.

THE VARIABILITY COMPRESSOR: TIME REDUCTION

We know that an option that has more time left until expiration is more valuable simply because the underlying stock has greater time to appreciate in value. As the time to expiration diminishes, the probability that a stock will advance beyond a particular price also diminishes. Figure 14–4 shows

*The probability of advance is known in statistics as the complementary cumulative normal density function.

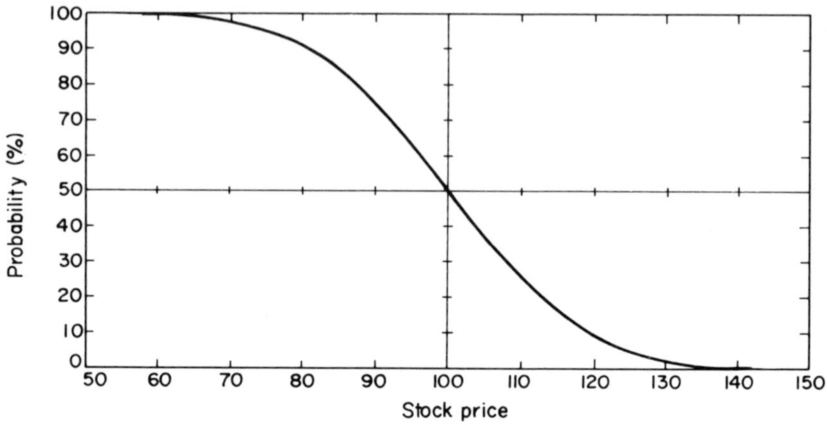

Figure 14–3. ***Probability that a stock will close above a particular price.***

the bell-shaped curves of probabilities for a particular stock for three time periods: nine, six, and three months. The shaded area represents 25 percent of the area under the curve. The stock has a 25 percent chance to close in this area by the end of the stated time period. As time diminishes, the curves become compressed. For a three-month period, the price beyond which the stock has a 25 percent chance to advance is less than that for longer periods. The shorter the time period, the smaller is the expected advance in price. The figure shows that in nine months there is a 25 percent chance that the stock will advance beyond 117½; in six months, beyond 114; and in three months, beyond 110.

The variability is a measure of the breadth of the curves. It decreases with decreasing time left until expiration. The chance is less that a stock will advance beyond a certain value if it is given less time to do so. Options with less time left until expiration cost less, since the underlying stock has less time to advance in price.

VARIABILITY: A STATISTICAL DEFINITION

The specific variability of a stock is a measure of the range within which a stock will close at the termination of a specific period of time. By definition, the probability is 68 percent that it will close within its variability range. If a stock is trading at 50 and has an *annual* price variability of 10

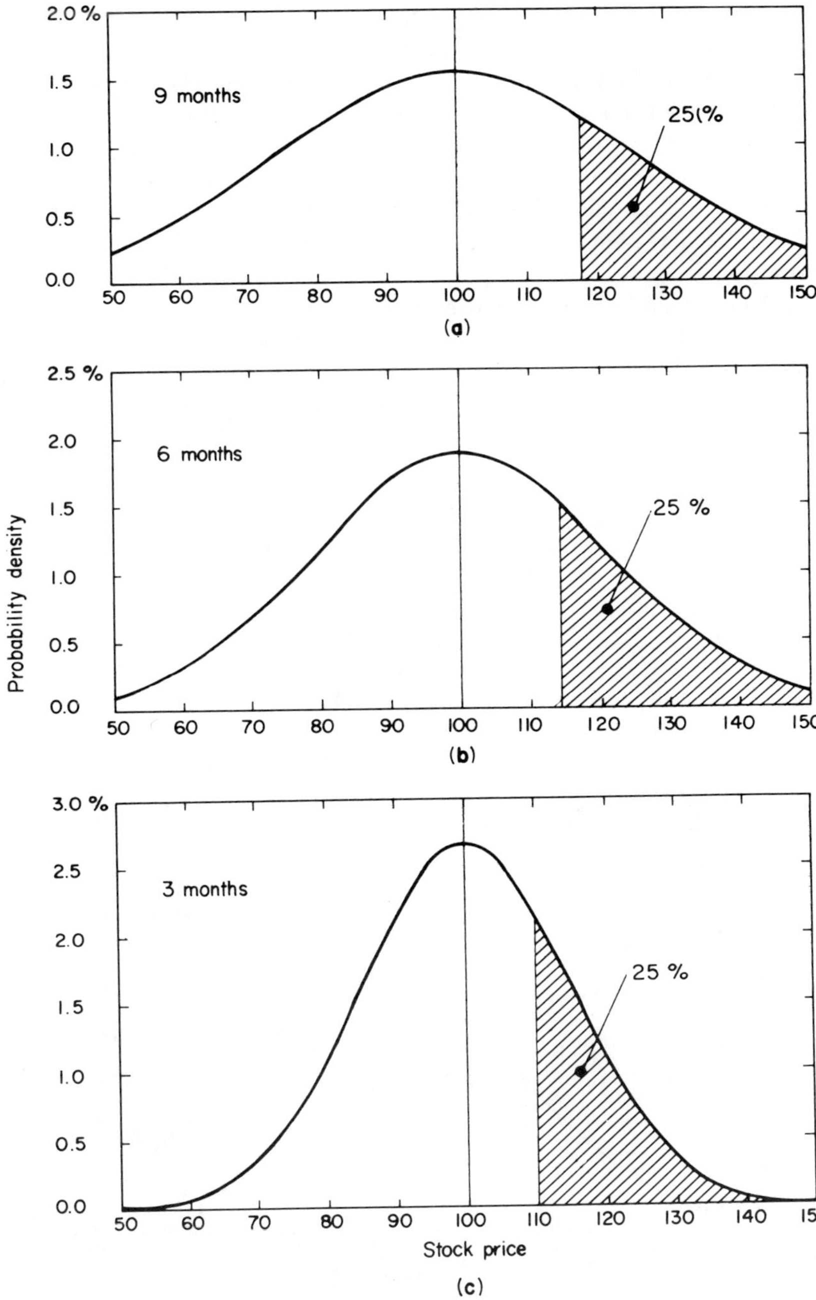

Figure 14–4. ***Probability densities for three time periods: (a) 9 months, (b) 6 months, and (c) 3 months.***

points, there is a 68 percent chance that in a year's time it will close somewhere between 40 and 60. Figure 14–5 represents the probability densities of low- and high-variability stocks. The figure depicts the price probabilities of two stocks for a two-month time period. The low-variability stock with a price variability of 8 points has a 68 percent chance of being within the range of 92 to 108 at the end of the two months. The high-variability stock has a price variability of 22 points. It has a 68 percent chance of staying within the range of 78 to 122. The high-variability stock has a wider breadth over which it can advance or decline.

Another way to look at variability is to inspect what it means in terms of a stock's closing above a particular price. This is what an option buyer is concerned with: What is the stock's chance of moving beyond the striking price and by how much? A stock always has a 16 percent chance to close above its price variability. If a stock is trading at 50 and has a price variabil-

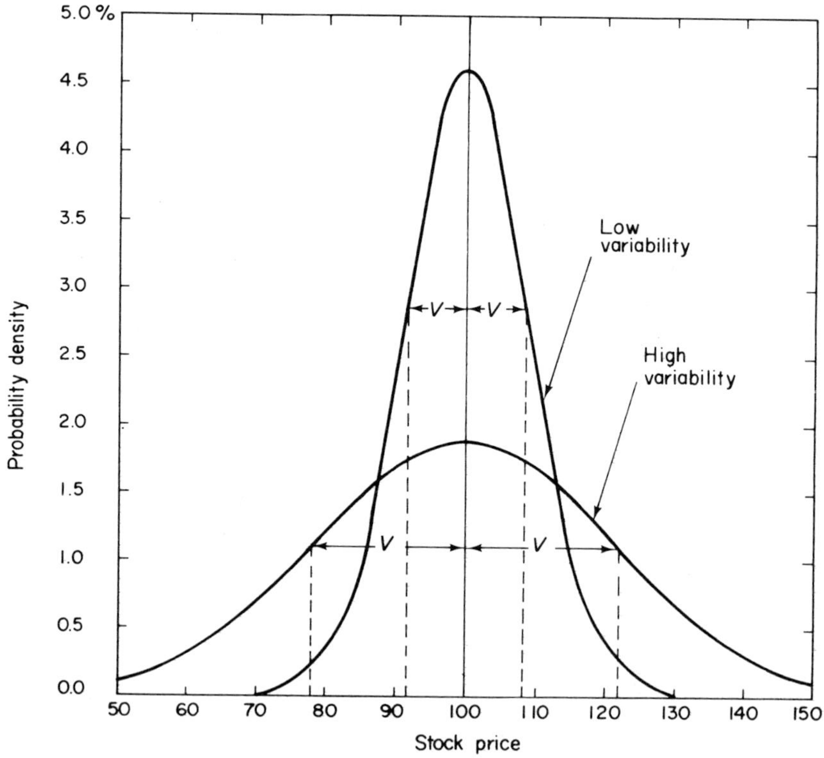

Figure 14–5. ***Probability densities of low- and high-variability stocks.***

ity of 10 points in a stated period of time, it has a 16 percent chance of closing above 60 at the end of that time period. Since it has a 68 percent chance to stay within its variability, there is a 32 percent chance that it will close above or below this range. Since the bell-shaped curve is symmetric, 16 percent of the time it will close above its variability and 16 percent of the time it will close below its variability. In Fig. 14–5 the low-variability stock has a 16 percent chance of closing above 108 at the end of two months. The high-variability stock has a 16 percent chance of closing above 122 at the end of the same time period. You can be sure that an option on the high-variability stock would cost more than an option on the low-variability stock, all other factors being the same. The high-variability stock has the same chance to advance to 122 as the low-variability stock has to advance to 108.

HOW VARIABILITY IS DETERMINED

Variability is basically a measure of how a particular stock has fluctuated in the past. A basic assumption is that the forces which caused fluctuations in the past will continue to cause fluctuations in the future. If we measure how the stock fluctuated in the past, we presume that it will fluctuate likewise in the future. Let us consider the closing price of a stock at the end of each week for a year. We can add up these 52 closing prices and get the average or mean weekly closing price. For each week we can inspect how much the weekly closing price deviates from the average. We would probably find that in nine of those weeks the stock closed within plus or minus one-fourth of a point from the average. In eight of those weeks it closed one-fourth to three-fourths of a point above the average and in another eight weeks one fourth to three-fourths below the average. Figure 14–6 shows the number of weeks that a particular deviation from the mean occurred. The total number of weeks under the curve adds up to 52. In 35 of the weeks the deviation from the mean was between $-1\frac{1}{4}$ and $+1\frac{1}{4}$ points. Thirty-five is approximately 68 percent of the 52 weeks. By definition, the probability is 68 percent that a stock closes within its variability range. Thus, the weekly price variability for this stock is $1\frac{1}{4}$ points, as is indicated in Fig. 14–6.

Often the variability of a stock is expressed as the price variability divided by the price of the stock. The weekly variability for the above case is $1\frac{1}{4} \div 50$, which equals 0.025.

A table of yearly variabilities for optionable stocks appears in Appendix C. The appendix also shows how to convert from the annual variability to any (weekly) time period and gives a more thorough discussion of how variabilities are obtained.

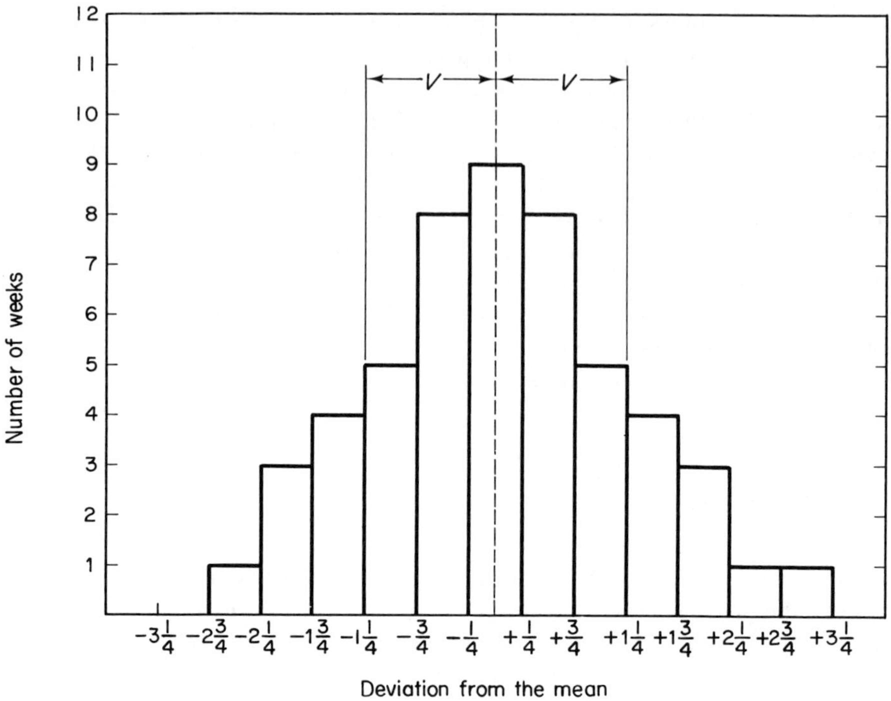

Figure 14–6. ***The number of weeks out of a year a particular point deviation from the mean occurred.***

The next chapter utilizes the concepts of variability and the bell-shaped curve in order to explain how the odds work.

15 | How the Odds Work

In the last chapter we discussed the random behavior of stock prices. We showed that if we could know the variability of a stock the bell-shaped curve would allow us to make some probabilistic estimates of how high or low it would go. The bell-shaped curve can also be referred to as the *odds curve*, since it gives the probability or odds that a stock will end up at a certain price. In addition to this information, we learned in Chapter 13 how to calculate the percentage of profit and loss (Fig. 13–2) from the purchase of an option as a function of the stock price at expiration. We thus have two important pieces of information, which can be combined to give us an idea of what our expected profit or loss would be if we purchased a particular option. We have: (1) the odds that a stock will end up at a particular price and (2) the profit or loss at that particular price. This is sufficient information for us to calculate what our expected return would be.

ROULETTE: WINNING AND LOSING

To show how expected return is calculated in a game of chance, let us consider two games of roulette, one that you will lose and one that you will win in the long run. Selecting the right option to buy is like being able to select which roulette wheel you would like to play. You can choose to play the winning or the losing wheel. One is fixed so that the house usually wins after many plays. You can play it and win occasionally in a big way. In the long run you will lose. The expected return on your investment in this wheel is negative or a loss. If you choose to play the other wheel, you can lose occasionally in a big way, but in the long run you will win. The expected return on your investment is positive or a profit.

The Losing Wheel

In a suitably designed roulette wheel each outcome is totally independent of the previous outcome or past history of outcomes. In gambling parlance, the roulette wheel has no memory. The relative frequency of each particular outcome is stable. Let us assume that we have a roulette wheel with ten trays or slots instead of the number that is commonly used in casinos. With each spin of the wheel there is a $1/10$ chance the ball will fall in a particular tray. The losing game has eight numbers on which you can bet. The remaining two are house numbers. You cannot bet on these. If the ball falls on one of these house numbers, the house wins the bet. If the ball falls on the number you select, the house pays you eight dollars for the dollar you bet. If it falls on a number you did not select, you lose your bet. We shall play 10,000 spins of the wheel and bet one dollar on each spin. We can shift to any number of the wheel on any bet. Since the wheel has no memory, it does not make any difference if we keep selecting the same number or switch numbers according to our hunches. Let us choose to play number four continuously. On any play our number (or any other number) has a $1/10$ chance of winning. On 10,000 plays we would invest \$10,000, betting one dollar at a

Table 15–1 Expected Return Calculation on the Losing Wheel

Wheel Number	*Odds (Probability)*	*Profit/Loss*	*Expected Profit/Loss*
1	0.1	−100%	−10%
2	0.1	−100%	−10%
3	0.1	−100%	−10%
4	0.1	+700%	+70%
5	0.1	−100%	−10%
6	0.1	−100%	−10%
7	0.1	−100%	−10%
8	0.1	−100%	−10%
House	0.1	−100%	−10%
House	0.1	−100%	−10%

Expected return = −20%

time. On 10,000 plays we can expect to win about $\frac{1}{10}$ of the times, or 1000 times. Since the house pays eight dollars (one dollar that we bet plus seven additional dollars), for each dollar winning bet, we can expect to win back $8000 of the $10,000 we bet. We lose $2000 in this game, so our return is −20 percent.

Table 15–1 shows how to calculate the expected profit and loss over all the outcomes of the losing game. The first eight numbers and the two house numbers each have a probability of $\frac{1}{10}$ of outcome. If any number other than four comes up, we lose 100 percent of our bet. If four turns up, we get back $8, a gain of 700 percent. To get the expected profit or loss for the outcome of each number on the wheel, we multiply the probability of occurrence of that number by the profit or loss we sustain if that number comes up. The sum of the expected profits and losses gives us an expected return of −20 percent, a losing game.

The Winning Wheel

In the winning game we again have a roulette wheel with ten trays. With each spin of the wheel there is a $\frac{1}{10}$ chance that the ball will fall in a particular tray. The winning game has only six numbers that you can select to bet on. However, in this game the remaining four trays are "freebies." You cannot bet on these, but if the ball falls in one of these trays you get your dollar back. If the ball falls on a number you did not select, you lose your bet. If the ball falls on the number you select, the house pays you eight dollars for the dollar you bet. Again we play 10,000 spins of the wheel and bet one dollar on each spin. Since the wheel has no memory, we again choose to play number four continuously. On 10,000 plays we can expect that number four will come up $\frac{1}{10}$ of the time, or 1000 times. We therefore get back $8000 from the house. In addition, we can expect the four "freebies" to come up $\frac{1}{10}$ of the time each, or 4000 times. We get back $4000. We lose on all the other outcomes. (We win a total of $12,000 having bet $10,000. We make $2000 in this game so our return is +20 percent.)

Table 15–2 shows how to calculate the expected profit and loss over all the outcomes of the winning game. The first six numbers and the four "freebies" each have an outcome probability of $\frac{1}{10}$. If any of the four "freebies" comes up, we get our dollar back for a 0 percent profit. If any number other than four comes up, we lose our dollar, or 100 percent of our bet. If four turns up, the house gives us back eight dollars for the dollar we bet, a gain of 700 percent. Again we obtain the expected profit or loss for the outcome of each occurrence by multiplying its probability by the profit or loss sustained by that occurrence. The sum of the expected profits and losses gives us an expected return of +20 percent, a winning game.

Table 15–2 Expected Return Calculation on the Winning Wheel

Wheel Number	*Odds (Probability)*	*Profit/Loss*	*Expected Profit/Loss*
1	0.1	−100%	−10
2	0.1	−100%	−10
3	0.1	−100%	−10
4	0.1	+700%	+70
5	0.1	−100%	−10
6	0.1	−100%	−10
Freebie	0.1	0%	0
Freebie	0.1	0%	0
Freebie	0.1	0%	0
Freebie	0.1	0%	0
		Expected return = −20%	

OPTION ROULETTE

We can apply the same probabilistic techniques demonstrated in the two roulette games to calculate our expected return prior to purchasing an option. In order to calculate the expected return in the roulette games, we only needed to know two things: (1) the odds that the ball would fall in a particular tray for all trays and (2) the profit or loss associated with the ball's falling in each tray.

In order to calculate the expected return from betting on an option we need to know: (1) the odds that the stock will end up at a particular price for all prices and (2) what our option profit or loss will be if it does end up at each price. We combine the data as we did with the roulette game to calculate the expected return. If the expected return is negative, we have a losing game. If the expected return is positive, we have a winning game. You can choose to play winning or losing option roulette. The losing option roulette game is fixed so that the writer of the option (the house) usually wins after many plays. You can play this game and occasionally win in a big way, but in the long run you will lose. The expected return in this game is negative for the buyer of options and positive for the writer or seller of options.

If you choose to play the winning game, you can occasionally lose in a big way, but in the long run you will win. The expected return in this game is positive for the buyer of options and negative for the writer or seller of options. The house loses.

CALCULATING THE ODDS

Let us assume that you are considering purchase of an option on fairly high-variability stock with the striking price and stock price at 10. The option is selling for only 1, and there are three months to expiration. It sounds attractive. Would you play this game? If you would, we would like to have the pleasure of your company at our casino, where we will wine and dine you, surround you with lovelies or dandies and let you play losing option roulette to your heart's content.

Let us calculate the expected return for the buyer of the option mentioned above. First multiply the prices given above by ten in order to make the subsequent presentation easier to follow. We are now talking about an option selling for 10 on a stock whose price and striking price are 100. The stock has a fairly high annual variability of 0.40. (This is equivalent to a three-month variability of 0.20.) Figure 15–1 gives the odds that the stock will end up within five-point intervals. This is just a bar chart of the familiar bell-shaped curve with a three-month variability of 0.20. The probability is 0.099 that the stock will end up between 100 and 105. The probability is 0.093 that the stock will end up between 105 and 110, etc. The sum of the probabilities of the stock prices between 50 and 150 is 1.0, or 100 percent. Figure 15–1 gives us the odds that the stock will end up in a particular price range for all reasonable prices of the stock (50 to 150).

To complete our information we need to know what our profit or loss

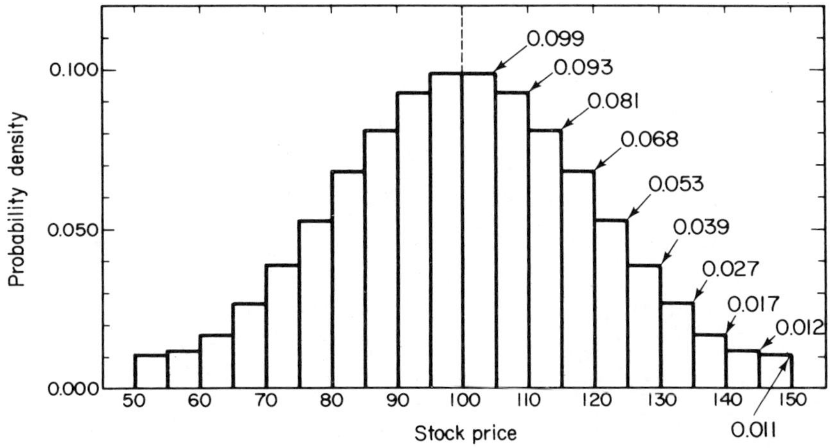

Figure 15–1. ***Probability of stock closing in five-point intervals. Three-month variability: 0.20.***

would be over the 50 to 150 price range of the stock. If the stock closes at 100 or below, the option expires worthless. We lose 100 percent of our investment. If the stock closes at 110 at expiration, the option is worth 10, and we get back our investment. If it closes at 120, our option is worth 20, a 100 percent gain. Figure 15–2 shows the percentage profits and losses over a wide price range of the stock.

Table 15–3 calculates the expected return for the option purchase being discussed. The expected profit or loss for each stock price interval is obtained by multiplying the percentage option profit or loss obtained from Fig. 15–2 by its probability of occurrence obtained from Fig. 15-1.

The expected return to the buyer of this option is −20.38 percent, which is as bad as the losing roulette game. Now you know why you were invited to the casino to play option roulette. The house odds were 20 percent against you.

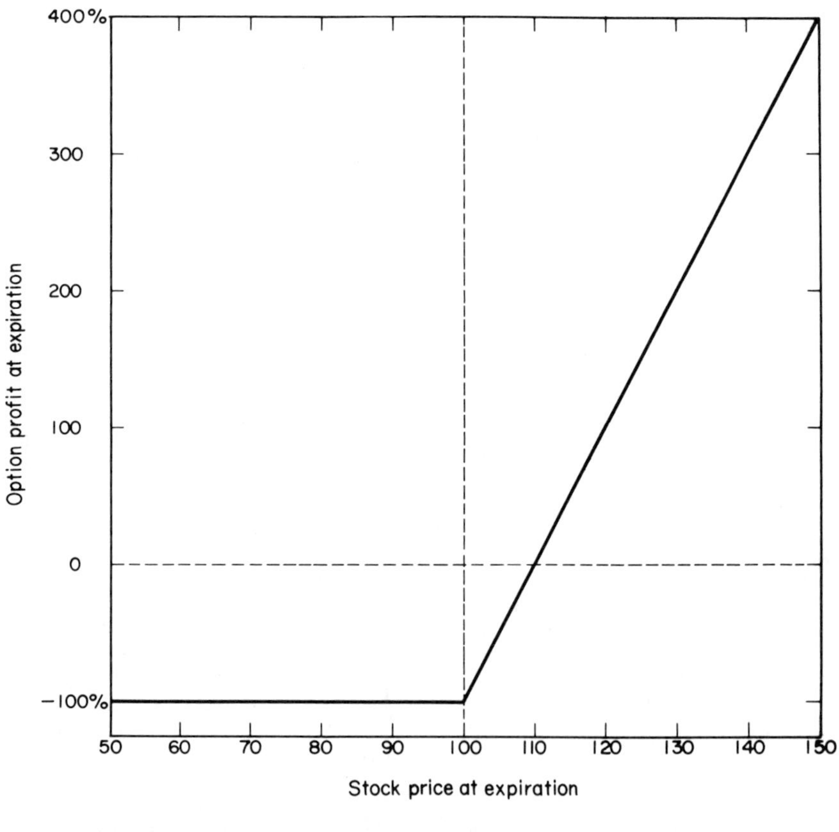

Figure 15–2. ***Percentage profit/loss on option over wide price range of stock.***

Table 15–3 The Expected Return on a Three-month Option

Option Price = 10
Stock Price = 100
Strike Price = 100
Annual Variability = 0.40

Stock Price Interval	*% Option Profit/Loss*	*Odds (Probability)*	*Expected Profit/Loss*
50–55	−100%	0.011	−1.10%
55–60	−100%	0.012	−1.20%
60–65	−100%	0.017	−1.70%
65–70	−100%	0.027	−2.70%
70–75	−100%	0.039	−3.90%
75–80	−100%	0.053	−5.30%
80–85	−100%	0.068	−6.80%
85–90	−100%	0.081	−8.10%
90–95	−100%	0.093	−9.30%
95–100	−100%	0.099	−9.90%
100–105	−75%	0.099	−7.43%
105–110	−25%	0.093	−2.33%
110–115	+25%	0.081	+2.03%
115–120	+75%	0.068	+5.10%
120–125	+125%	0.053	+6.63%
125–130	+175%	0.039	+6.83%
130–135	+225%	0.027	+6.08%
135–140	+275%	0.017	+4.68%
140–145	+325%	0.012	+3.90%
145–150	+375%	0.011	+4.13%
	Expected return = −20.38%		

In the options game you do not have to play when the odds are against you. With a little studying you can find a game where the expected return to you is much higher than 20 percent. In 1975 it was possible to find options with expected returns of 100 percent. This is equivalent to playing on a roulette wheel with ten trays. Two of the trays are house trays. If the ball lands in either of these, you lose your entire investment, a 100 percent loss. An additional two trays are freebies. If the ball lands in one of these, you get your bet back and can try again. If it lands in any of the other six trays, the house gives you three dollars for each dollar you invested, a 200 percent gain. For all the possible outcomes of the game this works out to a +100 percent expected return. If you play 10,000 spins, at the end of the game you should expect to have $20,000—ten that you started with plus ten that you won.

The following chapter tells you how to select options that are equivalent to playing on a winning roulette wheel, one which gives you a positive expected return. Buying an option with a positive expected return does not guarantee you a profit. You can still lose your investment. However, if you purchase options with a positive expected return over a long period of time, you will most likely profit.

16 | Improving the Odds

It would be extremely laborious if we had to go through the exercise presented in the previous chapter each time we wished to calculate the expected return on an option. We have devised a method that enables you quickly to determine whether an option is a winner or loser. It is essentially a two-step process that involves determining one factor from a graph and using another graph to see if that factor lies in an expected profit or loss zone. This enables you to know whether you are playing winning or losing option roulettte. First, however, we have to learn the concept of *normalization.*

NORMALIZATION

Normalization is a concept with which we are all familiar, but not necessarily by that name. If someone asks you the age of your stable paramour and you answer that he or she is young, you will get more questions. Young compared to what? To a woman who is 55, or her sister who is 45 or to her daughter who is 20? You are being asked to normalize the age to some standard reference of a specific time period. You are really being asked how old the person is compared to a one-year time period. This simplifies matters considerably. We can state ages of all kinds of things in terms of years rather than giving comparative answers with no standard of comparison.

It is helpful to normalize stock prices and option prices because this also simplifies matters considerably. What standard of reference should we use? We shall use the striking price as the standard of reference, because we are dealing with relationships between stock, option, and striking prices, and the stock and option prices change continuously, while the striking price remains stable.

Figure 16–1(a) shows how the actual option price varies as a function of the actual stock price. In this figure an option with a striking price of 50 was chosen for a medium-variability stock with about six months to expiration. In order to normalize the option and stock price, we simply divide these prices by the striking price. Figure 16–1(b) is the same as Fig. 16–1(a) except that the prices on the horizontal and vertical axes are normalized. You may be thinking that this is a lot of work to accomplish nothing, but you will see as we proceed that it cuts down on our work by a considerable factor. Instead of having to refer to charts or tables for 40 different striking prices, we shall have to refer to only one chart or table. Figure 16–1(b) can now be used to discuss options with any striking price. If we wish to use a normalized chart or graph, we obtain the normalized option price by dividing the actual stock and option price by the striking price under consideration. Let us assume that we are considering an option with the striking price of 100 and that the stock is selling at 90. The normalized stock price is 0.9. Figure 16–1(b) shows that the normalized option price is about 0.05. To get back the actual option price, we simply multiply the normalized price by the striking price to get 5.0. This is the price for which an option should sell if it is characterized by Fig. 16–1(b). The following rules are used to convert back and forth from actual prices to normalized prices:

Normalized stock (option) price = Actual stock (option) price ÷ (divided by) Striking price

Actual stock (option) price = Normalized stock (option) price × (times) Striking price

Let us work some more examples to become more familiar with how the normalized chart works. We would like to determine for which price an option should be selling if it has the variability and time characteristics similar to Fig. 16–1(b). The striking price of the stock is 40. If the stock is trading at 30, the normalized stock price, 0.75, is the true stock price divided by the striking price. From Fig. 16–1(b) we see that the normalized option price is 0.02. We multiply this by the striking price, 40, in order to get the true option price of 0.80. Let us next suppose that the stock is trading at 50. The normalized stock price, 1.25, is the actual stock price divided by the striking price. We see from Fig. 16–1(b) that this corresponds to a normalized option price of 0.30. To get the actual option price, we multiply the normalized option price of 0.30 by the striking price, 40, to get 12. This is the price for which the option should be selling if it is characterized by Fig. 16–1(b).

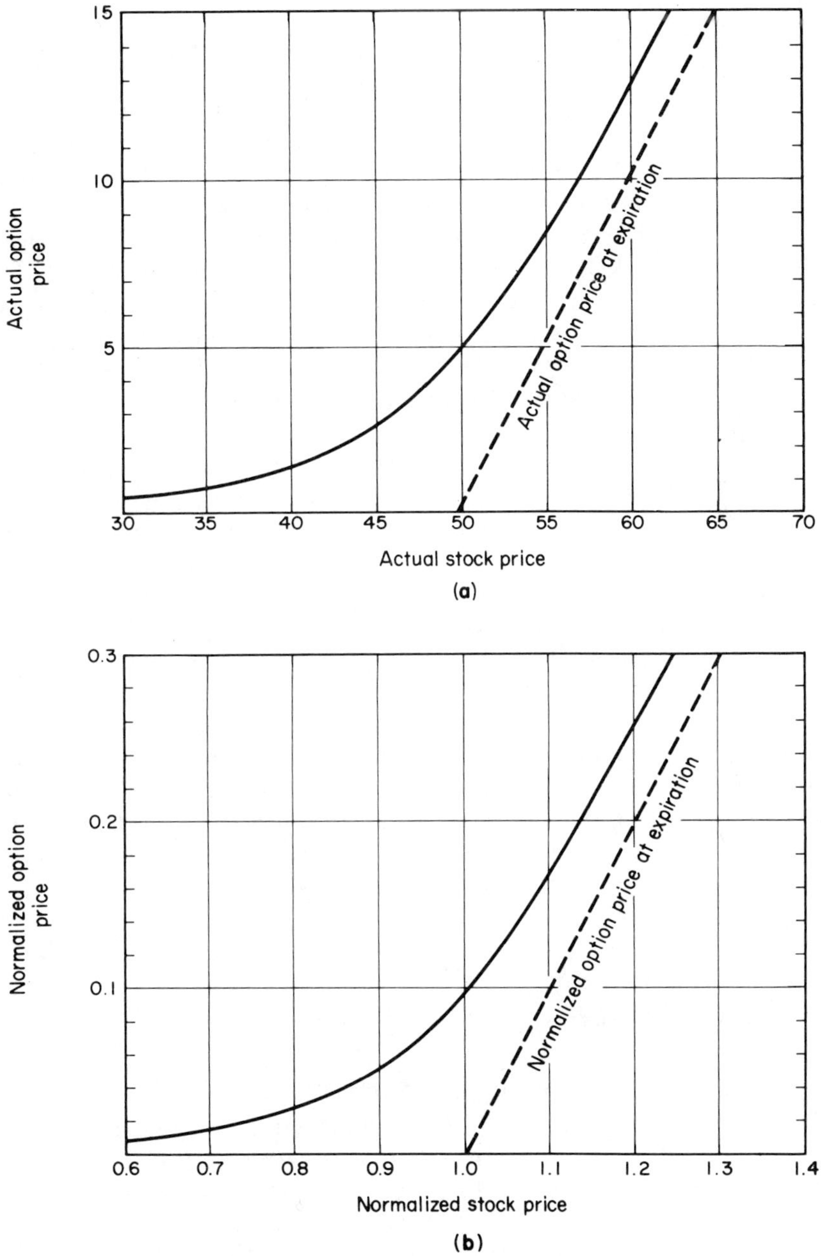

Figure 16–1. ***(a) Actual option price vs. actual stock price. (b) Normalized option price vs. normalized stock price.***

THE MASTER OPTION PRICE CHART

Using the master option price chart is the first step of the two-step process that is required in order to determine if an option has an expected profitability. Figure 16–2, the master option price chart, gives you the normalized option price as a function of the normalized stock price. The various curves labeled 0.05 through 0.15 are what we shall call the "D factors." The D factor is related* to the risk/leverage (R/L) factor discussed in Chapter 13. The major point that we made in that chapter was that if we were to buy an option with a particular expiration which had a few different striking prices, we should buy the option with the lowest R/L factor. The option with the lowest R/L factor was better than the other options on the same stock with the same expiration period. It did not tell us if we had a positive or negative expected return. We still did not know if we were playing winning or losing option roulette. Although it told us which option of a series was the best one to buy, it may only have been the best game selected from a series of losing games.

This chapter ties all the loose ends together. If you are interested in options on a particular stock, you can compare all the options on that stock regardless of striking price or expiration period and determine whether or not and to what degree the expected return is positive.

In order to evaluate an option we first calculate the normalized option and stock prices by dividing the actual option and stock price by the option's striking price. We then look at Fig. 16–2 to see where the intersection of the normalized option and stock price lies in order to determine the D factor for this option. Once the D factor is determined, we can go on to the second and final step, discussed next, in determining the expected profitability.

THE MASTER EXPECTED RETURN CHART

The master expected return chart, Fig. 16–3, was compiled by a process similar to that shown in Chapter 15 for calculating the expected return on an option. The profits and losses at each stock price stemming from the purchase of an option were multiplied by the probability that the stock closed at that price. The sum of these products gives us the expected profit or loss. Using higher mathematics, one can calculate the D factor of an option, which will

*The D factor is actually the square root of the risk/leverage factor.

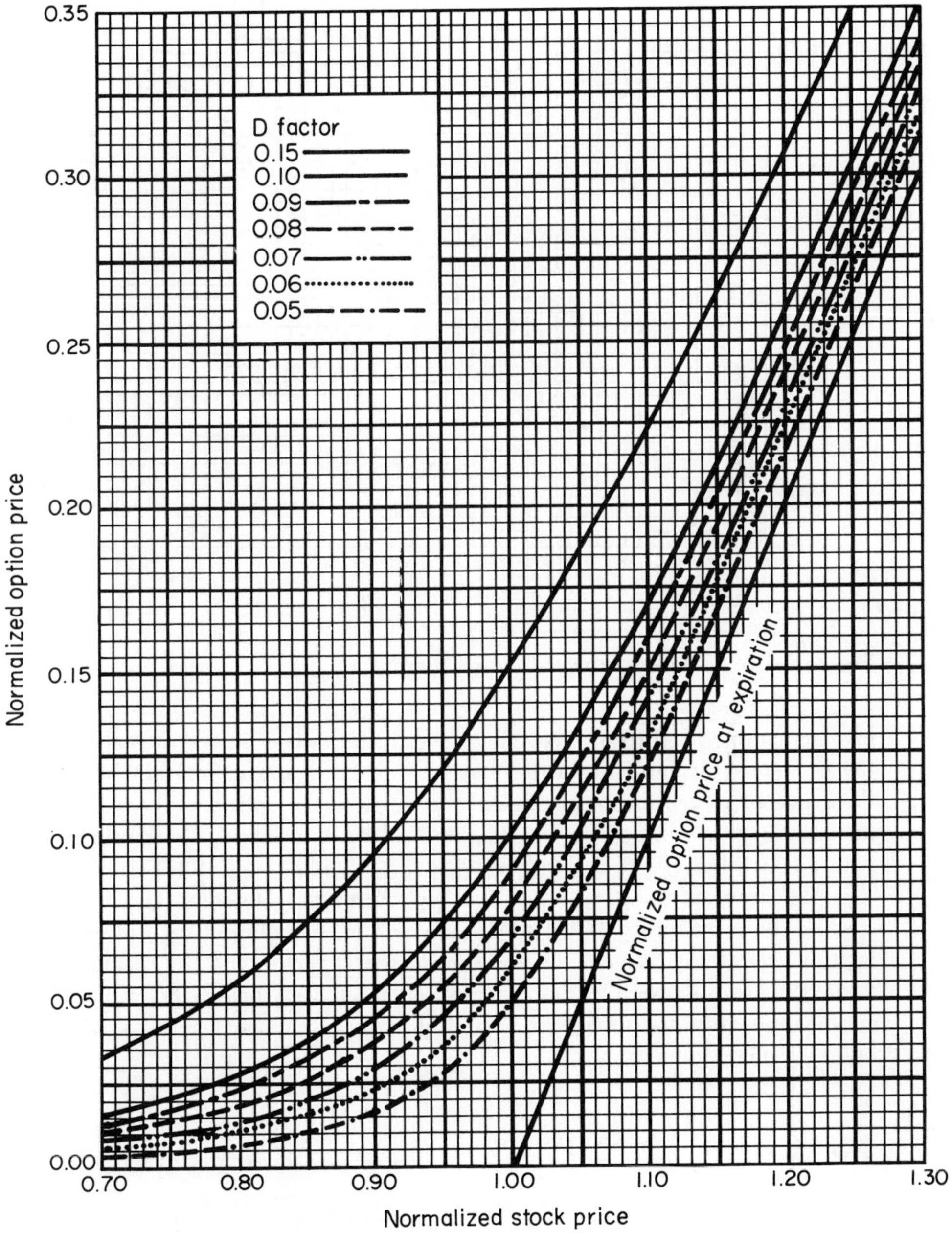

Figure 16–2. ***Master option price chart.***

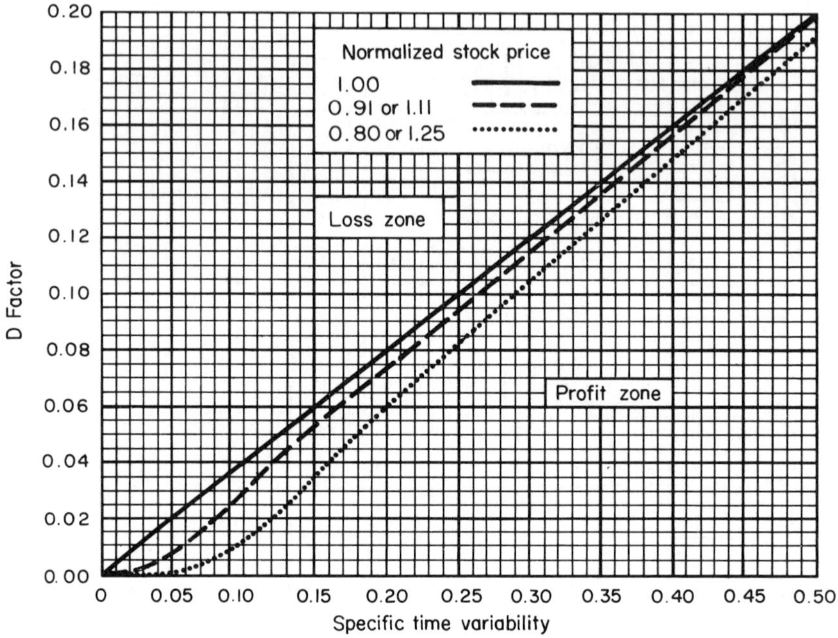

Figure 16–3. ***Master expected return chart.***

give an expected return of zero. The curves in Fig. 16–3 represent just that. If the D factor calculated from the first step outlined above falls on the curve, the expected return to the buyer and the seller of the option is zero. If the D factor falls above the curve, the expected return is a loss to the buyer and a gain to the seller.

To use Fig. 16–3 we must first determine the D factor and then the specific time variability of the stock on which we are purchasing options. We next determine the point of intersection of the D factor and the specific time variability in Fig. 16–3. If the intersection point falls below the appropriate curve, we have found ourselves, an option with an expected gain—a winning option roulette game.

TRAINING EXAMPLES

A number of examples are presented below in order to help train you in how to use the master option price and expected return charts. In each of the examples that follows, five basic bits of information are given from which we can determine whether an option has an expected loss or gain. These include the striking price, the option price, the stock price, the time until expiration, and the annual variability. The first three are obtained from newspaper quotes on options. You can calculate the time left until expiration by counting on a calendar the number of weeks until the option expires on the business Monday after the third Friday of its expiration month. The annual variability estimate can be obtained from Appendix C.

EXAMPLE 1 / BREAK EVEN

Striking price = 100	Stock price = 100	Annual
Option price = 8	Time (wks) = 13	variability = 0.40

The first step that is required in determining whether or not an option has an expected profit or loss is to determine the D factor from Fig. 16–2. The normalized stock and option prices are calculated by dividing the actual stock and option price by the striking price. The normalized stock and option prices are 1.00 and 0.08, respectively. These two prices intersect on the curve where the D factor is 0.08.

The second step involves determining the specific time variability and comparing this to the D factor in Fig. 16–3 to see if the intersection lies in a profit or loss zone. To obtain the specific time variability we must refer to Fig. C–1 in Appendix C. With 13 weeks left until expiration the time factor is 0.5. We multiply the time factor by the annual variability of the stock, 0.40, to obtain the specific time variability of 0.20.

We now have the two necessary bits of information to determine whether we shall play winning or losing option roulette. We have a D factor of 0.08 and a specific time variability of 0.20. There are three curves in Fig. 16–3. Since the striking price of the option that we are considering equals the stock price, we shall use the curve composed of the solid line which characterizes options with a normalized stock price of 1.00. We see that the intersection of the D factor and the specific time variability falls exactly on the curve. This means that the option falls exactly between the profit and loss zones. The expected return on this option is zero. We would expect neither to win nor to lose, but to make back our investment. Had the D factor been greater than 0.08, we would expect to experience a loss. The greater the distance that a point falls above the line, the greater is our expected loss. Likewise, the greater the distance that a point falls below the line, the greater is our expected gain.

EXAMPLE 2 / A SMALL EXPECTED PROFIT

Striking price = 50	Stock price = 50	Annual variability = 0.30
Option price = 4	Time (wks) = 25	

The normalized stock and option prices are 1.0 and 0.08, respectively. In Fig. 16–2 these intersect on the curve where the D factor is 0.08. With 25 weeks left until expiration, Fig. C–1 in Appendix C gives us a time factor of 0.69. We multiply the time factor by the annual variability, 0.30, to obtain the specific time variability 0.21. Again, since the stock price equals the striking price, we refer to the solid line in Fig. 16–3 to determine the zone of our expected return. The D factor of 0.08 and the specific time variability of 0.21 intersect just below the line in the profit zone. This particular option should, therefore, be slightly profitable. A warning is in order in a situation of this sort. Remember that the annual variabilities in Appendix C were calculated for a specific time period (June 1974 to June 1975). The variability of a stock changes slightly over a period of time and under different market conditions. If the variability of the stock that we considered in this example had been reduced slightly to give us a specific time variability of 0.19, instead of 0.21, the purchase of the option would represent a slight loss instead of a gain. In order to have greater confidence in an expected profit, you should buy options that fall substantially below the line in the profit zone.

EXAMPLE 3 / DETERMINING OPTION FAIR PRICE

Striking price = 50	Stock price = 45½	Annual variability = 0.48
Option price = ?	Time (wks) = 13	

The object of this example is to determine the price of an option for which there will be no gain or loss for the buyer or seller. This is referred to as the *fair price* of the option. If we know this price, we can compare the actual price of the option to the fair price to determine if the option is undervalued and therefore worth buying. We start by considering Fig. 16–3. Each of the three curves represents the fair prices (zero return) according to their D factors. The solid line represents options whose prices equal the striking prices. The dashed line represents options whose normalized stock prices are either 1.11 or 0.91. In this example, the normalized stock price is 45½ divided by 50, which equals 0.91; therefore, the dashed line is the zero return curve for this option. This means if the D factor falls on the dashed curve for any specific time variability, then the option characterized this way is fairly priced and will return neither a profit nor a loss to the buyer or seller. Since the option under consideration has 13 weeks left until expiration, the time factor obtained from Fig. C–1 in Appendix C is 0.50. The specific time variability, 0.24, is obtained by multiplying the time factor, 0.50, by the annual variability, 0.48. This intersects the dashed curve in Fig. 16–3 at D = 0.09. This D factor represents the fair price of the option, which now can be determined from Fig. 16–2. The normalized stock price, 0.91, and the 0.09 D factor curve intersect at the normalized option price of approximately 0.05. We get the actual fair option price, 2½, by multiplying the normalized option price, 0.05, by the striking price, 50. An option that sells above 2½ is overpriced and represents an expected loss to the buyer. An option that sells below 2½ is underpriced and represents an expected gain.

EXAMPLE 4 / DETERMINING WINNING OR LOSING OPTION ROULETTE

The method outlined above is basically the technique for determining the expected return on an option. If we determined the fair price of the option to be 2½ as in Example 3 and were able to purchase it at 1, our expected return would be (2½ − 1)/1, which equals 150 percent. This game would be better than the roulette game described in Chapter 15, which had an expected return of 100 percent.

If we were able to purchase the option for 4, our expected return would be (2½ − 4)/4, which equals −37.5 percent. This loss of 37.5 percent on an option purchased at 4 equals $150. The 150 percent gain on the option purchased at 1 also equals $150. It is important to relate the expected percentage gain or loss to actual dollars.

To summarize, in order to determine the expected return we must first calculate the fair price of the option as outlined in Example 3. To calculate the expected return, we obtain the difference between the fair option price and the actual option price and divide this by the actual option price. To get the dollar amount we would expect to gain or lose, we multiply the expected return by the amount invested in the option.

EXAMPLE 5 / EXTRAPOLATING

Striking price = 30	Stock price = 27⅛	Annual variability = 0.60
Option price = 2	Time (wks) = 19	

Occasionally you will encounter situations where you must make estimates from the master charts because the coordinates (prices, D factor, and variabilities) do not fall on a specific curve. In this example the normalized stock price is 0.90. We wish to use Fig. 16–3 in order to calculate the fair option price. There is no curve in the figure with a normalized stock price of 0.90, but the dashed curve for 0.91 is fairly close, so we shall use that one. With 19 weeks left until expiration, Fig. C–1 in Appendix C tells us that the time factor is 0.60. The time factor, 0.60, multiplied by the annual variability, 0.60, gives us the specific time variability, 0.36. In Fig. 16–3 the specific time variability of 0.36 intersects with the dashed curve at a D factor of 0.14. This represents the fair option price. We must next look at Fig. 16–2 to determine what the actual fair price is. Figure 16–2 does not have a curve with a D factor of 0.14, so we must extrapolate or make an approximation or educated guess. The normalized stock price is 0.90, so we shall work with points at that price. There are two curves, with D factors of 0.15 and 0.10, which bound the D factor of 0.14 in which we are interested. The normalized option prices on each of these curves are 0.094 and 0.054, respectively, at the normalized stock price of 0.90. The difference between these normalized option prices is 0.094 − 0.054, which equals 0.040. The D factor of the curve with which we are working, 0.14, is eight-tenths of the interval between the D factor curves of 0.15 and 0.10. The normalized fair option price, 0.086, is 0.054 plus 0.8 of the interval 0.040. The actual fair option price, 2.58, is obtained by multiplying the normalized price, 0.086, by the striking price, 30.

The option is actually selling for 2, while its fair price is 2.58. If we purchased this option for 2, we would expect a gain of 29 percent, that is (2.58 − 2)/2.

FOUR THOUSAND COULD HAVE GOTTEN YOU ONE HUNDRED THOUSAND PLUS

In Chapter 11 we discussed the half-blind strategy, which gave us a return of 26 percent. That strategy was given its name because we blindly bought and sold options at fixed intervals of time subject to certain criteria. We did not use any meaningful criteria in evaluating whether the options were over- or underpriced when bought or sold. We just purchased and sold options on a fixed day, paying no attention to whether or not the option was priced to our advantage.

We have just learned how to determine if an option is priced to our advantage. If the option falls in the profit zone of Fig. 16–3, it is underpriced and has a positive expected return and should be considered for purchase. If the option falls in the loss zone, it is overpriced and should be considered for sale.

The concept of positive and negative expected return could have been applied to parlay a $4000 investment to more than $110,000 in a year's time. We could have done this by investing in McDonalds options between June 14, 1974 and June 13, 1975, basing our actions on Friday's closing prices, by simply buying an option when its expected return was greater than 20 percent, and holding it until its expected return was less than −40 percent and simultaneously had a profit or until the normalized stock price dropped below 0.7 (a sure loss). Table 16–1 summarizes the transactions that could have

Table 16–1 Transaction Summary for Multiplying a $4000 Investment to $110,000

*Date**	*Stock Price*	*Action*	*Option Price*	*Expected (E) Return*	*Instantaneous Profit/Loss†*	*Round Trip Profit/Loss†*
6/14/74	61¼	Buy 3 Oct 60	7	36%	−2,100	
7/26/74	41	Sell 3 Oct 60	⅜	Px <.7 Pst	+112	−1,987
9/13/74	27⅛	Buy 10 Jan 30	2	35%	−2,000	
11/8/74	39	Sell 10 Jan 30	10¼	−52%	+10,250	+8,250
1/31/75	34¼	Buy 73 Apr 40	1⅜	28%	−10,037	
4/4/75	47¼	Sell 73 Apr 40	7⅜	−60%	+53,837	+43,800
4/4/75	47¼	Buy 90 Jul 45	6	21%	−54,000	
5/16/75	55⅞	Sell 90 Jul 45	12¾	−44%	+114,750	+60,750

Total profit = $110,813

*Prices are based on Fridays' closing prices.
†Commissions not included.

accomplished that feat. On June 14, 1974, McDonalds closed at 61¼, just below its high of 63¼ for the year. Despite the fact that it was trading close to its high for the year, the expected return on the October 60 option which closed at 7 was 36 percent.* We stated earlier that you should not buy an option whose striking price is below the stock price unless you have good reason to do so. We violated that rule with good reason because there were no October 70 options offered and October 60 had a high expected return. In the ensuing weeks bad news developed, and McDonalds plummeted. The price of the October 60 option, which we purchased at 7, went south even faster. By July 5, McDonalds had dropped to 47⅝, and the October 60 option had dropped 84 percent to 1⅛. The expected return on the option at the new low price was still a whopping 77 percent. There was no reason to sell the option and salvage some value. Besides, our rules told us not to sell the option until the expected return was less than −40 percent and had a simultaneous profit or until the price of the stock became less than 0.7 of the striking price.

On Sunday, July 7, 1974 an influential financial periodical published a report on McDonalds that apparently caused the stock to drop about 10 points on Monday, July 8. By Friday, July 12, the stock had recouped somewhat to 42⅜, and the October 60 option had declined to 7/16. It was not until July 26, when McDonalds closed at 41, that the normalized stock price dropped below 0.7. The option still had a positive expected return at its price of ⅜, but our alternative rule told us to sell. The normalized stock price was below 0.7.

From July 26 through September 6 the middle expiration month options did not sell at a price that would give an expected return greater than 20 percent. On September 13, McDonalds closed at 27⅛ and the January 30 option closed at 2. The expected return on this option was 35 percent. In three weeks' time, on October 4, McDonalds hit its low for the year, 21¼. The option we purchased at 2 had now declined to 1 3/16, but we did not sell, since the normalized stock price had not dropped below 0.7. McDonalds then staged a rally, which carried it to 39 on November 8. The January 30 option, which we bought at 2, made a spectacular rally to 10¼. For the first time we simultaneously had a profit and the expected return was more negative than −40 percent. This was our sell signal. Two thousand dollars had grown to more than $10,000.

McDonalds options continued to have negative expected returns. McDonalds dropped to 26¾, then rebounded to 34¼ on January 31, 1975, when

*An annual variability of 0.60 was assumed for the calculations presented in Tables 16–1 and 16–2. Prior to the big drop in McDonalds in June of 1974, the annual variability was less than 0.60. The expected return on the October 60 option would have been substantially less than 36 percent if the lower variability had been used.

the expected returns on many McDonalds options were positive. The middle expiration month, April 40, selling at 1⅜, had the highest expected return, 28 percent. This was a buy signal. By April 4, McDonalds had rallied to 47¼, and the April 40 option climbed more than five-fold to 7⅜. We had a substantial profit and simultaneously, for the first time since we purchased it, the expected return was more negative than −40 percent. This was our sell signal. Ten thousand dollars had grown to more than $50,000.

On the same day, April 4, the July 45 option selling at 6 had a positive expected return of 21 percent. This was marginal according to our guidelines, which cautioned to purchase only options with an expected return greater than 20 percent. Also, we again violated the rule that stated not to purchase options whose striking price is above the stock price unless we had good reason to do so. We violated that rule because we had two good reasons and one bad reason. First, we give the bad reason. We made so much money on the two previous transactions we were beginning to think that we were infallible. We forgot that in the first transaction when we violated this rule we lost practically all our money. Well, we violated that rule again for the same two good reasons. The expected return was sufficiently high, and there were no October 70 options offered.

McDonalds proceeded to climb from 47¼ on April 4 to 55⅞ on May 16, 1975. On that day the July 45 option closed at 12¾ with an expected return of −44 percent. The sell signal had been reached. We were able to double our money on that transaction to yield us more than $110,000.

We put up $4000 and had parlayed that to more than $110,000 by reinvesting all our gains. This is dangerous. Remember that the roulette wheel has no memory. Even with the roulette game described in Chapter 15, where the expected return was 100 percent, you could still lose your entire bet on any particular spin of the wheel. Likewise, if you had invested your total $110,000 in the next favorable option-buying opportunity, you would have lost back most of it. On June 20, 1975 McDonalds closed at 54, while the October 60 option closed at 3⅞. The option had an expected return of 30 percent. By September 5, McDonalds had dropped to 46⅛, and the October 60 option had dropped to ¼. Easy come, easy go! We lost 94 percent.

SAFER STRATEGY

Betting "double or nothing" in any game where there is a chance to lose will eventually get you nothing. It would have been far safer and in the long run more rewarding to invest a fixed dollar amount at each option-buying opportunity. Table 16–2 summarizes our results had we invested only $2000

Table 16–2 Transaction Summary for Minimizing Risk and Multiplying a $2000 Investment to $17,000

*Date**	*Stock Price*	*Action*	*Option Price*	*Expected (E) Return*	*Instantaneous Profit/Loss†*	*Round Trip Profit/Loss†*
6/14/74	61¼	Buy 3 Oct 60	7	36%	−2,100	
7/26/74	41	Sell 3 Oct 60	⅜	Px <.7	+112	−1,987
9/13/74	27⅛	Buy 10 Jan 30	2	35%	−2,000	
11/8/74	39	Sell 10 Jan 30	10¼	−52%	+10,250	+8,250
1/31/75	34¼	Buy 15 Apr 40	1⅜	28%	−2,062	
4/4/75	47¼	Sell 15 Apr 40	7⅜	−60%	+11,062	+9,000
4/4/75	47¼	Buy 3 Jul 45	6	21%	−1,800	
5/16/75	55⅞	Sell 3 Jul 45	12¾	−44%	+3,825	+2,025

Total profit = $17,288

*Prices are based on Friday's closing prices.
†Commissions not included.

at each option-buying opportunity. On the first transaction we lost $1987, but on the second transaction we made $8250. The remaining two transactions netted $9000 and $2025 for a total profit for the year of $17,288 (excluding commissions).

Even though we were $17,000 ahead, we stayed with our game plan and invested only $2000 on the next option-buying opportunity. That opportunity occurred on June 20, 1975, when the October 60 option closed at 3⅞ and had a 30 percent expected return. As noted above, by September 5, this option was worth ¼. We thus lost most of our $2000. We were still $15,000 ahead and ready to invest another $2000 at the next buying opportunity.

RECAP FOR IMPROVING THE ODDS

The crux of the previous two examples centered about being able to calculate the actual expected return on an option. In order to accomplish this, we must first calculate the fair price of the option, knowing the striking and stock prices, the annual variability, and the time left until expiration. We then determine the expected return by taking the difference between the fair option price and the actual option price and dividing this difference by the actual option price. Of course, to be more accurate, we should add the commissions to the actual option price. They can make a big difference in the expected return, especially if we are purchasing a single low-priced option. The seven steps for determining the fair option price are:

1 / *Look up the annual variability of the stock in Table C–1 in Appendix C.*

2 / *Determine the time factor from Fig. C–1 in Appendix C from the number of weeks left until expiration.*

3 / *Obtain the specific time variability by multiplying the time factor by the annual variability.*

4 / *Refer to the master expected return chart, Fig. 16–3, to obtain the D factor.*

5 / *Calculate the normalized stock price.*

6 / *Using Fig. 16–2, the master option price chart, find the intersection of the normalized stock price with the appropriate D factor curve to determine the normalized option price.*

7 / *Multiply the normalized option price by the striking price to obtain the fair price of the option.*

The fair option price represents that price for which the expected return is zero to both the buyer and the seller. If the option is priced below the fair option price, it has a positive expected return to the buyer and a negative expected return to the seller. If the option is priced above the fair option price, the results are reversed.

It cannot be overemphasized that the variability estimates in Table C–1 in Appendix C are subject to continuous change. It is possible to work the seven steps just mentioned in reverse to see what variability the market places on a particular stock. Use Friday's closing option prices for a few months. Calculate the normalized option price and stock prices and find the D factor line on which these two intersect in the master option chart. Now go to Fig. 16–3, the master expected return chart, and find where the D factor intersects the curve of the normalized stock price. Read down on this chart to obtain the specific time variability. Get the time factor from Fig. C–1 in Appendix C. The annual variability that the market places on the stock is the specific time variability divided by the time factor.

You can keep a running average of the annual variability that the options market places on a particular security. In this way you have an up-to-date market estimate of the variability of the stock you are following. Be sure to use at least a three-month average. Six months may be better. Once you have your current variability estimate, you can make better predictions of how high or low an option will go.

Use your own ingenuity. This is what makes the market competitive. Your instincts and knowledge are being pitted against those of the institutions and fat cats. They have more capital than you, but you outnumber them. Your ideas outnumber theirs. Some of you will make the fat cats heavier. Others of you will make them hungry and clawless only to metamorphose yourselves into Cheshire cats, competing against those from which you rose.

The following chapter discusses the importance of the option buyer in a free enterprise system—how his willingness to take on risk coupled with his desire for leveraged profit may be instrumental in providing a liquidity and stability in stock market investments that were not possible prior to the advent of viable option exchanges.

17 | Epilogue—Where Does It All Lead?

Over the years the institutions have been playing a larger role in the trading activities on the stock exchanges. In recent years the banks, insurance companies, pension funds, and investment counsellors, although controlling only one-third of the shares on the NYSE, accounted for about two-thirds of the trading activity. The small investors were unable to cope with these giants or with the increased costs of trading. Intimidated, and uninspired by the remote prospect of making it big, they slowly shrank away from the investment scene.

Where Are We Now? Inefficient Markets!

The concentration of huge assets in the hands of too few money managers has caused the stock marketplace to become a less efficient allocator of resources. The two-tiered and multitiered markets of the late 1960s and early 1970s were the result of the concentration of wealth in the hands of a few. The big institutions took big positions in many glamour stocks. The prices of these securities were run up and the public got interested in them also. When these securities seemed overpriced, the institutions had to sell. The liquidity was gone from the market. Who could absorb these large sales? Once the cork was popped, all the money managers tried to squeeze through the same bottleneck. Prices plummeted.

If the institutions had had an alternative, the liquidity might have been better and the variability might have been less. The money managers feared shortselling (selling borrowed stock with the hope it will decline in price) because of the great loss potential should the stock unexpectedly advance. If they had had a means for limiting their loss should the stock advance, many institutions might have shorted the stock. Their subsequent buy-backs would have provided brakes on the downswing.

The other alternative was to sell stock to the noninstitutional buyer. There were not enough of these types left to absorb the massive influx of sell orders. How can a vinegar bug get into a bottle of champagne after the bottle's been shaken and the cork has been popped?

The great volatility and loss of liquidity made the equity markets too risky, especially for pension funds. A sign of the times occurred in the Fall of 1975. The State of Connecticut decided to cut the amount of money that it invested in equities. In the fiscal year of 1976 it intended to put about $100 million into bonds and only about $6 million into stocks. It eventually hoped to have about 70 percent of its pension fund investments in fixed-income securities and the remaining 30 percent in stocks.

Where Can We Go? Improve Market Efficiency!

A full-fledged options market that trades both puts and calls can be instrumental in improving market efficiency. The liquidity would be greater and the variability less. This would make equities intrinsically more valuable, because they would have less risk. Pension funds would have a greater assurance of their total return on investment in equities.

The public has returned to trading securities once more, as evidenced by the phenomenal growth of the options markets. The options markets could have a major influence on the pricing mechanisms at the stock exchanges. If the public thought well of a stock, they would buy call options rather than the stock, because the calls are cheaper and the commissions are less. The premiums on call options would go up, making it attractive for institutions to sell (write) calls and buy more shares. The institutions could protect themselves from a sudden decline in the stock by purchasing puts. The public would spark the rise in the price of the stock.

If the public felt a stock would go down, they would buy put options rather than sell the stock short. The prices of puts would go up, making it attractive for institutions to short the stock and sell (write) puts. The institutions could protect themselves from an unexpected rise in the stock price by purchasing calls. The public again would be the prime mover in determining which way a stock should go. In the case above the public caused the stock to go down by buying puts. The institutions could lock in their profit on their short position as the stock declines by rolling over calls at lower and lower striking prices. The brakes would be put on the decline when the institutions repurchased the stock to close out their short position.

If an institution felt it was too heavily invested in a particular security, it could reduce its position by writing calls in an up market and buying puts in a down market. The shares would be distributed in a nondisruptive manner to the buyers of calls or the sellers of puts. There would not be a panic to unload large blocks of stock or the mania to bid prices so high.

The public would once again be responsible for the pricing function of the markets. The public would be responsible for making equities less variable and thus intrinsically more valuable as an investment. The public would be responsible for the reallocation of capital to the equity markets, where capital has become scarce. The voices of many people rather than few would be heard by the mechanisms that affect the market.

What Can We Do When We Get There? Relax and Enjoy!

A broad-based options market can serve the following economic funtions:

1 / *Transference of risk of stock ownership (or short position) to speculators.*

2 / *Reduction of variability and increased liquidity for the stock market.*

3 / *Determination of market behavior by the broad public.*

4 / *Participation in and determination of capital allocation by the broad public.*

These factors will be responsible for making the stock market a more serene entity to live with—no more ulcers for fund managers. The risks and rewards will be better defined so that reasonable goals will have a better chance of being met. There will be fewer wipeouts for the small investor, because fund managers will not panic and dump huge blocks of stock.

The best feature of all is that the small investor will not be shackled by the whims of a few money managers. Collectively, the small investor will be determining the major market moves once again. With a small amount of capital, many clever ones (and a few lucky ones) will multiply their coins through their new-found freedom and enjoy life.

APPENDIXES

A | The Half-Blind Strategy

In the half-blind strategy we are constricted to the following steps:

1 / *Buy the middle-month expiration option. For example, if January, April, and July options are being offered, we purchase the April option.*

2 / *Buy the option whose striking price is just above the price of the stock. If there is no such option, buy the option whose striking price is just below the price of the stock.*

Table A–1 summarizes the actions taken for a full year. The first transaction was made on May 31, 1974, when July, October, and January options on McDonalds were trading. According to Step 1, we selected for purchase the middle-month expiration option. Step 2 constricted us to buying the option whose striking price was just above the price of the stock. On that day McDonalds closed at 54½. There were no October 55 options available then, but there was an October 60, which we bought for 4½. Since we are investing at most only $1250 at three-month intervals, we could purchase only two October 60 options. Three months elapsed and McDonalds stock dropped to 35 on August 30, 1974. The October 60 options that we purchased at 4½ were trading at ⅛. We sold these and purchased three January 40 options for 3½. The remainder of the table is self-explanatory.

Table A–2 summarizes the cumulative profits and losses during the year for the half-blind strategy. In the first two round-trip transactions we lost $919 and $316. In the remaining two round-trip transactions we made $60 and $1689, for a net gain for the year of $514.

The cumulative cash outlay column totals the amount of cash we have expended at the end of each quarterly period. Our average outlay for the year was $1976. On this average outlay we reaped a gain of $514, or 26 percent.

Table A–1 Summary of Option Rollover

Date	Stock Price Px	Action/Option/Price											
		Oct			Jan			Apr			Jul		
		A	*Pst*	*Pxo*	*A*	*Pst*	*Pxo*	*A*	*Pst*	*Pxo*	*A*	*Pst*	*Pxo*
May 31, 1974	54½	B	60	4½									
Aug 30, 1974	35	S	60	⅛	B	40	3½						
Nov 29, 1974	33⅞				S	40	2¾	B	35	6⅛			
Feb 28, 1975	40¾							S	35	6⅞	B	40	6⅛
May 30, 1975	54										S	40	15⅛

A = action: Buy or Sell Pxo = option price
Pst = striking price Px = stock price

Table A–2 Profit and Losses from Half-blind Strategy with McDonalds Options

Date	*Stock Price*	*Action*	*Option Price*	*Com-missions (Approx.)*	*Investment Cost*	*Cumulative Cash Outlay*	*Profit/Loss per Transaction*	*Cumulative Profit/Loss*
May 31 1974	54½	Buy 2 Oct 60	4½	39	−939			
Aug 30	35	Sell 2 Oct 60	⅛	5	+20	−939	−919	−919
1974		Buy 3 Jan 40	3½	48	−1098			
Nov 29	33⅞	Sell 3 Jan 40	2¾	43	+782	−2017	−316	−1235
1974		Buy 2 Apr 35	6⅛	44	−1269			
Feb 28	40¾	Sell 2 Apr 35	6⅞	46	+1329	−2504	+60	−1175
1975		Buy 2 Jul 40	6⅛	44	−1269			
May 30	54	Sell 2 Jul 40	15⅛	67	+2958	−2444	+1689	+514
1975								

Average Cash Outlay = $1976 Profit = +$514

B | Risk and Leverage: How to Calculate Them

The risk in your purchasing an option and holding it until expiration is related to how much the stock has to advance in order for you to get your investment back. Let us consider an option with a striking price of 55 with the stock at 50. If we purchase this option at $2\frac{1}{2}$, the breakeven or intrinsic premium is the striking price minus the stock price plus the option price, or $7\frac{1}{2}$. The stock has to advance $7\frac{1}{2}$ points, or 15 percent, by expiration for us to break even. If we purchase the option for $3\frac{1}{2}$, the stock has to advance $8\frac{1}{2}$ points, or 17 percent, to break even. Risk is the percentage rise a stock must make in order for us to recapture our investment. The higher the intrinsic premium, the higher is our risk. The breakeven or intrinsic premium Pi is given by Pi equals $Pst - Px + Pxo$, where Pst equals striking price, Px equals stock price, and Pxo equals option price.

To calculate the risk factor R, we simply divide the intrinsic premium by the stock price:

$$R = \frac{Pi}{Px} \quad \text{(risk factor)} \qquad \text{(B–1)}$$

The leverage of an option at expiration is zero if the stock closes below the striking price. The leverage is always greater than zero when the stock price is above the striking price. Let us calculate what the leverage is for an option with a striking price of 55 selling at $2\frac{1}{2}$ when the stock is at 50. If the stock closes at 55 or lower by expiration, we lose 100 percent of our investment. If the stock closes at the breakeven price, we gain or lose nothing. We just get back our initial investment. The breakeven premium is $7\frac{1}{2}$ points. The stock has to rise from 50 to $57\frac{1}{2}$ in order for us to recoup all (100 percent) of our investment of 2½. The five-point stock rise from 50 to 55 adds nothing to the value of the option premium. It is worthless in this range at expiration. The stock has to rise 2½ points from 55 to 57½, for us to recoup 100 percent of our investment. A 2½-point rise represents a 5 percent gain when compared to the original price of the stock, 50. Leverage is the percentage change in price of the option divided by the percentage change in price of the stock *to produce that change in the option.* We recoup 100 percent of our option investment when the stock moves from 55 to 57½. Thus, leverage is

$$\text{L} = \frac{\%\text{ change in option price}}{\%\text{ change in stock price}} = \frac{100\%}{5\%} = 20$$

The leverage is obtained by dividing the stock price by the option price:

$$L = \frac{Px}{Pxo} \quad \text{(leverage factor)} \tag{B–2}$$

where Px = stock price

Pxo = option price.

The risk/leverage (R/L) factor is obtained by dividing the risk by the leverage:

$$R/L = \frac{R}{L} = \frac{Pi/Px}{Px/Pxo}$$

$$R/L = \frac{PiPxo}{Px^2} = \frac{(Pst - Px + Pxo)Pxo}{Px^2} \tag{B–3}$$

To calculate the R/L factor for an option with a striking price of 55, stock price of 50, and option price of 2½, we substitute in Eq. (B–3) to get

$$R/L = \frac{(55 - 50 + 2.5)\ 2.5}{(50)^2} = 0.0075$$

It should be pointed out that the R/L factor is proportional to the time left until expiration and the square of the annual variability. You should purchase options only when R/L is less than

$$\frac{0.16\ ts^2}{365} \tag{B–4}$$

where t is the number of days to expiration and s is the annual variability of the stock. Annual variability can be found in Appendix C.

Let us assume that a stock has three options outstanding with 90 days to expiration. The stock is trading at 50. The striking and option prices are as follows: the 45 option sells for 7½; the 50 option sells for 4; the 55 option sells for 2. Which of these options has the lowest risk/leverage factor and thus is the best one to buy? Substituting into Eq. (B–3) we find the *R/L* factors, respectively, to be 0.0075, 0.0064, and 0.0056. The 55 striking price option selling for 2 has the lowest R/L factor (0.0056).

Is the *R/L* factor less than what Eq. (B–4) dictates? The stock variability is 0.40 and there are 90 days to expiration. According to Eq. (B–4), the *R/L* factor must be less than 0.0063. The 45 and 50 striking price options have *R/L* factors greater than 0.0063, and therefore should not be purchased unless you can withstand a negative expected return. The 55 striking price option has a *R/L* factor lower than 0.0063 and therefore may be purchased to provide you with a positive expected return.

C | Variability Estimates

Variability estimates can be arrived at in a number of ways. Some people get an estimate of volatility by calculating the difference between the stock's high and low for the year and dividing by its mean price. This is at most very crude, but gives a ballpark estimate of volatility which is good for comparative purposes.

It is possible to obtain annualized variabilities by considering stock price fluctuations from shorter periods of time. This is so because statistical analysis tells us that the weekly price fluctuation of a stock is independent of the monthly or yearly price fluctuation. We can thus calculate the weekly variability of a stock and convert this to obtain the annual variability.

The annual variabilities of optionable stocks appear in Table C–1. These variabilities were obtained from the weekly stock price closes between June of 1974 and June of 1975. It must be remembered when one is using this table that variabilities change slightly with time. The variability estimates made from that time period will differ from present estimates made from the last twelve months.

Variabilities were calculated from data available for the most recent one-year time period. The results were computed in such a way that the most recent weeks were considered more heavily than the more distant weeks. This is known as a time-weighted calculation. This was done because it is felt that the most recent action of a stock is more indicative of how the stock will behave in the near future. Price fluctuations in the stock, say, five years ago, have a more remote connection with how the stock will behave in the next few months.

Figure C–1 gives the time factor that enables us to convert the annual variabilities to shorter periods of time. A stock has an annual variability of

Table C–1 Annual Variability Estimates

June 1974 to June 1975

	Ticker Symbol	*Stock*	*Annual Variability*
CBOE	AA	ALUMINUM CO AMER	0.44
	AEP	AMERICAN ELEC PWR	0.34
	AHS	AMERICAN HOSP SUPPLY	0.44
	T	AMERICAN TEL & TEL	0.24
	ARC	ATLANTIC RICHFIELD	0.31
	AVP	AVON PRODS	0.54
	BAX	BAXTER LABS	0.43
	BS	BETHLEHEM STL	0.36
	BDK	BLACK & DECKER	0.42
	BA	BOEING	0.42
	BC	BRUNSWICK	0.49
	CBS	CBS	0.38
	FNC	CITICORP	0.44
	KO	COCA COLA	0.44
	CL	COLGATE PALMOLIVE	0.45
	CWE	COMMONWEALTH EDISON	0.28
	CDA	CONTROL DATA	0.48
	DAL	DELTA AIRLINES	0.42
	DOW	DOW CHEM	0.35
	EK	EASTMAN KODAK	0.37
	XON	EXXON	0.30
	FNM	FEDERAL NATL MTG ASSN	0.40
	F	FORD	0.34
	GD	GENERAL DYN	0.47
	GE	GENERAL ELEC	0.42
	GF	GENERAL FOODS	0.36
	GM	GENERAL MTRS	0.32
	GWF	GREAT WESTN FINL	0.49
	GW	GULF & WESTN	0.35
	HAL	HALLIBURTON	0.37
	HWP	HEWLETT PACKARD	0.38
	HIA	HOLIDAY INNS	0.49
	HM	HOMESTAKE MNG	0.46
	HON	HONEYWELL	0.52
	INA	INA	0.36
	IBM	INTL BUSINESS MACHINES	0.34
	IFF	INTL FLAV & FRAG	0.38
	HR	INTL HARVESTER	0.35
	IGL	INTL MIN & CHEM	0.41
	IP	INTL PAPER	0.38
	ITT	INTL TEL & TEL	0.38
	JWC	JIM WALTER CORP	0.40
	JM	JOHNS MANVILLE	0.36
	JNJ	JOHNSON & JOHNSON	0.34
	KN	KENNECOTT COPPER	0.37
	KMG	KERR MCGEE	0.40

	Ticker Symbol	Stock	Annual Variability
	KG	KRESGE	0.48
	LTR	LOEWS	0.46
	MCD	MCDONALDS	0.57
	MRK	MERCK & CO	0.45
	MMM	MINNESOTA MNG & MFG	0.40
	MOB	MOBIL OIL	0.35
	MTC	MONSANTO	0.37
	NSM	NATL SEMICONDUCTOR	0.51
	NWA	NORTHWEST AIRLINES	0.50
	OXY	OCCIDENTAL PETE	0.50
	PZL	PENNZOIL	0.44
	PRD	POLAROID	0.60
	RTN	RAYTHEON	0.48
	RCA	RCA	0.42
	RJR	REYNOLDS R. J.	0.30
	SLB	SCHLUMBERGER	0.37
	S	SEARS	0.38
	SKY	SKYLINE	0.51
	SO	SOUTHERN CO	0.33
	SY	SPERRY RAND	0.43
	SN	STANDARD OIL IND	0.34
	SYN	SYNTEX	0.51
	TSO	TESORO PETE	0.45
	TG	TEXAS GULF	0.36
	TXN	TEXAS INSTRS	0.41
	UAL	UAL INC	0.47
	UPJ	UPJOHN	0.53
	UC	UTAH INTERNATIONAL	0.40
	WY	WEYERHAEUSER	0.43
	WMB	WILLIAMS CO	0.43
	XRX	XEROX	0.49
AMEX	AET	AETNA LIFE & CAS	0.45
	ACY	AMERICAN CYANAMID	0.33
	AHP	AMERICAN HOME PRODS	0.43
	AMF	AMF	0.45
	ASA	ASA LTD	0.43
	AR	ASARCO	0.35
	BRY	BEATRICE FOODS	0.37
	BGH	BURROUGHS	0.40
	CAT	CATERPILLAR TRACTOR	0.34
	CMB	CHASE MANHATTAN	0.40
	CTC	CONTINENTAL TEL	0.35
	DE	DEERE & CO	0.46
	DEC	DIGITAL EQUIP	0.49
	DIS	DISNEY	0.55
	DD	DU PONT	0.38
	ELG	EL PASO CO	0.31
	FCF	FIRST CHARTER FINL	0.54

	Ticker Symbol	*Stock*	*Annual Variability*
	GTE	GENERAL TEL & ELECTRS	0.30
	GS	GILLETTE	0.39
	GT	GOODYEAR	0.34
	GRA	GRACE W. R.	0.34
	G	GREYHOUND	0.35
	GO	GULF OIL	0.32
	HPC	HERCULES	0.44
	HFC	HOUSEHOLD FINANCE	0.33
	MER	MERRILL LYNCH	0.46
	MSA	MESA PETE	0.60
	MOT	MOTOROLA	0.45
	NSI	NORTON SIMON	0.45
	JCP	PENNEY J. C.	0.37
	PFE	PFIZER	0.47
	PD	PHELPS DODGE	0.38
	MO	PHILIP MORRIS	0.42
	P	PHILLIPS PETE	0.44
	PG	PROCTOR & GAMBLE	0.30
	SRL	SEARLE G. D.	0.60
	SYP	SIMPLICITY PATTERN	0.55
	SD	STANDARD OIL CALIF	0.38
	STY	STERLING DRUG	0.47
	TGT	TENNECO	0.30
	TX	TEXACO	0.32
	TGR	TIGER INTL	0.53
	UK	UNION CARBIDE	0.38
	X	UNITED STATES STL	0.34
	WLA	WARNER LAMBERT	0.43
	WX	WESTINGHOUSE	0.46
	ZE	ZENITH	0.54
PWB			
	ABT	ABBOTT LABS	0.39
	ACD	ALLIED CHEM	0.39
	AHC	AMERADA HESS	0.44
	BCC	BOISE CASCADE	0.45
	CLX	CLOROX	0.48
	CLL	CONTINENTAL OIL	0.36
	ENG	ENGELHARD	0.40
	FIR	FIRESTONE TIRE & RUB	0.34
	HJ	HOWARD JOHNSON	0.50
	LLX	LOUISIANA LND & EXPL	0.48
	VEL	VIRGINIA ELECTRIC	0.34
	WU	WESTERN UNION	0.40
	Z	WOOLWORTH	0.38

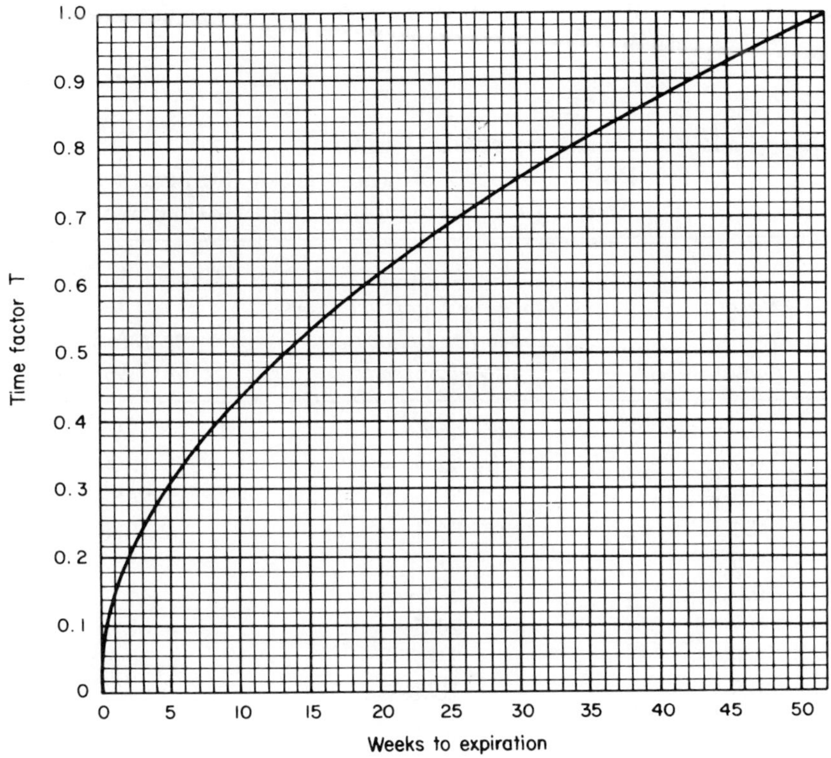

Figure C–1. ***Time factor T vs. weeks to expiration.***

0.40, and we wish to determine its variability for a 15-week period. The time factor for 15 weeks is 0.54. We simply multiply the annual variability by the time factor to get the 15-week variability of 0.216.

Knowing the variability, we can make some probabilistic predictions of what the stock will do in the future. Table C–2 lists the percentage chance that a stock has to close so many points beyond its current trading price at the end of the time period characterized by its variability and point spread factor.

Assume that a stock is currently trading at 50 and has a variability of 0.216 for a particular time period, say 18 weeks. The point spread is obtained by multiplying the variability by the price of the stock times the point spread factor. If the point spread factor is 0.1, the stock has a 46 percent chance to close 1.08 points (0.216 × 50 × 0.1) or higher at the end of the 18-week time period. If the point spread factor is 0.5, the stock has a 31 percent chance to close 5.40 points (0.216 × 50 × 0.5) or higher at the end of the 18-week time period.

Table C–2 Point Spread Odds
Point spread is obtained from the product of point spread factor, variability, and stock price.

Point Spread Factor	*Chance for Stock to Close Above (or Below) its Point Spread*	*Chance for Stock to Close Within its Point Spread*
0.1	46%	8%
0.2	42%	16%
0.3	38%	24%
0.4	34%	32%
0.5	31%	38%
0.6	27%	46%
0.7	24%	52%
0.8	21%	58%
0.9	18%	64%
1.0	16%	68%

D | Statistical and Fundamental Information on Selected Optionable Stocks

AVON PRODUCTS, INC.

LISTED	SYMBOL	INDICATED DIV.	RECENT PRICE	PRICE RANGE (1975)	YIELD
NYSE	AVP	$1.60	43	51 - 28	3.7%

INTRINSIC INVESTMENT QUALITY: UPPER MEDIUM GRADE. EXPANSION INTO NEW FIELDS TO MAINTAIN HIGH GROWTH HAS BEEN DISAPPOINTING.

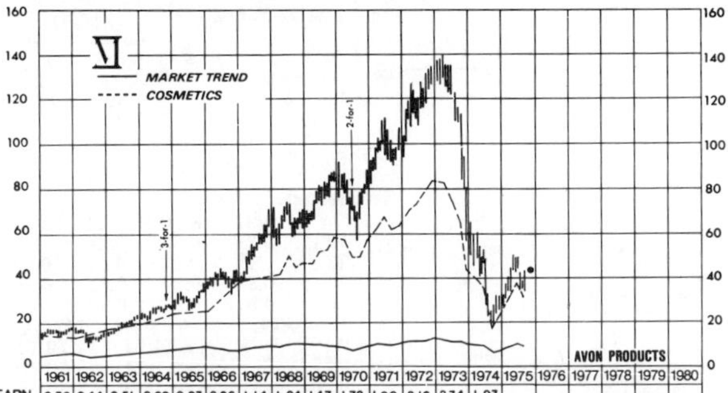

	1961	1962	1963	1964	1965	1966	1967	1968	1969	1970	1971	1972	1973	1974	1975	1976	1977	1978	1979	1980
EARN.	0.36	0.44	0.51	0.69	0.83	0.96	1.14	1.24	1.47	1.72	1.90	2.16	2.34	1.93						
DIV.	0.19	0.23	0.32	0.37	0.45	0.58	0.70	0.80	0.90	1.08	1.25	1.35	1.40	1.48						

CAPITALIZATION:

	(12/31/74) (000)	(%)
Debt	$ 35,646	6.9
Defer.inc.tax	7,727	1.5
Com. & Surp.	471,599	91.6
Total	$514,972	100.0%

Shs. ($0.50)-57,991,239

INTERIM EARNINGS:

Qu.	3/31	6/30	9/30	12/31
72	0.29	0.46	0.46	0.95
73	0.35	0.50	0.48	1.01
74a	0.29	0.38	0.40	0.86
75	0.29	0.47	0.52	

DIVIDENDS:	RECORD	PAYABLE
0.37Q	8/15/74	9/1/74
0.37Q	11/15	12/1
0.37Q	2/18/75	3/1/75
0.37Q	5/15	6/2
0.37Q	8/18	9/1

BACKGROUND:

Avon sells cosmetic and toiletry items including fragrances, make-up, creams, lotions, bath products, deodorants and household products. In addition to the steady broadening of traditional product lines, the Company has been expanding into new product areas, as well as new geographic areas. Distribution is directly to customers at home through more than 450,000 representatives in the United States and foreign countries. Most of domestic sales are in products manufactured by the Company. Foreign operations, excluding Canada, are conducted in 15 countries. In 1974, foreign operations contributed about 38% to consolidated sales and were responsible for 23% of consolidated earnings.

RECENT DEVELOPMENTS:

Sales for the nine months ended 9/30/75 rose 2.9% to $851 million and net income advanced 19.4% to $74.4 million. For the third quarter, sales advanced 1.7% to $300.6 million and net income increased 29.3% to $30.2 million. The profit gains reflect continuing substantial improvement in gross margin. Sales results were good in Latin America and Pacific areas. Sales in the U.S. and Europe were sluggish. Foreign exchange fluctuations helped third quarter earnings by 1c a share, compared with a gain of 3c a share in the prior year period.

PROSPECTS:

Even the stronger contenders in the highly competitive cosmetics and toiletries industry have been finding it increasingly difficult to forge ahead. This trend is likely to continue. Avon is diversifying into areas which, at least for now, are much more demanding than its basic business. Over the long run, new ventures in other areas of consumer products may not be as rewarding. The outlook remains cloudy.

STATISTICS:

YEAR	GROSS REVS. ($ MILL.)	OPER. PROFIT MARGIN %	NET INCOME ($ 000)	WORK CAP. ($ MILL.)	SENIOR CAPITAL ($ MILL.)	NO. SHS. OUT. (000)	EARN. PER SH. $	DIV. PER SH. $	DIV. PAY. %	PRICE RANGE	PRICE X EARN.	AVG. YIELD %
65	352.0	25.5	47,569	71.3	2.5	57,387	0.83	0.45	54	38^{2} - 26^{4}	39.0	1.4
66	408.2	26.2	55,328	85.0	17.8	57,399	0.96	0.58	60	44^{6} - 33	40.5	1.5
67	474.8	26.6	65,383	98.5	16.9	57,429	1.14	0.70	61	71^{2} - 38	47.9	1.3
68	558.6	26.6	71,310	122.8	28.7	57,473	1.24	0.80	65	72 - 55	51.2	1.3
69	656.7	25.9	84,293	132.1	32.9	57,496	1.47	0.90	61	87^{6} - 62^{5}	51.1	1.2
70	759.2	25.9	99,988	164.9	34.8	57,547	1.72	1.08	63	92^{2} - 59^{1}	44.0	1.4
71	873.2	25.3	124,900	185.8	36.1	57,652	1.90	1.25	66	112 - 82^{1}	51.1	1.3
72	1,005.3	25.3	124,929	227.4	37.5	57,845	2.16	1.35	63	139^{6} - 94	54.1	1.2
73	1,150.7	23.3	135,700	273.6	31.7	57,991	2.34	1.40	60	140 - 57^{2}	42.1	1.4
74	1,260.3	18.9	a111,755	292.1	35.6	57,991	a1.93	1.48	77	65 - 18^{5}	21.7	3.5

Note: Adjusted for 2-for-1 stock split, 6/70. a-Reflects change to LIFO accounting.

INCORPORATED: Jan. 27, 1916 - N.Y.

PRINCIPAL OFFICE: 9 West 57th St., New York, N.Y. 10019

ANNUAL MEETING: Last Tuesday in April

NUMBER OF STOCKHOLDERS: 36,000

TRANSFER AGENT: Chase Manhattan Bank, N.Y.

REGISTRAR: Chase Manhattan Bank, N.Y.

INSTIT. HOLDINGS: NO.: 248 SHS.: 7,956,983

OFFICERS

CHAIRMAN: F.G. Fusee

PRESIDENT: D.W. Mitchell

SECRETARY: M. Williams

TREASURER: H.R. Fandl

BOEING COMPANY

LISTED	SYMBOL	INDICATED DIV.	RECENT PRICE	PRICE RANGE (1975)	YIELD
NYSE	BA	$0.95	26	32 - 15	3.7%

INTRINSIC INVESTMENT QUALITY: SPECULATIVE GRADE. DEMAND FOR MILITARY AIRCRAFT AND WEAPONS SYSTEMS IS OFFSETTING SOFTNESS IN JET TRANSPORT ORDERS. DECLINE IN 727 ORDERS.

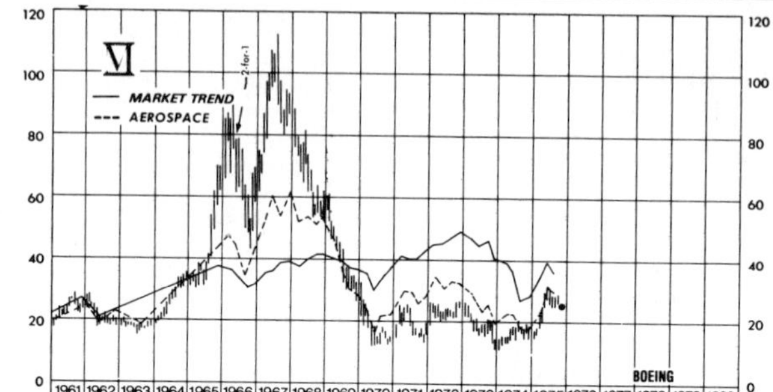

	1961	1962	1963	1964	1965	1966	1967	1968	1969	1970	1971	1972	1973	1974	1975	1976	1977	1978	1979	1980
EARN.	2.24	1.70	1.36	2.82	4.78	3.90	3.89	3.83	0.47	1.02	1.04	1.40	2.38	3.42						
DIV.	0.85	1.00	1.00	1.00	1.25	1.10	1.20	1.20	1.20	0.40	0.40	0.40	0.40	0.75						

CAPITALIZATION: (12/31/74)

	(000)	(%)
Debt	$ 149,039	13.2
Def.inc.tax	23,000	2.1
Com. & Surp.	954,967	84.7
Total	$1,127,006	100.0%

Shs. ($5)-21,171,488

INTERIM EARNINGS:

Qu.	3/31	6/30	9/30	12/31
72	0.31	0.33	0.24	0.52
73	0.49	0.67	0.57	0.65
74	0.83	0.87	0.81	0.91
75	0.87	0.94	0.82	

DIVIDENDS:	RECORD	PAYABLE
0.15Q	11/14/74	12/10/74
0.15 Sp.	11/14	12/10
0.20Q	2/13/75	3/10/75
0.20Q	5/15	6/10
0.20Q	8/14	9/10

BACKGROUND:

Boeing is the largest manufacturer of commercial airliners; current production includes the 707, 727, 737 and 747 aircraft series. For the government, Company is modifying a large fleet of B-52 bombers and producing Sea Knight and Chinook helicopters. In 1974, transportation equipment (primarily aircraft) accounted for 81% of sales and 71% of earnings, with the remainder coming from missiles/space and other activities. In December, 1970, Company established its computer services business as a separate subsidiary. Boeing was the prime contractor for development of the Super Sonic Transport (SST) program. $19,780,000 was recovered from the government for the termination of the program.

RECENT DEVELOPMENTS:

In the third quarter of 1975, despite a 13% decline in sales to $794.6 million, net income increased fractionally to $17.3 million. For the nine months, sales of $2.67 billion were down 2% from a year earlier, but net income was up 5% to $55.8 million. The favorable earnings reflected continued good performance of major programs, lower employment, lower interest costs and higher other income.

PROSPECTS:

Overcapacity in the airline industry will restrict the short-term order rate for 727's. However, the long-term outlook for 727's remains bright. The demand for the Comany's military aircraft and weapon systems including, airborne warning and control system aircraft, short range attack missiles, air-launched cruise missiles and 747 superjets remains strong. Government contracts, including modification of the B-52 bomber fleet, NASA developmental work will add stability to earnings.

STATISTICS:

YEAR	GROSS REVS. ($ MILL.)	OPER. PROFIT MARGIN %	NET INCOME ($ 000)	WORK CAP. ($ MILL.)	SENIOR CAPITAL ($ MILL.)	NO. SHS. OUT. (000)	EARN. PER SH. $	DIV. PER SH. $	DIV. PAY. %	PRICE RANGE	PRICE X EARN.	AVG. YIELD %
65	2,023.4	6.8	78,268	260.3	98.3	16,374	4.78	1.25	26	70^{2} - 30^{1}	10.5	2.5
66	2,356.6	5.5	76,133	434.3	466.5	19,497	3.90	1.10	28	91 - 44^{4}	17.4	1.6
67	2,879.7	5.1	83,938	358.3	480.5	21,597	3.89	1.20	31	112^{3} - 61^{6}	22.4	1.4
68	3,274.0	4.7	82,972	467.0	470.5	21,647	3.83	1.20	31	90^{2} - 52^{4}	18.6	1.7
69	2,834.6	0.1	10,230	610.5	632.5	21,683	0.47	1.20	—	61^{1} - 27^{2}	94.0	2.7
70	3,677.1	1.2	22,090	656.6	623.8	21,683	1.02	0.40	39	31^{7} - 12	21.5	1.8
71	3,039.8	0.8	a22,430	694.8	527.6	21,683	a1.04	0.40	38	25^{2} - 13^{4}	18.6	2.1
72	2,369.6	1.8	30,405	738.5	502.6	21,689	1.40	0.40	29	26^{6} - 19	16.3	1.7
73	3,335.2	1.6	51,215	463.8	164.8	21,296	2.38	0.40	17	26^{7} - 11^{6}	8.1	2.1
74	3,730.7	1.9	72,432	502.1	149.0	21,171	3.42	0.75	22	20^{4} - 11^{5}	4.7	4.7

Note: Adjusted for 2-for-1 stock split 5/66. a-Excl. special items; 1971, $19.8 mill. ($0.91 a share) credit.

INCORPORATED: July 19, 1934—Delaware

PRINCIPAL OFFICE: 7755 E. Marginal Way So. Seattle, Washington 98124

ANNUAL MEETING: First Monday in May

NUMBER OF STOCKHOLDERS: 72,053

TRANSFER AGENT: First National City Bank, N.Y.

REGISTRAR: Bankers Trust Co., N.Y.

INSTIT. HOLDINGS: NO.: 59 SHS.: 4,783,000

OFFICERS

CHAIRMAN: T.A. Wilson

PRESIDENT: M.T. Stamper

SECRETARY: J.E. Prince

TREASURER: J.B.L. Pierce

BURROUGHS CORPORATION

LISTED	SYMBOL	INDICATED DIV.	RECENT PRICE	PRICE RANGE (1975)	YIELD
NYSE	BGH	$0.60	82	111 - 61	0.7%

INTRINSIC INVESTMENT QUALITY: HIGH GRADE. AN EXPANDING PRODUCT RANGE AND BROADENING RENTAL BASE HAVE CONTRIBUTED TO THE STRONG EARNINGS UPTREND.

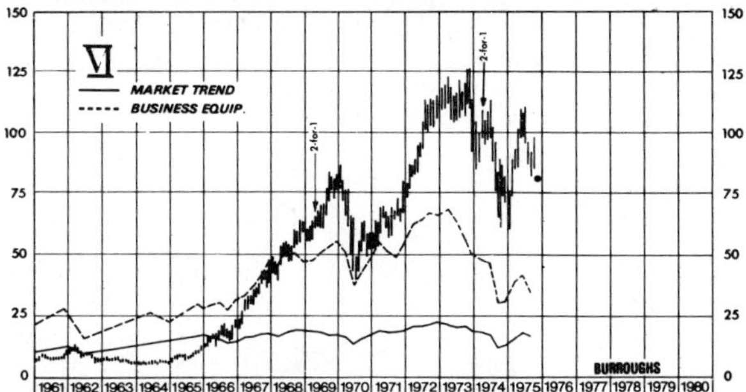

	1961	1962	1963	1964	1965	1966	1967	1968	1969	1970	1971	1972	1973	1974	1975	1976	1977	1978	1979	1980
EARN.	0.40	0.36	0.29	0.35	0.59	0.91	1.07	1.31	1.66	1.81	2.02	2.36	3.01	3.66						
DIV.	0.25	0.25	0.25	0.25	0.25	0.25	0.25	0.25	0.29	0.30	0.30	0.32	0.36	0.48						

CAPITALIZATION:

	(12/31/74) (000)	(%)
Debt	g$ 150,004	11.7
Com. & Surp.	1,133,526	88.3
Total	$1,283,530	100.0%

Shs. ($5)-39,260,258

INTERIM EARNINGS:

Qu.	3/31	6/30	9/30	12/31
72	0.33	0.55	0.44	1.04
73	0.50	0.68	0.54	1.29
74	0.55	0.87	0.66	1.58
75	0.65	0.97	0.69	

DIVIDENDS:	RECORD	PAYABLE
0.125Q	9/20/74	10/21/74
0.125Q	12/20	1/20/75
0.15Q	4/9/75	5/7
0.15Q	7/9	8/7
0.15Q	10/8	11/7

BACKGROUND:

Burroughs Corp. is a leading producer of business equipment with a broad line which covers most major sectors of the data processing market. Products range from very small to giant systems. In addition, the Company offers a full range of peripherals, terminals and data entry equipment. Computer products are supported by an extensive library of application programs which are sold primarily to small users who do not have their own programming capability. Products are designed so that customers can easily move up to larger equipment as their needs expand. The Business Machines Group accounted for 47% of 1974 revenues; International, 37%; Federal and Special Systems, 7%; Business Forms and Supplies, 8%; and other income, 1%.

RECENT DEVELOPMENTS:

In the first nine months of 1975, on 10% increase in revenues to $1.15 billion, net income rose 13% to $91.6 million. Total world-wide orders for the period increased 3%, despite the recession. Backlogs continued at a high level and were up 20% over the beginning of the year, as of September 30, even after adjustment for recent declines in dollar values of certain foreign currencies. Third-quarter net income was up 7% to $27.5 million, on a 6% rise in revenues to $367.7 million.

PROSPECTS:

Burroughs is expected to continue to show good progress. Company objectives call for revenue growth of 15% annually, a realistic expectation. This represents a long term average, however, rather than a minimum expectation in a given year. An expanding product line combined with an effective research and development program should help achieve or exceed this goal. Earnings should rise somewhat faster than sales as the Company benefits increasingly from the economies of higher volume. Earnings should continue to rise in 1976.

STATISTICS:

YEAR	GROSS REVS. ($ MILL.)	OPER. PROFIT MARGIN %	NET INCOME ($ 000)	WORK CAP. ($ MILL.)	SENIOR CAPITAL ($ MILL.)	NO. SHS. OUT. (000)	EARN. PER SH. $	DIV. PER SH. $	DIV. PAY. %	PRICE RANGE	PRICE X EARN.	AVG. YIELD %
65	456.7	8.9	17,528	130.0	91.8	29,540	0.59	0.25	42	12^{7} - 6^{2}	16.1	2.6
66	489.7	13.2	a29,607	174.1	114.4	32,696	a0.91	0.25	28	23^{7} - 12^{3}	19.9	1.4
67	550.6	13.2	34,831	175.6	116.9	32,800	1.07	0.25	24	48 - 20^{2}	31.9	0.7
68	650.8	15.3	43,301	210.0	212.5	33,033	1.31	0.25	19	64 - 39^{2}	39.4	0.5
69	751.8	16.8	55,199	196.0	236.2	34,464	1.66	0.29	17	83^{6} - 55^{1}	41.8	0.4
70	884.6	19.1	66,542	283.9	352.1	36,716	1.81	0.30	17	86^{3} - 39^{3}	34.7	0.5
71	932.7	17.8	74,151	338.2	383.4	36,990	2.02	0.30	15	80 - 52^{2}	32.7	0.5
72	1,040.8	16.5	87,541	410.3	391.0	37,349	2.36	0.32	13	114^{6} - 73	39.9	0.3
73	1,263.6	16.9	115,890	459.5	261.5	38,988	3.01	0.36	12	126^{3} - 92	36.3	0.3
74	1,510.8	17.5	142,937	349.5	150.0	39,260	3.66	0.48	13	113 - 61^{3}	23.8	0.6

Note: Adjusted for 2-for-1 stock splits 4/69, and 4/74. a-Excl. $1.3 mill. (4c a share) capital gain in 1966. g-Incl. $3.7 mill. debentures convertible into common at $70 a share and $14.4 mill. debentures convertible into common at $95 a share.

INCORPORATED: Jan. 16, 1905—Michigan

PRINCIPAL OFFICE: Burroughs Place, Detroit, Mich. 48232

ANNUAL MEETING: Fourth Wed. in March

NUMBER OF STOCKHOLDERS: 53,636

TRANSFER AGENT: Bankers Trust Co., New York; National Bank, Detroit, Mich.

REGISTRAR: Morgan Guaranty Trust Co., N.Y.; Detroit Bank & Tr. Co., Detroit, Mich.

INSTIT. HOLDINGS: NO.: 363; SHS.: 8,935,927

OFFICERS

CHAIRMAN: R.W. MacDonald

PRESIDENT: P.S. Mirabito

SECRETARY: K.L. Miller

TREASURER: L.W. Bowen

CITICORP.

LISTED	SYMBOL	INDICATED DIV.	RECENT PRICE	PRICE RANGE (1975)	YIELD
NYSE	FNC	$0.88	29	39 - 25	3.0%

INTRINSIC INVESTMENT QUALITY: HIGH GRADE. HOLDING COMPANY FOR THE NATION'S SECOND LARGEST BANK.

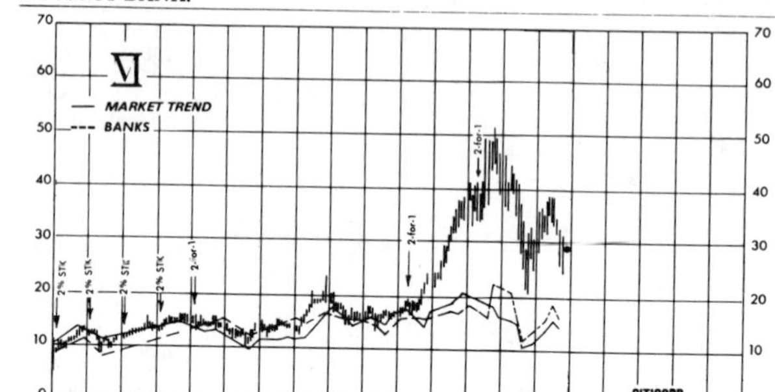

	1961	1962	1963	1964	1965	1966	1967	1968	1969	1970	1971	1972	1973	1974	1975	1976	1977	1978	1979	1980
EARN.	0.69	0.70	0.72	0.82	0.88	0.99	1.06	1.17	1.20	1.32	1.54	1.78	2.14	2.55						
DIV.	0.35	0.36	0.37	0.37	0.40	0.43	0.46	0.51	0.56	0.62	0.66	0.66	0.71	0.78						

CAPITALIZATION: (12/31/74)

	(000)	(%)
Total Deposits	$44,741,706	83.7
Total Debt	b 6,348,806	11.9
Com. & Surp.	2,074,544	3.9
Loan Val. Res.	262,473	0.5
Total	$53,427,529	100.0%

Shs.($6.75)-123,467,046

INTERIM EARNINGS:

Qu.	3/31	6/30	9/30	12/31
72	0.42	0.45	0.43	0.48
73	0.50	0.54	0.54	0.56
74	0.60	0.65	0.65	0.65
75	0.70	0.77	0.75	

DIVIDENDS:	RECORD	PAYABLE
0.20Q	9/30/74	11/1/74
0.20Q	12/31	2/1/75
0.22Q	3/31/75	5/1
0.22Q	6/30	8/1
0.22Q	9/30	11/1

BACKGROUND:

Citicorp is a diversified financial services organization whose principal asset is Citibank. The reorganization of Citibank in 1968, which resulted in the acquisition of Citibank's shares by Citicorp, created an organization which offers a broad range of financially-oriented services. In addition to general banking, Citicorp's subsidiaries and affiliates are engaged in asset-based financing, merchant banking, consumer businesses and investment management and trust services. Altogether Citicorp and its subsidiaries and affiliates have 1,625 offices in 103 countries around the world. Company's divestiture of Advance Mortgage Corp., the nation's third largest mortgage company, which was acquired in 1970, was ordered by the FRB to be completed by 1980.

RECENT DEVELOPMENTS:

Operating earnings for the first nine months of 1975 rose 18% to a record $374.7 million. International earnings were up 26% to $182.8 million. The jump in net interest revenue was partially offset by increases in the provision for loan losses and a $26 million charge for Citicorp's share of losses of its U.K. affiliate. The valuation portion of the loan loss reserve has been increased to $305 million after write-offs of $180 million (including $35 million related to $97 million loan to W.T. Grant).

PROSPECTS:

Aggressive and innovative management has made Citicorp a leader in entering new areas for bank holding companies. Overseas operations have been growing rapidly; these operations should continue to benefit both from the economic growth of overseas markets and from further penetration of those markets. Domestic geographic expansion also enhances prospects. Results for 1975 should be helped by a better gross interest spread domestically during the early part of the year as well as the high level of average earnings assets added during the past two years.

STATISTICS:

YEAR	DEPOSITS ($ MILL.)	LOANS ($ MILL.)	GROSS INCOME ($ MILL.)	NET OPERATING EARNINGS ($000)	PROFIT MARGIN %	SHARES (000)	EARNINGS PER SHARE	DIVIDEND PER SHARE	DIV. PAY. %	BOOK VALUE PER SHARE	PRICE RANGE	PRICE EARN. RATIO	AVG. YIELD %
65	11,949	8,326	g 486.4	93,729	19.3	106,559	0.88	0.40	45	9.42	15^{6} - 13^{1}	16.4	2.8
66	12,940	8,985	571.5	104,890	18.4	106,595	0.99	0.43	43	9.76	14^{5} - 10^{1}	12.5	3.4
67	15,201	10,147	632.0	112,756	17.8	106,820	1.06	0.46	44	10.11	15^{2} - 12^{5}	13.2	3.3
68	16,643	11,544	760.6	124,789	16.4	107,736	1.17	0.51	44	10.49	21^{1} - 13^{6}	15.0	2.9
69	19,142	13,571	958.0	c130,580	13.6	108,525	1.20	0.56	47	10.87	20^{6} - 14^{4}	14.6	3.2
70	21,013	15,267	1,703 5	143,781	8.4	109,055	1.32	0.62	47	11.32	18^{6} - 13^{6}	12.3	3.8
71	24,260	18,503	1,788.6	168,198	9.4	110,080	1.54	0.66	43	12.22	23^{6} - 16^{4}	13.1	3.3
72	27,704	21,573	1,954.6	201,801	10.3	116,055	1.78	0.66	37	13.44	38^{4} - 21^{5}	16.9	2.2
73	34,942	27,971	3,091.6	254,820	8.2	121,966	2.14	0.71	33	14.89	51^{4} - 33^{5}	19.9	1.7
74	44,742	35,294	4,988.3	313,027	6.3	123,467	2.55	0.78	31	16.80	46^{2} - 20^{7}	13.2	2.3

Note: Adjusted for 2-for-1 stock splits 1/65, 4/71 and 3/73. b-Convertible into common at $16.67 a share. c-Reflects accounting change, 1968 restated to $120.5 mill. ($1.13 a share). g-Incl. funds sold.

INCORPORATED: 1967—Delaware

PRINCIPAL OFFICE: 399 Park Avenue, New York, N.Y. 10022

ANNUAL MEETING: Last Tues. in March

NUMBER OF STOCKHOLDERS: 75,000

TRANSFER AGENT: First National City B,nk, N.Y.; Bank of America, San Francisco, Calif.

REGISTRAR: U.S. Trust Co., N.Y.; Wells Fargo Bank, San Francisco, Calif.

INSTIT. HOLDINGS: NO.: 432; SHS.: 18,609,009

OFFICERS

CHAIRMAN: W.B. Wriston

PRESIDENT: W.I. Spencer

SECRETARY: C.W. Desch

TREASURER: C.W. Desch

COLGATE-PALMOLIVE COMPANY

LISTED	SYMBOL	INDICATED DIV.	RECENT PRICE	PRICE RANGE (1975)	YIELD
NYSE	CL	$0.76	28	35 - 22	2.7%

INTRINSIC INVESTMENT QUALITY: INVESTMENT GRADE. THIS IS A LEADING PRODUCER OF SOAP AND TOILET ARTICLES THROUGHOUT THE WORLD.

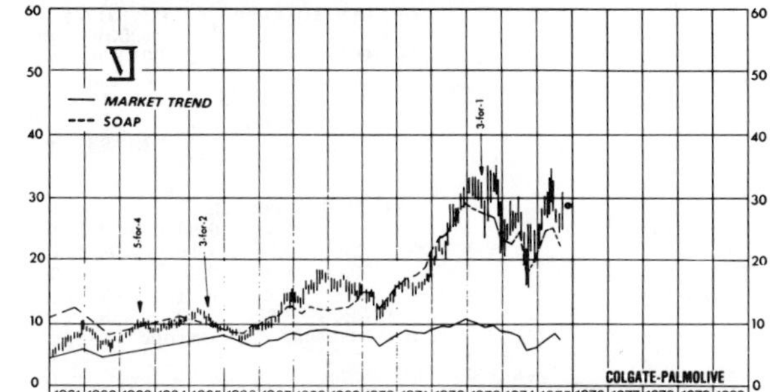

	1961	1962	1963	1964	1965	1966	1967	1968	1969	1970	1971	1972	1973	1974	1975	1976	1977	1978	1979	1980
EARN.	0.47	0.49	0.51	0.55	0.61	0.67	0.75	0.82	0.86	0.92	1.04	1.07	1.31	1.52						
DIV.	0.25	0.25	0.26	0.27	0.28	0.30	0.33	0.37	0.40	0.43	0.47	0.49	0.52	0.60						

CAPITALIZATION: (12/31/74)

	(000)	(%)
Debt	$ 84,607	10.3
Minority Int.	1,743	0.2
Pfd.	g 12,732	1.5
Defer.inc.tax	38,705	4.7
Com. & Surp.	686,224	83.3
Total	$824,011	100.0%

Shs. ($1)-(3/31/75)-68,514,157

INTERIM EARNINGS:

Qu.	3/31	6/30	9/30	12/31
72b	0.20	0.26	0.31	0.30
73c	0.24	0.33	0.38	0.36
74h	0.27	0.40	0.45	0.40
75	0.32	0.46	0.51	

DIVIDENDS:	RECORD	PAYABLE
0.17Q	10/25/74	11/15/74
0.17Q	1/24/75	2/15/75
0.17Q	4/25	5/15
0.17Q	7/25	8/15
0.19Q	10/24	11/15

BACKGROUND:

Colgate-Palmolive is the third largest soap maker in terms of sales. Foreign operations are of major importance, and account for more than half of sales and an even larger percentage of consolidated earnings. Company makes a line of soaps and detergents including Vel, Fab, Ajax, Cold Power, Cashmere Bouquet and Palmolive soaps. Toilet goods include Lustrecreme and Halo Hair Shampoos, toothpastes and shaving cream. Among the Company's nonsoap household products are Florient air freshener, Baggies disposable bags and Handy Wipes disposable towels. Acquisitions have contributed importantly to diversification. Dividends have been paid since 1895.

RECENT DEVELOPMENTS:

Sales for the nine months ended 9/30/75 advanced 7% to $2.14 billion while net income was up 15% to $89 million. Net income for the third quarter advanced 14% to $35 million on a sales gain of 8% to $730.2 million. The results primarily reflect growth in overseas markets, where the Colgate, Kendall and Helena Rubenstein divisions all contributed. The results include the operations of Ram Golf Corp. and Bancroft Sporting Goods Co. The quarterly cash dividend was increased 2c to 19c a share.

PROSPECTS:

Strong consumer acceptance of Colgate's products in both domestic and foreign markets will help the Company to continue its sales and earnings growth trend in coming years. Growth will come from expansion of present product lines and expansion into new markets, both domestically and overseas. A third source is through improvement of existing products as well as development of new ones through extensive research. Acquisitions, such as Kendall and Helena Rubenstein, further enhance prospects. Higher earnings are anticipated in 1976.

STATISTICS:

YEAR	GROSS REVS. ($ MILL.)	OPER. PROFIT MARGIN %	NET INCOME ($ 000)	WORK CAP. ($ MILL.)	SENIOR CAPITAL ($ MILL.)	NO. SHS. OUT. (000)	EARN. PER SH. $	DIV. PER SH. $	DIV. PAY. %	PRICE RANGE	PRICE X EARN.	AVG. YIELD %
65	862.1	6.6	28,020	169.1	50.5	45,357	0.61	0.28	46	12^4 - 8^7	17.5	2.6
66	931.6	7.5	30,475	181.8	45.9	44,718	0.67	0.30	45	10 - 7^4	13.0	3.4
67	1,025.4	7.4	33,511	187.8	40.9	44,244	0.75	0.33	44	15^1 - 9	16.1	2.8
68	1,098.1	7.5	36,590	199.3	39.9	44,202	0.82	0.37	45	18^3 - 12^2	18.7	2.4
69	1,141.6	7.4	37,802	215.3	38.8	43,683	0.86	0.40	47	17^4 - 13^3	18.0	2.6
70	1,210.2	7.0	40,312	223.6	26.2	43,221	0.92	0.43	47	15^7 - 10^4	14.3	3.3
71	1,309.6	7.5	44,940	249.1	34.5	42,942	1.04	0.47	45	20^3 - 14^3	16.8	2.7
b72	1,807.6	7.7	67,541	356.0	73.8	62,979	1.07	0.49	46	31^5 - 19^1	23.7	1.9
c73	2,195.3	7.7	88,769	429.7	81.7	67,685	1.31	0.52	40	35^1 - 21	21.4	1.9
74	2,615.4	7.6	h104,160	475.1	97.3	68,705	h1.52	0.60	39	30^2 - 15^6	15.1	2.6

Note: Adjusted for stock splits: 3-for-2, 7/65; 3-for-1, 5/73. b-Incl. acquisition of Kendall Co. for entire period. c-Incl. acquisition of Helena Rubenstein. g-Incl. 2,107 shares each convertible into 10.05 common shares. h-Before $14.5 mill. (21c a share) gain.

INCORPORATED: July 25, 1923--Delaware

PRINCIPAL OFFICE: 300 Park Avenue, New York, N.Y. 10022

ANNUAL MEETING: Fourth Wed. in April

NUMBER OF STOCKHOLDERS: 41,400

TRANSFER AGENT: Morgan Guaranty Trust Co., N.Y.; First National Bank of Boston

REGISTRAR: Chase Manhattan Bank, N.Y.; First National Bank of Boston

INSTIT. HOLDINGS: NO.: 130; SHS.: 5,839,010

OFFICERS

CHAIRMAN: D.R. Foster

PRESIDENT: K. Crane

SECRETARY: R. Cantwell

TREASURER: W.R. Schantz, Jr.

CONTROL DATA CORPORATION

LISTED	SYMBOL	INDICATED DIV.	RECENT PRICE	PRICE RANGE (1975)	YIELD
NYSE	CDA	...	19	24 - 11	...

INTRINSIC INVESTMENT QUALITY: SPECULATIVE GRADE. COMPANY IS A MAJOR FACTOR IN BOTH ELECTRONIC DATA PROCESSING AND FINANCIAL SERVICES.

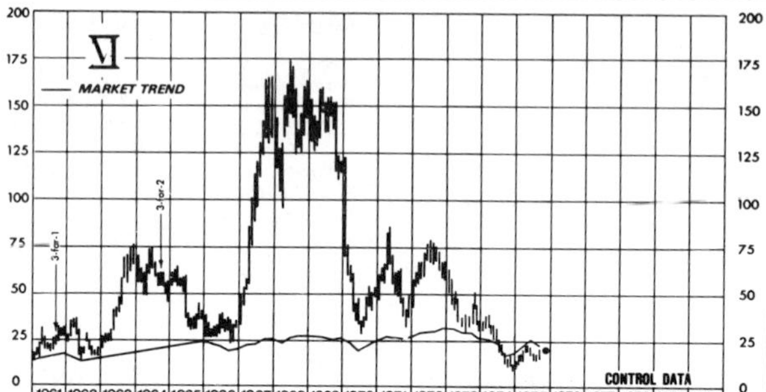

	1961	1962	1963	1964	1965	1966	1967	1968	1969	1970	1971	1972	1973	1974	1975	1976	1977	1978	1979	1980
EARN.	0.16	0.26	0.50	0.88	1.07	d	0.96	3.23	3.20	d	2.38	3.93	3.70	0.09						
DIV.	—	—	—	—	—	—	—	—	—	—	—	—	—	—						

CAPITALIZATION: (12/31/74)

	(000)	(%)
Debt	b$ 261,896	21.5
Defer.inc.tax	67,255	5.5
4½% pfd. ($100)	37,113	3.0
Com. & Surp.	853,634	70.0
Total	$1,219,898	100.0%

Shs. ($1)-15,952,528

INTERIM EARNINGS:

Qu.	3/31	6/30	9/30	12/31
72n	0.70	1.10	1.04	1.09
73n	1.01	0.95	0.82	0.92
74n	0.89	0.71	d0.47	d1.04
75n	0.66	0.69	0.58	

DIVIDENDS: **RECORD** **PAYABLE**

None Paid

BACKGROUND:

Control Data's principle businesses are in large scale computer systems, computer services, peripheral products, and financial services. Company manufactured computer systems and computer services are marketed worldwide to users in government, education, process control, petroleum, utilities, nuclear power, manufacturing, brokerage, finance, transportation and health care. Company's data services offerings include time-sharing, remote batch and traditional batch processing for both commercial and engineering applications. Company also produces a broad line of disk drives and disk packs. Financial services are offered through the Commercial Credit subsidiary and include consumer and business loans, and casualty and life insurance.

RECENT DEVELOPMENTS:

In the third quarter of 1975, Control Data achieved a profit of $9.6 million, in contrast with a year-earlier loss of $7.1 million. Computer operations recovered strongly from a loss of $13.9 million to a profit of $5.1 million. Revenues from that source rose 9% to $310.2 million. However, Profits from Commercial Credit's business declined 30% to $5 million. Shipments of the first computers in the Cyber 170 family were made in the quarter, but demand for peripherals to other systems slowed.

PROSPECTS:

Company is in a gradual transition from its earlier strategy of emphasizing large computers to that of data services. In computer operations, data services and peripheral products have good long-range potential. Profits from the systems business have been under pressure as a result of inflation as well as high development and interest costs. Increased Cyber 170 shipments should help near-term results. In the financial services subsidiary, earnings are tied to interest rates. Lower rates are helping the performance of these operations.

STATISTICS:

YEAR	GROSS REVS. ($ MILL.)	OPER. PROFIT MARGIN %	NET INCOME ($ 000)	WORK CAP. ($ MILL.)	SENIOR CAPITAL ($ MILL.)	NO. SHS. OUT. (000)	EARN. PER SH. $	DIV. PER SH. $	DIV. PAY. %	PRICE RANGE	PRICE X EARN.	AVG. YIELD %
e66	167.6	1.4	d1,912	67.4	100.1	7,558	d0.38	Nil	—	39^{2} - 23^{5}	—	—
e67	245.2	11.2	8,406	168.8	201.6	7,730	0.96	Nil	—	165^{5} - 33^{4}	—	—
e68	387.4	13.4	18,464	197.2	189.7	8,950	2.04	Nil	—	-	--	—
68	438.0	12.7	c45,509	194.7	184.6	13,815	3.23	Nil	—	174 - 95^{1}	41.7	—
69	570.8	10.0	47,196	255.9	190.3	14,251	m3.20	Nil	—	159^{2} - 110	42.1	—
70	539.5	d	d 3,209	133.5	185.2	14,299	d0.34	Nil	—	122^{4} - 28^{6}	—	—
71	571.2	1.8	n35,781	204.3	326.4	14,363	n2.38	Nil	—	85 - 32^{2}	24.6	—
72	663.7	7.3	n60,506	228.7	287.7	15,706	n3.93	Nil	—	79^{3} - 42^{4}	15.5	—
g73	936.0	7.8	n60,362	280.9	281.4	15,894	n3.70	Nil	—	62 - 30^{3}	12.5	—
74	1,080.6	d	n2,991	281.2	299.0	15,953	n0.09	Nil	—	39^{1} - 9^{4}	—	—

b-Incl. $28.2 mill. debs. conv. into common at $85.80 a share. $15.0 mill. conv. at $136.80 a sh. and $1.1 mill. conv. at $87.65 a share. c-Incl. Commercial Credit. n-Before special credit; 1971, $0.07 mill. ($0.01 a share); 1972, $1.9 mill. ($0.13 a share); 1973, $0.5 mill. (3c a share); 1974, $0.7 mill. (4c a share) 1975 $0.2 mill. (1c a share).

INCORPORATED: May 31,1912—Delaware

PRINCIPAL OFFICE: P.O. Box 0, Minneapolis, Minn. 55440

ANNUAL MEETING: First Wed. In May

NUMBER OF STOCKHOLDERS: 50,730

TRANSFER AGENT: First National Bank, Minneapolis, Minn.; Chase Manhattan Bank, N.Y.; Royal Trust Co., Toronto, Ca

REGISTRAR: Northwestern National Bank Minneapolis, Minn.; Chemical Bank, N.Y.

INSTIT. HOLDINGS: NO.: 81; SHS.: 2,373,775

OFFICERS

CHAIRMAN: W.C. Norris

PRESIDENT:

SECRETARY: R.B. Hawkins

TREASURER: W.B. Quackenbush

DELTA AIR LINES, INC.

LISTED	SYMBOL	INDICATED DIV.	RECENT PRICE	PRICE RANGE (1975)	YIELD
NYSE	DAL	$0.60	33	41 - 25	1.8%

INTRINSIC INVESTMENT QUALITY: MEDIUM GRADE. COMPANY HAS SHOWN CONSISTENT PROFITABILITY BECAUSE OF CAPABLE MANAGEMENT AND SOUND ROUTE STRUCTURE.

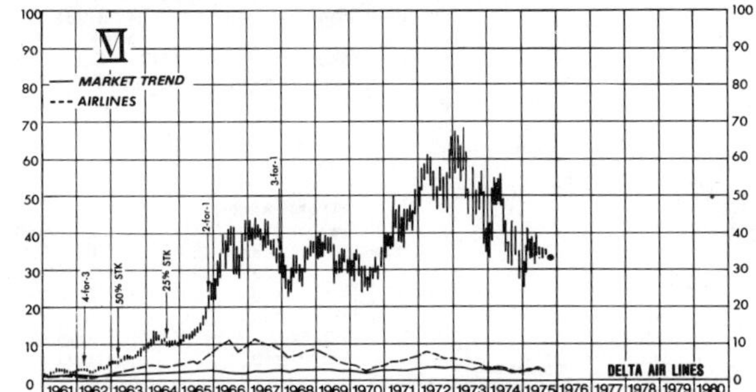

	1961	1962	1963	1964	1965	1966	1967	1968	1969	1970	1971	1972	1973	1974	1975	1976	1977	1978	1979	1980
EARN.	0.28	0.37	0.72	0.82	1.20	1.81	2.57	1.89	2.05	2.33	1.57	2.20	3.32	4.56	2.48					
DIV.	0.08	0.10	0.16	0.23	0.28	0.33	0.37	0.40	0.40	0.45	0.50	0.50	0.55	0.60						

CAPITALIZATION:

	(6/30/75) (000)	(%)
Debt	$395,673	34.6
Defer. inc. tax	267,361	23.4
Com. & Surp.	481,176	42.0
Total	$1,144,210	100.0%

Shs. ($3)-19,880,577

INTERIM EARNINGS:

Qu.	9/30	12/31	3/31	6/30
73	0.74	0.94	0.64	1.00
74	0.88	1.15	1.07	1.46
75	1.24	0.62	0.21	0.41
72	0.31			

DIVIDENDS:	RECORD	PAYABLE
0.15Q	11/8/74	12/1/74
0.15Q	2/7/75	3/1/75
0.15Q	5/9	6/1
0.15Q	8/8	9/1
0.15Q	11/7	12/1

BACKGROUND:

Delta's major routes extend from N.Y. to Atlanta, New Orleans and Houston; Chicago-Atlanta-Miami; Chicago-St. Louis-New Orleans; Atlanta-Dallas-Ft. Worth-Los Angeles and San Francisco; New Orleans-San Juan, and Caracas. After acquisition of Northeast Airlines in 1972, the combined airline ranks as the sixth largest U.S. carrier, with new routes throughout the Northeast, and to Bermuda, Nassau and Florida. The present fleet consists of 178 owned and leased aircraft, which includes L-1011's and B-747 jumbo jets, DC-8's, DC-9's and both B-727-100 and B-727-200 aircraft.

RECENT DEVELOPMENTS:

Revenues in the first three months of fiscal 1976 declined 3% to $349.6 million, while net income dropped 75% to $6.2 million. Total operating revenues for fiscal 1975 rose 12% to $1.38 billion, but net income declined 46% to $49.2 million including a gain of $4.0 million from the sale of aircraft. As of June 30, 1975 debt included $260.0 million under the 1973 bank credit agreement and $41.8 million due insurance companies.

PROSPECTS:

Domestic operations have reflected reduced business and leisure-time travel. Earnings in fiscal 1976 are expected to decline further. Long-term outlook remains satisfactory with improved profit margins and above average revenue growth expected over the longer run; however, profit margins will remain under pressure if jet fuel costs continue to rise. Capital expenditures of approximately $680 mill. have been allocated for fleet expansion during fiscal years 1974 through 1977.

STATISTICS:

YEAR	GROSS REVS. ($ MILL.)	OPER. PROFIT MARGIN %	NET INCOME ($000)	WORK. CAP. ($ MILL.)	SENIOR CAPITAL ($ MILL.)	NO. SHS. OUT. (000)	EARN. PER SH. $	DIV. PER SH. $	PASS. LOAD FACT. %	PRICE RANGE	PRICE X EARN.	AVG. YIELD %
6/30												
66	318.9	20.6	34,554	39.9	88.4	19,125	1.81	0.33	61.0	43^{1} - 22^{1}	18.1	1.0
67	397.8	22.4	49,190	20.7	86.3	19,125	2.57	0.37	66.2	44^{2} - 29	14.2	1.0
68	431.6	15.8	36,134	24.1	132.4	19,125	1.89	0.40	59.4	38^{1} - 23^{2}	16.2	1.3
69	516.1	15.9	39,191	16.0	214.9	19,125	2.05	0.40	55.9	40^{7} - 26^{1}	16.2	1.2
70	622.1	14.9	44,527	13.9	214.9	19,125	2.33	0.45	50.6	34 - 24	12.4	1.6
71	661.2	8.0	29,994	d25.4	188.9	19,125	1.57	0.50	47.3	51^{3} - 33^{2}	27.0	1.2
72	757.6	10.0	42,169	d 4.7	167.4	19,160	2.20	0.50	48.0	65^{6} - 45^{1}	25.2	0.9
b73	1,049.7	11.5	65,995	d24.1	168.0	19,867	3.32	0.55	51.7	68^{3} - 35^{2}	15.6	1.1
74	1,227.1	12.8	90,649	d24.4	345.1	19,879	4.56	0.60	54.8	56^{1} - 27^{7}	9.2	1.4
75	1,377.0	6.9	49,223	d31.3	395.7	19,881	2.48	0.60	54.0			

Note: Adjusted for stock splits: 2-for-1, 12/65; 3-for-1, 12/67. b-Incl acquisitions.

INCORPORATED: June 28, 1967—Delaware

PRINCIPAL OFFICE: Hartsfield Airport, Atlanta, Georgia 30320

ANNUAL MEETING: Fourth Thursday in Oct.

NUMBER OF STOCKHOLDERS: 23,638

TRANSFER AGENT: Citizens & Southern National Bank, Atlanta, Ga.

REGISTRAR: Citizens & Southern National Bank, Atlanta, Ga.

INSTIT. HOLDINGS: NO.: 124 SHS.: 5,226,447

OFFICERS

CHAIRMAN: W.T. Beebe

PRESIDENT: D.C. Garrett, Jr.

SECRETARY: R.S. Maurer

TREASURER: R. Oppenlander

DIGITAL EQUIPMENT CORPORATION

LISTED	SYMBOL	INDICATED DIV.	RECENT PRICE	PRICE RANGE (1975)	YIELD
NYSE	DEC	- - -	129	136 - 45	- - -

INTRINSIC INVESTMENT QUALITY: MEDIUM GRADE. THROUGH AGGRESSIVE PRODUCT DEVELOPMENT AND MARKETING, COMPANY HAS BECOME AN IMPORTANT COMPUTER MAKER.

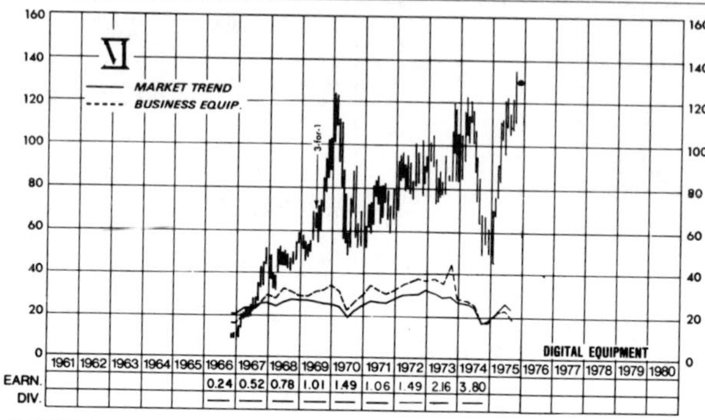

CAPITALIZATION: (6/29/75)

	(000)	(%)
Debt	$ 85,215	17.8
Com. & Surp.	394,385	82.2
Total	$479,600	100.0%

Shs. ($1)-12,021,793-(adj.)

INTERIM EARNINGS:

Qu.	9/30	12/31	3/31	6/30
73	0.33	0.42	0.56	0.85
74	0.58	0.85	1.01	1.36
75	0.63	0.81	0.95	1.46
76	0.95			

DIVIDENDS:	RECORD	PAYABLE
3-for-1 split	5/23/69	6/27/69

BACKGROUND:

Digital Equipment is a leading manufacturer of mini-computers, with a broad line of small, general purpose digital computers. Sizes range from a suit-case size table top model to larger ones used in time-sharing functions. Applications include scientific, medical, industrial, and educational uses. With R&D expenditures averaging over 10% of sales, Company has developed a variety of peripheral equipment including magnetic tape systems, disc and drum storage readers, printers, plotters, cathode-ray-tube display and data communication interfacing terminals. Software is designed both for broad and specific market applications. Most of its computers are sold rather than leased, making Company more vulnerable to economic fluctuations.

RECENT DEVELOPMENTS:

Revenues in the first quarter of fiscal 1976 increased 20% to $140.5 million and net income rose 34% to $11.4 million. In June, 1975 the Company announced plans to construct a plant in Phoenix, Arizona. Sales increased 27% to $533.8 million in fiscal 1975 and net income rose 4% to $46 million. There was a relative lack of strength in the original equipment, industrial and large-scale computer markets due to the recession. However, the rate of incoming orders remained strong, helped by the introduction of new products.

PROSPECTS:

Heavy expenditures for R&D should continue to provide the impetus for long-term growth. The pattern of growth, however, is not expected to be smooth because of the rapidly changing nature of the computer industry and the uneven flow of technological progress. Growth overseas will probably be somewhat faster than in domestic markets. Over the near term, some parts of the Company's business will reflect the effects of the recession while others will continue to show good growth. Higher earnings are expected in fiscal 1976.

STATISTICS:

YEAR	GROSS REVS. ($ MILL.)	OPER. PROFIT MARGIN %	NET INCOME ($ 000)	WORK CAP. ($ MILL.)	SENIOR CAPITAL ($ MILL.)	NO. SHS. OUT. (000)	EARN. PER SH. $	DIV. PER SH. $	DIV. PAY. %	PRICE RANGE	PRICE X EARN.	AVG. YIELD %
6/30												
67	38.9	21.3	4,541	14.0	0.1	8,730	0.52	Nil	—	52$_5$ - 9^6	59.4	—
68	57.3	22.1	6,857	19.8	Nil	8,780	0.78	Nil	—	59^5 - 31$^6_1$	58.6	—
69	87.9	18.9	9,329	40.5	Nil	9,216	1.01	Nil	—	103 - 46$^1_6$	73.8	—
70	135.4	19.4	14,400	56.1	Nil	9,673	1.49	Nil	—	124$_4$ - 48$^6_4$	58.0	—
71	146.8	12.3	10,600	96.1	Nil	10,239	1.06	Nil	—	85^4 - 52$^4_4$	65.1	—
72	187.5	13.4	15,300	87.2	Nil	10,343	1.49	Nil	—	103$_2$ - 69$^4_2$	57.9	—
73	265.5	13.8	23,500	152.7	Nil	11,079	2.16	Nil	—	119$^2_6$ - 73^2	44.6	—
74	421.9	15.4	44,400	238.7	10.6	11,932	3.80	Nil	—	122^6 - 49	22.6	—
75	533.8	14.0	46,000	333.2	85.2	12,022	3.85					

Note: Adjusted for 3-for-1 split 6/69.

INCORPORATED: August 23, 1957—Mass.

PRINCIPAL OFFICE: 146 Main Street
Maynard, Mass. 01754

ANNUAL MEETING: Last Tuesday in October

NUMBER OF STOCKHOLDERS: 14,393

TRANSFER AGENT: National Shawmut Bank, Boston
Morgan Guaranty Trust, N.Y.

REGISTRAR: National Shawmut Bank, Boston
Chase Manhattan Bank, N.Y.

INSTIT. HOLDINGS: NO.: 148
SHS.: 3,616,588

OFFICERS

CHAIRMAN:

PRESIDENT:
K.H. Olsen

SECRETARY:
E.A. Schwartz

TREASURER:
A.M. Bertocchi

DISNEY (WALT) PRODUCTIONS

LISTED	SYMBOL	INDICATED DIV.	RECENT PRICE	PRICE RANGE (1975)	YIELD
NYSE	DIS	\$0.12	50	56 - 21	0.2%

INTRINSIC INVESTMENT QUALITY: MEDIUM GRADE. THE ABOVE AVERAGE EARNINGS RECORD OF THIS COMPANY REFLECTS GOOD CONSUMER ACCEPTANCE OF ITS ENTERTAINMENT PRODUCTS.

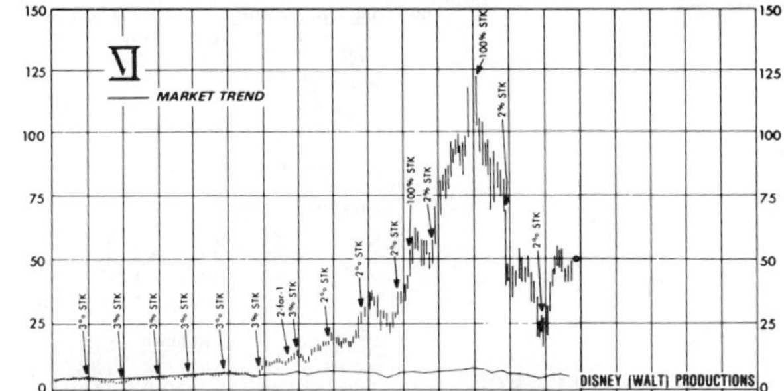

	1961	1962	1963	1964	1965	1966	1967	1968	1969	1970	1971	1972	1973	1974	1975	1976	1977	1978	1979	1980
EARN.	0 25	0 29	0 36	0 39	0 62	0 66	0 54	0 68	0.75	0.88	0 98	1 39	1 61	1 63						
DIV.	0.04	0.04	0.04	0 04	0.04	0 04	0.04	0 07	0 08	0.07	0 09	0. 10	0. 14	0 12						

CAPITALIZATION: (9/30/74)

	(000)	(%)
Debt	\$ 60,801	9.0
Defer. inc. tax	63,144	9.3
Com. & Surp.	552,478	81.7
Total	\$676,423	100.0%

Shs. (\$1.25)-29,738,563-(adj.)

INTERIM EARNINGS:

Qu.	12/31	3/31	6/30	9/30
72	0.18	0.30	0.35	0.56
73	0.18	0.35	0.46	0.62
74	0.20	0.31	0.42	0.70
75	0.24	0.47	0.53	

DIVIDENDS:	RECORD	PAYABLE
0.03Q	12/5/74	1/1/75
2% stk	12/5	1/1
0.03Q	3/10/75	4/1
0.03Q	7/7	8/5
0.03Q	10/6	11/5

BACKGROUND:

Walt Disney produces and distributes motion pictures including animated cartoon-type, live-action and nature films; operates Disneyland, an amusement park (opened in 1955) in Anaheim, Cal., near Los Angeles; produces films for television; and conducts other activities including licensing of its characters, publishing, music and records. In the fiscal 1974, entertainment and recreational activities contributed 66% to total revenues, film rentals 21% and other activities 13%. Walt Disney World, a large recreation complex in Florida opened in October, 1971. The Company's film library contains 114 full-length features and over 500 short subjects and other films.

RECENT DEVELOPMENTS:

Revenues for the nine months ended 6/30/75 advanced 24% to \$347.1 million. Net income for the period increased 33% to \$37.0 million. Operating profit margins for entertainment and recreational activities widened to 15.4% as compared to 11.1% a year earlier. The wider profit margins were achieved despite a \$3.8 million write-off for the abandonment of certain projects and imagineering concepts. Attendence levels at Disneyland and Walt Disney World were ahead of year earlier levels, 4.7% and 20.8%, respectively.

PROSPECTS:

Disney derives about 75% of total revenues from its two entertainment parks and earnings should be helped by the price increases implemented at them and by higher room rates at the Disney World hotels. Prospects are clouded due to moves that may be taken to curtail gasoline consumption, but the cutbacks in consumer spending may benefit the Company's motion picture business as consumers switch to lower cost entertainment. Earnings in fiscal 1976 should move to higher levels.

STATISTICS:

YEAR	GROSS REVS. ($ MILL.)	OPER. PROFIT MARGIN %	NET INCOME ($ 000)	WORK CAP. ($ MILL.)	SENIOR CAPITAL ($ MILL.)	NO. SHS. OUT. (000)	EARN. PER SH. $	DIV. PER SH. $	DIV. PAY. %	PRICE RANGE	PRICE X EARN.	AVG. YIELD %
9/30												
65	109.9	20.2	11,379	21.6	8.0	18,409	0.62	0.04	7	6^{3}_{1} - 4^{4}_{2}	8.9	0.7
66	116.5	20.1	12,392	16.9	6.5	18,674	0.66	0.04	6	9^{1} - 4^{2}_{1}	10.0	0.6
67	117.5	16.7	a10,367	21.4	13.7	19,054	a0.54	0.04	8	14_{2} - 8^{1}_{2}	20.3	0.3
68	137.1	18.4	13,106	52.6	47.0	19,168	0.68	0.07	10	21^{2}_{2} - 9^{2}_{6}	22.3	0.4
69	148.4	21.9	15,804	94.4	51.7	22,152	0.75	0.07	9	31^{2}_{4} - 15^{6}_{6}	31.6	0.3
70	167.1	26.2	21,759	56.6	1.7	24,844	0.88	0.07	8	36^{4}_{6} - 20^{6}_{5}	32.7	0.2
71	175.6	27.6	26,721	36.9	102.8	27,416	0.98	0.09	9	68^{6}_{7} - 32^{5}_{6}	5.2	0.2
72	328.8	22.6	40,293	23.7	53.5	29,701	1.39	0.10	7	113^{7}_{1} - 63^{6}_{7}	63.8	0.1
73	385.1	23.4	47,768	1.6	44.4	29,739	1.61	0.14	9	119^{1}_{3} - 38^{7}_{5}	48.3	0.2
74	429.9	26.1	48,328	33.7	60.8	29,755	1.63	0.12	7	53^{3} - 16^{5}	21.4	0.3

Note: Adjusted for 2-for-1 stock split 11/67; also stock dividends: 1965-68, 3%; 1969, 70, 72, 74 and 75 2%; 1971, 100% and 2%; and 1973, 100%. a-Before \$0.9 mill. (5c a share) non-recurring gain.

INCORPORATED: 1938—California

PRINCIPAL OFFICE: 500 South Buena Vista St. Burbank, California 91505

ANNUAL MEETING: Second Wed. in Feb.

NUMBER OF STOCKHOLDERS: 55,000

TRANSFER AGENT: Bank of America, Los Angeles, Cal. Bankers Trust Co., N.Y.

REGISTRAR: Bank of America, Los Angeles, Cal. Morgan Guaranty Trust Co., New York

INSTIT. HOLDINGS: NO.: 125 SHS.: 4,240,206

OFFICERS

CHAIRMAN: D.B. Tatum

PRESIDENT: E.C. Walker

SECRETARY: L.R. Marr

TREASURER: O.V. Melton

GENERAL ELECTRIC COMPANY

LISTED	SYMBOL	INDICATED DIV.	RECENT PRICE	PRICE RANGE (1975)	YIELD
NYSE	GE	$1.60	48	53 - 32	3.3%

INTRINSIC INVESTMENT QUALITY: HIGH GRADE. COMPANY HAS SUBSTANTIAL POSITIONS IN ELECTRIC EQUIPMENT, ELECTRONICS, POWER GENERATING EQUIPMENT AND CONSUMER PRODUCTS.

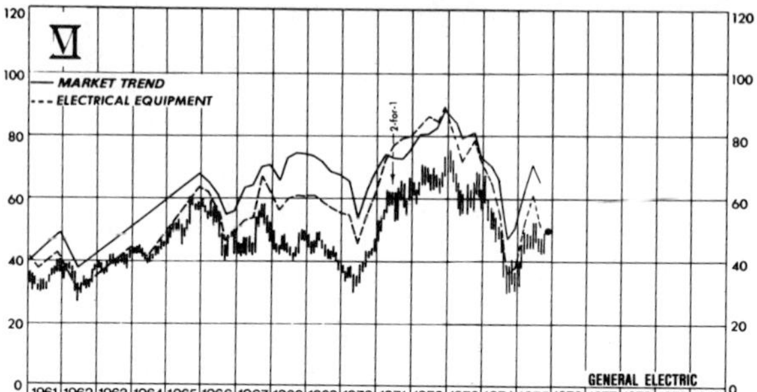

	1961	1962	1963	1964	1965	1966	1967	1968	1969	1970	1971	1972	1973	1974	1975	1976	1977	1978	1979	1980
EARN.	1.36	1.49	1.57	1.72	1.96	1.87	1.95	1.96	1.54	1.81	2.60	2.91	3.21	3.24						
DIV.	1.00	1.00	1.00	1.10	1.15	1.30	1.30	1.30	1.30	1.30	1.35	1.40	1.45	1.60						

CAPITALIZATION: (12/31/74)

	(000)	(%)
Debt	a$1,195,200	24.0
Minority int.	71,200	1.4
Com. & Surp.	3,704,300	74.6
Total	$4,970,700	100.0%

Shs. ($2.50)-182,651,032

INTERIM EARNINGS:

Qu.	3/31	6/30	9/30	12/31
72	0.57	0.66	0.71	0.97
73	0.63	0.75	0.78	1.05
74	0.67	0.82	0.80	1.05
75	0.41	0.71	0.85	

DIVIDENDS:	RECORD	PAYABLE
0.40Q	9/23/74	10/25/74
0.40Q	12/9	1/25/75
0.40Q	3/6/75	4/25
0.40Q	6/11	7/25
0.40Q	9/22	10/25

BACKGROUND:

General Electric is the largest and most diversified producer of electrical and electronic equipment. GE operates within a broadly decentralized framework under which its business is carried on by 175 product departments. It produces utility apparatus, appliances, home entertainment products, operates a time sharing network, produces lamps, plastics, electrical and medical products, jet engines, electronic components, missile and radar systems. Its major groups account for the following proportions of sales: consumer, 21%; industrial power equipment, 18%; industrial components and systems, 29%; and aerospace, 12%. International sales were 20% of the total.

RECENT DEVELOPMENTS:

Despite a 2% decline in sales to $3.28 billion in the third quarter of 1975, net income increased 7% to $156.1 million. Higher profits were generated in the consumer good area, mainly as a result of improving cost/price relationships. Sales have picked up since the beginning of the year, but remain below year-earlier levels. Earnings from foreign operations failed to keep pace with sales growth because of somewhat lower export margins. Earnings of GE Credit Corp. climbed to $13.4 million, for a gain of 25% over a year earlier.

PROSPECTS:

Results over the near term should continue to improve, helped by better control over costs and more favorable price structure. Although sales and profits from industrial power equipment are recovering, they remain depressed. Reduced shipments of power generating equipment to utilities, which have cut back sharply their plans for expansion, will continue to retard growth. Recovery overseas may be slower than in the U.S. GE Credit should continue to be an important factor in overall growth over the longer term.

STATISTICS:

YEAR	GROSS REVS. ($ MILL.)	OPER. PROFIT MARGIN %	NET INCOME ($ 000)	WORK CAP. ($ MILL.)	SENIOR CAPITAL ($ MILL.)	NO. SHS. OUT. (000)	EARN. PER SH. $	DIV. PER SH. $	DIV. PAY. %	PRICE RANGE	PRICE X EARN.	AVG. YIELD %
65	6,213.6	10.4	355,122	1,275.6	364.1	181,558	1.96	1.15	59	60^{1} - 45^{4}	27.0	2.2
66	7,177.3	8.8	338,861	1,129.8	476.5	181,196	1.87	1.30	70	60 - 40	26.7	2.6
67	7,741.2	8.3	g361,389	1,230.3	724.1	181,157	1.95	1.30	67	58 - 41^{2}	25.4	2.6
68	8,381.6	6.9	357,107	1,206.8	749.1	182,051	1.96	1.30	66	50^{2} - 40^{1}	23.0	2.9
69	8,448.0	4.5	278,015	921.1	673.3	180,813	1.54	1.30	85	49^{1} - 37	28.1	3.0
70	8,726.7	5.2	328,480	683.8	573.5	181,627	1.81	1.30	72	47^{2} - 30^{1}	21.4	3.4
71	9,425.3	7.2	471,800	798.6	787.3	182,123	2.60	1.35	52	66^{4} - 46^{4}	21.7	2.4
72	10,239.5	6.5	530,000	1,109.6	947.3	182,348	2.91	1.40	48	73 - 58^{2}	22.6	2.1
73	11,575.3	6.3	585,100	993.0	917.2	182,147	3.21	1.45	45	75^{7} - 55	20.4	2.2
74	13,413.1	7.4	608,100	1,343.1	1,195.2	182,651	3.34	1.60	48	65 - 30	14.2	3.4

Note: Adjusted for 2-for-1 stock split, 3/71. a-Incl. $48.8 mill. debentures convertible into common at $65.50 a share and $50.0 mill. convertible into common at $80.75 a share. b-Before antitrust charges, 0.41c a share. basis. g-Incl. special items.

INCORPORATED: April 15, 1892—N.Y.

PRINCIPAL OFFICE: 3135 Easton Turnpike, Fairfield, Conn. 06431

ANNUAL MEETING: Fourth Wed. in April

NUMBER OF STOCKHOLDERS: 530,000

TRANSFER AGENT: Company office; Old Colony Trust Co., Boston, Mass.

REGISTRAR: Morgan Guaranty Trust Co., N.Y.; First National Bank, Boston, Mass.

INSTIT. HOLDINGS: NO.: 673; SHS.: 17,722,340

OFFICERS

CHAIRMAN: R.H. J[illegible]es

PRESIDEN[illegible]

SECRET[illegible]Y: R.M. Estes

TREASURER: R.E. Whitmyer

GREAT WESTERN FINANCIAL CORPORATION

LISTED	SYMBOL	INDICATED DIV.	RECENT PRICE	PRICE RANGE (1975)	YIELD
NYSE	GWF	$0.44	14	19 - 11	3.1%

INTRINSIC INVESTMENT GRADE; MEDIUM GRADE. A SAVINGS AND LOAN HOLDING COMPANY WHOSE EARNINGS REFLECT SWINGS IN INTEREST COSTS.

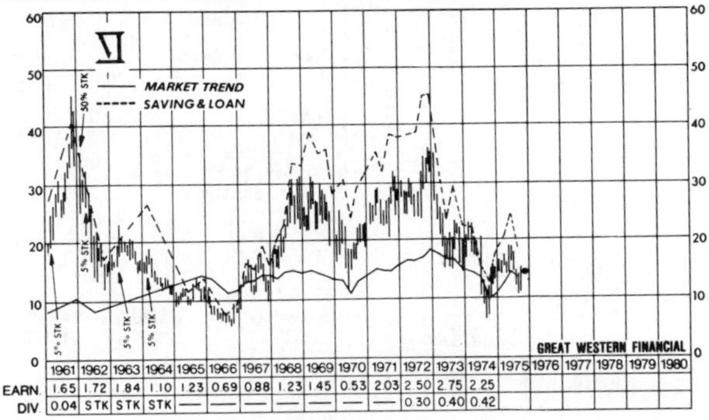

CAPITALIZATION:

	(12/31/74) (000)	(%)
Debt.	c$ 17,000	4.4
Com. & Surp.	367,427	95.6
Total	$384,427	100.0%

Shs. ($1)-14,922,886

INTERIM EARNINGS:

Qu.	3/31	6/30	9/30	12/31
72h	0.53	0.61	0.66	0.70
73h	0.65	0.79	0.70	0.61
74h	0.60	0.60	0.57	0.48
75	0.49	0.48	0.41	

DIVIDENDS:	RECORD	PAYABLE
0.20S	11/1/73	11/30/73
0.20S	5/1/74	5/31/74
0.22S	11/1	11/29
0.22S	5/1/75	5/30/75
0.22S	11/3/75	11/28/75

BACKGROUND:

Great Western merged with LFC Financial Corp. in December, 1970, making it the second largest publicly-owned savings and loan holding company in the nation. The Company now has a statewide network of 75 branch offices, the largest in California. Principal activities include furnishing savings investment media and home financing. Through affiliated subsidiary companies, Great Western also offers escrow and reconveyance services as well as Fire & Hazard insurance. The Company operates offices throughout California servicing 99% of the state's population.

RECENT DEVELOPMENTS:

For the nine months ended September 30, 1975 net income was $20.5 million compared with $28.0 million (including a $1.6 million tax credit) for the nine onths ended September 30, 1974. NFor the first half of 1975, net income was $14.4 million vs. $18.8 million. Provision for losses was $2 million vs. $985,000. Operating results for the four quarters of 1974 continued to be affected by the rising costs of funds. Net income for the period, before an extraordinary item, amounted to $33.5 million compared to $41.1 million a year ago.

PROSPECTS:

A reduced level of loan volume in 1974 will hinder revenue flows in the future. Short term interest rates declined during the final quarter of 1974, producing an improved savings situation. Savings for the first half of 1975 produced a net inflow. The broadly based branch office network provides the Company with the opportunity to tape all potential savings markets in California.

STATISTICS:

YEAR	DEPOSITS ($ MILL.)	LOANS ($ MILL.)	GROSS INCOME ($ MILL.)	OPERATING EARNINGS ($ 000)	PROFIT MARGIN %	SHARES (000)	EARNINGS PER SHARE	DIVIDEND PER SHARE	DIV. PAY. %	BOOK VALUE PER SHARE	PRICE RANGE	PRICE EARN. RATIO	AVG. YIELD %
65	1,236.4	1,412.5	100.9	10,573	12.2	8,589	1.23	Nil	—	13.80	13^{7} - 9	9.3	—
66	1,227.2	1,405.8	101.6	5,923	7.1	8,589	0.69	Nil	—	14.49	11^{7} - 5^{6}	12.8	—
67	1,380.1	1,407.6	103.8	7,752	8.5	9,152	0.88	Nil	—	15.34	18^{2} - 8^{5}	15.3	—
68	1,526.0	1,574.2	119.0	12,971	14.7	11,264	a1.23	Nil	—	15.84	30^{7} - 12^{7}	17.8	—
69	1,674.2	1,911.0	142.0	18,458	13.0	12,780	1.45	Nil	—	16.14	31^{2} - 19^{2}	17.4	—
b70	2,459.8	3,029.0	230.6	g7,905	3.4	14,895	g0.53	Nil	—	15.92	25^{2} - 11^{5}	34.8	—
71	2,905.2	3,382.5	258.4	h30,289	11.7	14,901	h2.03	Nil	—	17.97	31^{6} - 20^{3}	12.8	—
72	3,422.4	3,877.8	291.6	h37,325	12.8	14,920	h2.50	0.30	12	20.24	36 - 24	12.0	1.0
73	3,575.2	4,175.4	343.7	h41,087	12.0	14,923	h2.75	0.40	15	22.68	34^{6} - 14^{5}	9.0	1.6
74	3,591.3	4,251.4	380.5	h33,524	8.8	14,923	h2.25	0.42	19	24.62	23 - 6^{3}	6.5	2.9

a-On average shares. b-Incl. acquisitions. c-Convertible into common at $40 a share. g-Excl. special items. h-Excl. special items: 1971, $0.2 mill. (1c a share) credit; 1972, $1.0 mill. (7c a share) credit; 1973, $1.3 mill. (9c a share) credit; 1974 $1.8 mill. (11c a share) credit.

INCORPORATED: June 22, 1955—Delaware

PRINCIPAL OFFICE: 8484 Wilshire Blvd. Beverly Hills, Calif. 90211

ANNUAL MEETING: Third Tuesday in April

NUMBER OF STOCKHOLDERS: 35,000

TRANSFER AGENT: First National City Bank, N.Y.

REGISTRAR: Bankers Trust Co., New York

INSTIT. HOLDINGS: NO.: 63 SHS.: 5,526,625

OFFICERS

CHAIRMAN: S. Davis

PRESIDENT. J.F. Montgomery

SECRETARY: J. Simons

TREASURER: M. Morgan

GULF & WESTERN INDUSTRIES, INC.

LISTED	SYMBOL	INDICATED DIV.	RECENT PRICE	PRICE RANGE (1975)	YIELD
NYSE	GW	$0.70	21	22 - 18	3.3%

INTRINSIC INVESTMENT QUALITY: SPECULATIVE GRADE. ACQUISITIONS ACCOUNTED FOR THIS CONGLOMERATE'S RAPID GROWTH.1

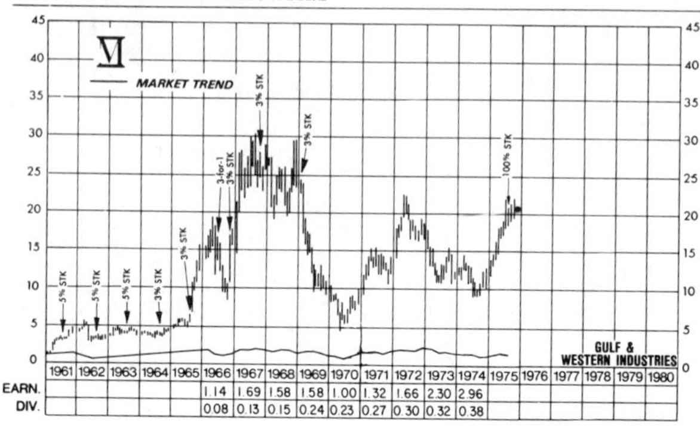

CAPITALIZATION: (7/31/74)

	(000)	(%)
Debt	c$1,174,979	60.0
Minority int.	75,960	3.9
Pfd.	g 37,455	1.9
Com. & Surp.	668,830	34.2
Total	$1,957,224	100.0%

Shs. ($1)-15,552,786

INTERIM EARNINGS:

Qu.	10/31	1/31	4/30	7/31
72	0.41	0.38	0.41	0.46
73	0.49	0.55	0.63	0.63
74	0.64	0.69	0.80	0.83
75	1.00	1.06	1.21	p1.22

DIVIDENDS:	RECORD	PAYABLE
0.25Q	2/28/75	4/1/75
0.25SP	2/28	4/1
0.275Q	5/30	7/1
100% stk.	7/30	8/22
0.15Q	9/5	10/1

BACKGROUND:

Gulf & Western's operations are diversified and are derived as follows: financial services (18% sales 9% operating income before corporate expenses and inter-company items), leisure time (11%-8%), food products (6%-26%), consumer products (8%-6%), manufacturing (29%-24%), paper and building products (14%-15%), auto replacement parts (8%-7%), and natural resources (6%-18%). Some of the larger operating units include Associates Corp. of North America, Paramount Pictures Corp., Consolidated Cigar Corp., E.W. Bliss Co., New Jersey Zinc Co., Brown Co. (78% owned) and A.P.S. Inc. (82% owned). Outstanding convertible securities provide a potential 9-1/2% dilution to per share earnings.

RECENT DEVELOPMENTS:

In October the Company announced plans to jointly develop three new zinc mines and build a zinc refinery with Union Miniere, S.A. The Company also announced in October that it plans to offer $20 million of Eurodollar notes in the international market. Net income for fiscal 1975 rose 39% to $140.1 million on a 13% increase in revenues to $2.6 billion.

PROSPECTS:

Despite cutbacks in capital spending and a weak U.S. economy, further earnings improvement appears likely this year to about $8 a share. The manufacturing operations outlook is favorable, helped by high backlogs which reflect increased demand for energy related products. Financial services operations may show some improvement later in the year aided by lower interest rates. Helped by strong demand, natural resources should continue to improve. Paper and forest products could slow down because of economic conditions.

STATISTICS:

YEAR	GROSS REVS. ($ MILL.)	OPER. PROFIT MARGIN %	NET INCOME ($ 000)	WORK CAP. ($ MILL.)	SENIOR CAPITAL ($ MILL.)	NO. SHS. OUT. (000)	EARN. PER SH. $	DIV. PER SH. $	DIV. PAY. %	PRICE RANGE	PRICE X EARN.	AVG. YIELD %
7/31												
b67	644.9	9.9	46,199	163.2	312.1	23,928	1.69	0.13	7	30^2 - 14^3	13.3	0.5
k67	1,189.0	8.9	59,054	358.9	407.3	24,094	a1.34	-	-	-	-	-
b68	1,313.9	8.4	69,842	469.6	965.4	30,876	a1.58	0.15	9	32^1 - 18^6	18.3	5.6
b69	1,563.6	4.5	72,050	576.5	1,009.3	32,620	a1.58	m0.24	15	25^1 - 8^6	10.7	1.4
70	1,629.6	4.6	44,771	417.0	968.3	29,928	a1.00	0.23	23	10^3 - 4^6	7.5	3.0
71	1,566.3	5.0	55,252	478.4	1,035.5	31,096	1.32	0.27	20	15^4 - 9^4	9.5	2.7
72	1,669.7	5.6	69,601	559.9	1,085.5	32,774	1.66	n0.30	18	22^3 - 14	11.8	1.6
73	1,927.2	6.9	89,216	545.6	1,115.5	27,890	2.30	0.32	13	17^7 - 10^5	6.2	2.2
74	2,295.5	8.5	100,646	585.8	1,212.4	31,104	2.96	0.38	12	14^4 - 9	3.1	3.2
p75	2,602.1		140,055			30,058	4.49					

Note: Adjusted for all stock dividends and splits through 100% stock dividend 8/75. a-On average common & common equivalent shares. b-Incl. acquisitions. c-Incl. $416.7 mill. debentures and notes convertible into common. g-Incl. 1,107,677 shares convertible into common. k-Pro-forma. m-Plus 1/20th. share G&W Land Dev. Corp. n-Plus 1/10th share Athena Communications Corp.

INCORPORATED: April 18, 1967—Delaware

PRINCIPAL OFFICE: 1 Gulf & Western Plaza, New York, N.Y. 10023

ANNUAL MEETING: Second Tuesday in Dec.

NUMBER OF STOCKHOLDERS: 44,000

TRANSFER AGENT: Chase Manhattan Bank, N.Y.; Fidelity Union Trust Co., Newark, N.J.

REGISTRAR: Manufacturers Hanover Tr. Co., N.Y.

INSTIT. HOLDINGS: NO.: 49; SHS.: 6,124,924

OFFICERS

CHAIRMAN: C.G. Bluhdorn

PRESIDENT: D.N. Judelson

SECRETARY:

TREASURER: N.R. Forson

HEWLETT-PACKARD COMPANY

LISTED	SYMBOL	INDICATED DIV.	RECENT PRICE	PRICE RANGE (1975)	YIELD
NYSE	HWP	$0.30	100	121 - 56	0.3%

INTRINSIC INVESTMENT QUALITY: INVESTMENT GRADE. GROWTH HAS RESULTED FROM LEADERSHIP IN ELECTRONIC INSTRUMENTS THROUGH STRONG RESEARCH.

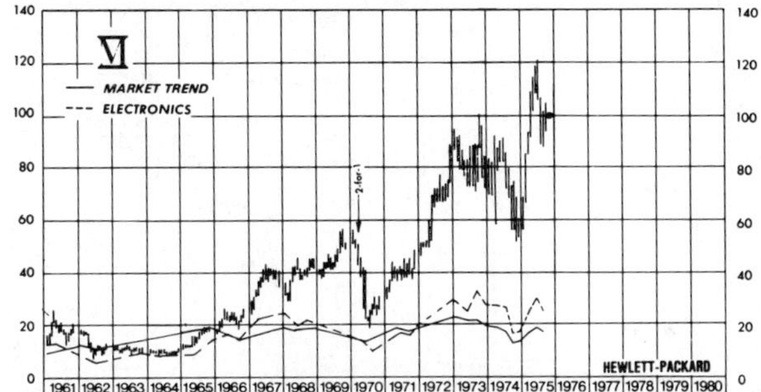

	1961	1962	1963	1964	1965	1966	1967	1968	1969	1970	1971	1972	1973	1974	1975	1976	1977	1978	1979	1980
EARN.	0.26	0.31	0.30	0.39	0.56	0.71	0.81	0.83	1.01	0.90	0.88	1.40	1.89	3.08						
DIV.	—	—	—	—	0.10	0.10	0.10	0.10	0.10	0.20	0.20	0.20	0.20	0.20						

CAPITALIZATION:

	(10/31/74) (000)	(%)
Debt	$ 2,899	0.6
Com. & Surp.	457,679	99.4
Total	$460,578	100.0%

Shs. ($1)-27,298,474

INTERIM EARNINGS:

Qu.	1/31	4/30	7/31	10/31
72b	0.25	0.33	0.35	0.47
73	0.33	0.54	0.39	0.63
74	0.54	0.76	0.84	0.94
75	0.67	0.87	0.73	

DIVIDENDS:	RECORD	PAYABLE
0.10S	9/24/74	10/15/74
0.10S	3/25/74	4/15/74
0.10S	9/24	10/15
0.10S	3/24/75	4/15/75
0.15S	9/24	10/15

BACKGROUND:

Hewlett-Packard is the largest and most diversified producer of electronic instruments in the world. Contributions to sales (and pretax earnings) in 1974 were as follows: test, measuring and related items, 50% (46%); electronic data products, 37% (47%); medical electronic equipment, 9% (5%) and analytical instrumentation, 4% (2%). Heavily research oriented, the Company has spent close to 8% of sales during recent years for product development and a number of important new products have recently been introduced. International orders account for over 40% of the Company total. The proportion of government orders is 17%.

RECENT DEVELOPMENTS:

Profits declined in the third quarter of 1975 due to increased pressure of profit margins, particularly for calculators. Net income fell 12% to $20.3 million. For the nine months, however, sales were up 10% to $706.3 million and net income was up 8% to $62.7 million. New orders for the nine-month period totaled $753.2 million, 9% ahead of a year earlier. International markets have displayed notable strength, with orders up 18% to $381.5 million. Domestic orders were up only 1.5%.

PROSPECTS:

Successful diversification through development of new instrument products, a strengthened management structure and stronger technical and marketing capabilities has enhanced long term prospects for this leading instruments manufacturer. Business will likely show good improvement over the near term in both domestic and foreign markets. Continued good growth is expected to follow the strong historical performance, aided by high backlogs which reflect a substantial increase in new orders and major additions to capacity.

STATISTICS:

YEAR	GROSS REVS. ($ MILL.)	OPER. PROFIT MARGIN %	NET INCOME ($ 000)	WORK CAP. ($ MILL.)	SENIOR CAPITAL ($ MILL.)	NO. SHS. OUT. (000)	EARN. PER SH. $	DIV. PER SH. $	DIV. PAY. %	PRICE RANGE	PRICE X EARN.	AVG. YIELD %
10/31												
a65	163.7	15.9	13,907	43.2	0.5	24,258	0.56	0.10	18	19^{4} - 11^{2}	27.5	0.7
66	203.3	15.6	17,445	47.6	0.8	24,601	0.71	0.10	14	27^{7} - 17^{4}	32.0	0.4
67	243.4	15.3	20,117	58.7	2.0	24,863	0.81	0.10	12	44^{7} - 24^{3}	42.7	0.3
68	268.8	14.9	20,825	76.3	1.2	25,128	0.83	0.10	12	45^{6} - 29^{4}	45.3	0.3
69	323.8	16.3	25,585	89.3	0.9	25,299	1.01	0.10	10	57^{3} - 37^{5}	47.2	0.2
70	347.3	12.0	23,103	104.6	1.0	25,649	0.90	0.20	22	55^{2} - 19^{3}	41.5	0.5
71	375.1	11.0	b22,780	133.6	1.3	26,038	b0.88	0.20	23	49^{5} - 29^{4}	45.0	0.5
72	479.1	14.2	b37,250	166.8	1.9	26,450	b1.40	0.20	14	88^{3} - 45^{4}	47.9	0.3
73	661.3	13.2	50,749	174.4	2.2	26,816	1.89	0.20	11	100^{5} - 71	45.4	0.2
74	884.1	16.3	84,022	237.3	3.0	27,298	3.08	0.20	6	92^{4} - 52	23.5	0.3

Note: Adjusted for 2-for-1 stock split, 2/70. a-Incl. acquisitions for entire year. b-Excl. $1.1 mill. (4c a share) credit in 1971 and $1.2 mill. (5c a share) credit in 1972.

INCORPORATED: Aug. 18, 1947—Calif.

PRINCIPAL OFFICE: 1501 Page Mill Road, Palo Alto, Calif. 94304

ANNUAL MEETING: Fourth Tues. in Feb.

NUMBER OF STOCKHOLDERS: 21,941

TRANSFER AGENT: Crocker National Bank, San Francisco, Calif.; Chase Manhattan Bank, N.Y.

REGISTRAR: Crocker National Bank, San Francisco, Calif.; Chase Manhattan Bank, N.Y.

INSTIT. HOLDINGS: NO.: 130 SHS.: 3,009,065

OFFICERS

CHAIRMAN: D. Packard

PRESIDENT: W.R. Hewlett

SECRETARY: W.F. Cavier

TREASURER: E.E. van Bronkhorst

HOLIDAY INNS, INC.

LISTED	SYMBOL	INDICATED DIV.	RECENT PRICE	PRICE RANGE (1975)	YIELD
NYSE	HIA	$0.35	14	15 - 5	2.5%

INTRINSIC INVESTMENT QUALITY: MEDIUM GRADE. CHANGES IN THE RATE OF EARNINGS GAINS AND INVESTOR EVALUATIONS HAVE CAUSED WIDE STOCK PRICE SWINGS.

	1961	1962	1963	1964	1965	1966	1967	1968	1969	1970	1971	1972	1973	1974	1975	1976	1977	1978	1979	1980
EARN.	0.12	0.15	0.18	0.21	0.28	0.43	0.58	0.62	1.15	1.30	1.36	1.38	1.50	1.06						
DIV.	STK	STK	0.01	0.06	0.08	0.11	0.13	0.16	0.19	0.22	0.24	0.27	0.29	0.32						

CAPITALIZATION: (12/31/74)

	(000)	(%)
Debt	$336,250	41.9
Defer.inc.tax	40,627	5.1
Pfd.	g 856	0.1
Com. & Surp.	424,238	52.9
Total	$801,971	100.0%

Shs. ($1.50)-29,877,812

INTERIM EARNINGS:

Qu.	3/31	6/30	9/30	12/31
72s	0.22	0.39	0.48	0.29
73	0.24	0.46	0.57	0.23
74	0.09	0.30	0.53	0.14
75	0.23	0.32	0.56	

DIVIDENDS:	RECORD	PAYABLE
0.08125Q	9/27/74	11/1/74
0.08125Q	12/27	2/1/75
0.0875Q	3/27/75	5/1
0.0875Q	6/27	8/1
0.0875Q	9/26	11/1

BACKGROUND:

The Holiday Inn System has over 1,650 Inns with 250,000 rooms (with some 300 Inns with 52,000 rooms owned and operated by Holiday Inns, Inc.) in 50 states, Canada and overseas. For future expansion and greater efficiency, Holiday Inns, Inc. has added the following integrated divisions and subsidiaries: National Institutional Sales Division, institutional supplies; and Holiday Industries, plastic laminated furniture. Revenue distribution in 1974 was: Food and Lodging, 51%; Travel and Transportation, 28% and Products division 20%. All of the outstanding 5% preferred stock is held by Gulf Oil Corp. (to be redeemed 2½% annually from 6/30/68; also, sinking fund requirement of 5% of consolidated net from 12/31/68).

RECENT DEVELOPMENTS:

Revenues for the nine months ended 10/3/75 advanced 3% to $696.1 million, while net income posted a 27% gain to $34.4 million. Food and lodging revenues and pre-tax income for the third quarter were up. Occupancy rates at company-operated inns were down. Higher revenues and pre-tax income were posted in transportation operations reflecting improved results by Continental Trailways. A reduced volume of furnishing and equipment sales for new construction contributed to lower sales and pre-tax income in the product division.

PROSPECTS:

Company is aggressively expanding its inns systems with a program to add over 15,000 rooms at 14 existing and 70 new licensed inns under construction in 19 countries throughout the world. Business travel is expected to improve in 1976 in response to a stronger economy. The prospects for leisure are also bright as increased consumer spending is anticipated. Divesture of food processing operatons will enable the Company to more effectively expand food service and lodging operations. Higher earnings are expected in 1976.

STATISTICS:

YEAR	GROSS REVS. ($ MILL.)	OPER. PROFIT MARGIN %	NET INCOME ($ 000)	WORK CAP. ($ MILL.)	SENIOR CAPITAL ($ MILL.)	NO. SHS. OUT. (000)	EARN. PER SH. $	DIV. PER SH. $	DIV. PAY. %	PRICE RANGE	PRICE X EARN.	AVG. YIELD %
6/30												
66	100.8	16.7	7,101	8.8	74.3	15,352	0.43	0.11	25	11^{2} - 6^{3}	20.7	1.2
b67	157.2	11.9	9,945	7.9	126.9	15,961	0.58	0.13	23	29_{4} - 10_{5}	33.6	0.7
68	204.1	14.2	f11,735	14.2	127.3	18,862	f0.62	0.16	25	40^{4} - 19^{5}	48.4	—
m68	404.9	13.3	f25,722	24.8	192.0	22,855	f1.01	—	—	-	—	—
m69	538.7	13.9	32,012	19.1	236.5	25,068	n1.15	0.19	17	47^{3} - 32^{4}	34.7	0.5
70	604.6	10.9	36,971	38.3	297.6	26,367	n1.30	0.22	17	42^{7} - 19^{6}	24.1	0.7
71	707.9	10.4	s40,601	33.2	293.1	27,984	s1.36	0.24	18	50^{5} - 34^{5}	31.3	0.6
72	775.2	10.1	42,024	55.7	347.7	29,296	1.38	0.27	20	55^{5} - 36^{1}	33.2	0.6
73	885.7	8.5	46,403	42.7	346.7	29,877	1.50	0.29	19	42^{7} - 10^{6}	17.9	1.1
74	986.1	5.8	32,641	42.9	337.2	29,878	1.06	0.32	30	18^{3} - 4^{2}	10.7	2.8

Note: Adjusted for all stock splits thru 2-for-1, 5/69. a-From operations. b-Incl. Nat. Buring Packing Co., Phenix Carpet Mills and two re-acquired inns. f-Excl. special items. g-Incl. 761,834 shares each convertible into 1.5 common shares. m-Incl. T.C.O. Industries & other acquisitions as reported; fiscaı year changed to end 12/31. n-As reported. s-Excl. $1.5 mill. (5c a share) credit.

INCORPORATED: April 30, 1954—Tennessee

PRINCIPAL OFFICE: 3742 Lamar Avenue, Memphis, Tennessee 38118

ANNUAL MEETING: Third Wednesday in May

NUMBER OF STOCKHOLDERS: 37,934

TRANSFER AGENT: First National Bank, Memphis, Tenn.
First National City Bank, N.Y.
Bank of America, L.A., Calif.

REGISTRAR: Nat. Bk. of Commerce, Memphis, Tenn.
Bank of New York, New York, N.Y.
United Calif. Bank, Los Angeles, Calif.

INSTIT. HOLDINGS: NO.: 78
SHS.: 2,511,781

OFFICERS

CHAIRMAN: K. Wilson

PRESIDENT: L.M. Clymer

SECRETARY: W.C. Marsh

TREASURER: E.J. House

HOMESTAKE MINING COMPANY

LIS. ED	SYMBOL	INDICATED DIV.	RECENT PRICE	PRICE RANGE (1975)	YIELD
NYSE	HM	$1.25	37	56 - 32	3.4%

INTRINSIC INVESTMENT QUALITY: MEDIUM GRADE. THIS STOCK HAS HAD AN ERRATIC EARNINGS AND DIVIDEND RECORD. PRICE 'CTION HAS BEEN SENSITIVE TO INVESTOR INTEREST IN GOLD 'S A HEDGE.

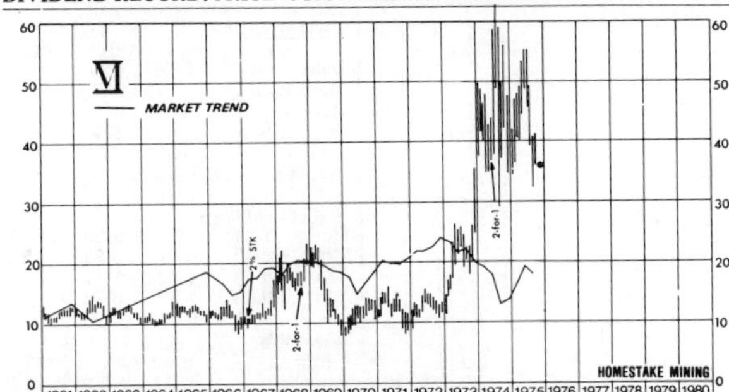

	1961	1962	1963	1964	1965	1966	1967	1968	1969	1970	1971	1972	1973	1974	1975	1976	1977	1978	1979	1980
EARN.	0.63	0.68	0.49	0.55	0.49	0.42	0.34	0.27	0.27	0.31	0.27	0.64	2.00	3.01						
DIV.	0.49	0.39	0.39	0.39	0.39	0.39	0.20	0.20	0.20	0.20	0.20	0.20	0.20	1.25						

CAPITALIZATION: (12/31/74)

	(000)	(%)
Debt	$ 5,153	3.8
Defer. inc. tax	6,200	4.6
Com. & Surp.	122,664	91.6
Total	$134,017	100.0%

Shs. ($1)-11,299,590

INTERIM EARNINGS:

Qu.	3/31	6/30	9/30	12/31
72g	0.09	0.20	0.20	0.15
73	0.32	0.60	0.51	0.56
74	0.81	0.92	0.73	0.55
75	0.70	0.73	0.36	

DIVIDENDS:	RECORD	PAYABLE
0.25Q	12/2/74	12/16/74
0.25E	12/2	12/16
0.25Q	2/24/75	3/10/75
0.25Q	5/28	6/16
0.25Q	8/18	9/15

BACKGROUND:

Homestake, largest gold producer in the Western Hemisphere, owns mining claims in the Black Hills near Lead, S.D. Measured gold ore reserves were 8.8 million tons on 12/31/74. In 1953-54 it began developing uranium properties in Wyoming and Utah. In 1956, in partnership with others, interests in large uranium properties in New Mexico were acquired for full development at a cost of $25 million. Of 1974 revenues, about 48% came from gold, 41% lead and zinc, 5% silver and 2% forest products. Dividends have been paid each year since 1879 except in 1920 and 1943-45. In April, 1969, a rights offering (at $17 a sh. adjusted) of 1,113,770 shares was made for expansion.

RECENT DEVELOPMENTS:

In the first six months of 1975, net income declined 16% to $16.2 million and sales eased 4% to $66.5 million. In 1974, net income increased 47% and revenues gained 25%. The Homestake gold mine in South Dakota returned a far greater profit in 1974 than it did in 1973, although both tonnage and grade of ore were down slightly. The jointly owned Buick lead-zinc mine in Missouri also generated record income. All of Homestake's uranium activities have been combined under one management in a newly organized Uranium Division.

PROSPECTS:

Any further rises in the price of gold will result in increased earnings for Homestake Mining. Improvements in Company's milling process should boost recovery of the metal from the ore mined. Benefits in the future should be realized from the expanded production at Homestake's lead and zinc mines. Long-term prospects are brightened by Company's varied mineral diversification programs as well as its plan to mine ore from the deep levels of the Homestake mine. High silver prices should boost earnings from Company's mine in Colorado.

STATISTICS:

YEAR	GROSS REVS. ($ MILL.)	OPER. PROFIT MARGIN %	NET INCOME ($ 000)	WORK CAP. ($ MILL.)	SENIOR CAPITAL ($ MILL.)	NO. SHS. OUT. (000)	EARN. PER SH. $	DIV. PER SH. $	DIV. PAY. %	PRICE RANGE	PRICE X EARN.	AVG. YIELD %
65	32.2	14.0	4,951	24.2	3.0	10,041	a b0.49	0.39	80	13^{3}_{6} - 10^{5}_{5}	24.2	3.3
66	30.7	8.9	4,210	17.5	28.9	10,040	0.42	0.39	93	13_{2} - 8^{4}	26.5	3.5
67	28.0	6.1	3,384	13.4	35.4	10,024	0.34	0.20	59	17_{2} - 9^{4}	39.3	1.5
68	25.7	4.5	2,684	10.7	37.6	10,024	0.27	0.20	74	23^{2} - 12^{4}	66.1	1.1
69	29.4	d	c2,991	28.8	14.4	11,138	c0.27	0.20	74	23 - 8_{1}	57.4	1.3
70	57.5	0.7	3,393	28.1	19.4	11,138	0.31	0.20	65	14 - 8^{1}_{3}	36.1	1.8
71	46.2	2.3	2,949	19.3	13.6	11,138	0.27	0.20	75	16 - 8^{3}	45.1	1.6
72	58.4	16.2	g7,151	25.6	10.9	11,138	g0.64	0.20	31	15_{4} - 9_{5}	18.8	1.6
73	107.1	26.2	23,209	54.3	8.0	11,207	2.00	0.20	10	35^{4}_{5} - 11^{5}_{2}	11.7	0.9
74	121.8	40.0	34,100	67.5	5.2	11,300	3.01	1.25	42	69^{5} - 29^{2}	16.4	2.5

Note: Adjusted for 2-for-1 stock split, 9/68, 5/74 and 2% stock dividend 3/67. a-Before "percentage" depletion. b-$0.57 on average number of shares. c-Excl. special items. g-Excl. $1.0 mill. (9c a share) special credit.

INCORPORATED: November 5, 1877—Calif.

PRINCIPAL OFFICE: 650 California Street, San Francisco, Calif. 94108

ANNUAL MEETING: Second Tuesday in May

NUMBER OF STOCKHOLDERS: 22,607

TRANSFER AGENT: Bankers Trust Co., N.Y.

REGISTRAR: Banker Trust Co., N.Y.

INSTIT. HOLDINGS: NO.: 25 SHS.: 273,050

OFFICERS

CHAIRMAN: J.K. Gustafson

PRESIDENT: P.C. Henshaw

SECRETARY: H.C. Harvey

TREASURER: H.C. Harvey

HONEYWELL, INC.

LISTED	SYMBOL	INDICATED DIV.	RECENT PRICE	PRICE RANGE (1975)	YIELD
NYSE	HON	$1.40	35	41 - 21	4.0%

INTRINSIC INVESTMENT QUALITY: MEDIUM GRADE. ALTHOUGH COMPUTERS COULD EVENTUALLY ADD MORE STABILITY TO EARNINGS, SOME CYCLICALITY PERSISTS.

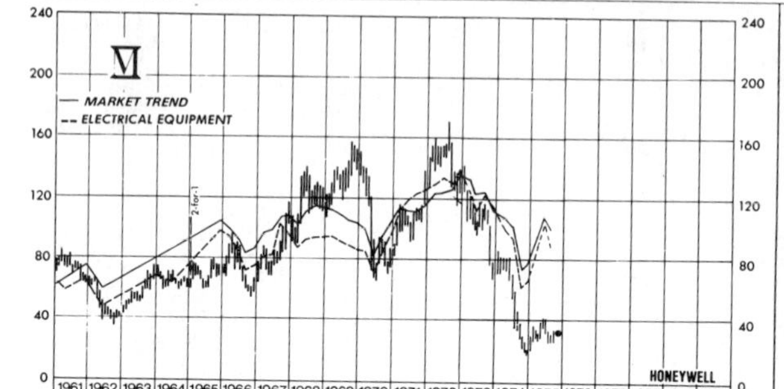

	1961	1962	1963	1964	1965	1966	1967	1968	1969	1970	1971	1972	1973	1974	1975	1976	1977	1978	1979	1980
EARN.	1.74	1.86	2.42	2.89	2.61	3.07	2.85	3.40	4.10	3.55	3.88	4.38	5.46	3.93						
DIV.	1.00	1.00	1.00	1.03	1.10	1.10	1.10	1.10	1.18	1.30	1.30	1.35	1.40	1.40						

CAPITALIZATION: (12/31/74)

		(000)	(%)
Debt	c$	435,956	27.0
Minority int.		184,038	11.4
Defer.inc.tax		54,060	3.4
Com. & Surp.		938,227	58.2
Total		$1,612,281	100.0%

Shs. ($1.50)-19,533,412

INTERIM EARNINGS:

Qu.	3/31	6/30	9/30	12/31
72b	0.60	0.81	0.85	2.12
73b	0.89	1.10	1.17	2.30
74b	0.85	1.07	0.58	1.43
75g	0.31	0.55	0.75	

DIVIDENDS:	RECORD	PAYABLE
0.35Q	8/30/74	9/16/74
0.35Q	11/29	12/16
0.35Q	2/28/75	3/17/75
0.35Q	5/30	6/16
0.35Q	8/29	9/15

BACKGROUND:

Honeywell is engaged generally in the design, manufacture, sale and service of automation equipment and systems which utilize inputs of various kinds to produce some type of output, control or display. Honeywell Information Systems (81.5% owned by Honeywell and the remainder owned by GE), ranks as the second largest factor in the computer industry.

Honeywell's 1974 revenues (and profits) were as follows: computers, 47% (28%); home and building automation systems and controls, 19% (61%); aerospace and defense, 16% (18%); industrial automation systems and controls, 16% (22%); and photographic products, 2% (slightly unprofitable).

RECENT DEVELOPMENTS:

Third quarter revenues increased 8% to $666.2 million and produced a 30% gain in net income to $14.8 million. Though this represents a significant improvement over the heavily depressed year-earlier quarter as well as the weakness earlier in 1975, the Company has a long way to go to restore former profit levels. A positive element in third quarter results was good demand for cost-and-energy-saving systems for commercial buildings, which more than offset low new-construction activity.

PROSPECTS:

Near term prospects are clouded by the effect of substantially higher costs on margins and the influence of economic activity on some portions of the Company's business. Over the longer term, potential growth of computer operations offer the promise of helping to stabilize the cyclical sensitivity. It will take some time, however, for earnings to reflect the substantial current investment in this area.

STATISTICS:

YEAR	GROSS REVS. ($ MILL.)	OPER. PROFIT MARGIN %	NET INCOME ($ 000)	WORK CAP. ($ MILL.)	SENIOR CAPITAL ($ MILL.)	NO. SHS. OUT. (000)	EARN. PER SH. $	DIV. PER SH. $	DIV. PAY. %	PRICE RANGE	PRICE X EARN.	AVG. YIELD %
65	700.4	10.2	37,500	215.0	157.9	14,069	2.61	1.10	42	79^{7} - 58^{2}_{4}	26.5	1.6
66	914.4	10.4	45,280	237.3	186.1	14,516	3.07	1.10	36	96_{7} - 53_{4}	24.3	1.5
67	1,044.9	7.2	42,270	298.5	246.2	14,568	2.85	1.10	39	117_{6} - 63_{3}	31.8	1.2
68	1,281.3	8.9	50,545	313.5	250.1	14,869	3.40	1.10	32	139_{2} - 89_{6}	33.7	1.0
69	1,426.0	9.9	62,481	350.8	271.5	15,238	4.10	1.18	29	157^{2} - 107_{5}	32.3	0.9
a70	1,921.2	7.9	61,650	278.0	477.7	17,376	3.55	1.30	37	152_{6} - 65^{5}	30.7	1.2
71	1,946.1	8.8	b72,139	420.8	404.6	18,609	b3.88	1.30	34	138^{6} - 82_{4}	28.4	1.2
72	2,125.4	8.6	b82,327	430.8	408.5	18,961	b4.38	1.35	31	170_{3} - 115_{4}	32.7	0.9
73	2,390.6	8.9	b103,885	509.0	436.5	19,172	b5.46	1.40	26	140_{2} - 67^{4}	19.0	1.4
74	2,625.7	6.8	b75,768	516.8	436.0	19,533	b3.93	1.40	36	86^{2} - 17^{4}	13.2	2.7

a-Incl. acquisitions for entire year. b-Incl. tax loss carry-forward but excl. special item. c-Incl. $15.6 mill. foreign subsidiaries debentures convertible into common at $103.00 a share and $50.0 mill. convertible at $120 a share. g-Before extraordinary income of $1.2 mill. (6c a share).

INCORPORATED: Oct. 27, 1927—Delaware

PRINCIPAL OFFICE: 2701 Fourth Ave. South, Minneapolis, Minn. 55408

ANNUAL MEETING: First Tuesday in May

NUMBER OF STOCKHOLDERS: 49,252

TRANSFER AGENT: Morgan Guaranty Trust Co., N.Y.; Northwestern National Bank, Minneapolis, Minn.

REGISTRAR: Manufacturers Hanover Trust Co., N.Y.; First National Bank, Minneapolis, Minn.

INSTIT. HOLDINGS: NO.: 193; SHS.: 2,391,568

OFFICERS

CHAIRMAN: S.F. Keating

PRESIDENT: E.W. Spencer

SECRETARY: R.L. Post

TREASURER: L.E. Navin

INTERNATIONAL BUSINESS MACHINES CORPORATION

LISTED	SYMBOL	INDICATED DIV.	RECENT PRICE	PRICE RANGE (1975)	YIELD
NYSE	IBM	$7.00	217	227 - 157	3.2%

INTRINSIC INVESTMENT QUALITY: HIGH GRADE. AGGRESSIVE RESEARCH AND STRONG MARKETING STRONGLY SUGGEST THAT COMPANY'S OUTSTANDING GROWTH WILL CONTINUE.

	1961	1962	1963	1964	1965	1966	1967	1968	1969	1970	1971	1972	1973	1974	1975	1976	1977	1978	1979	1980
EARN.	1.57	1.81	2.72	3.20	3.52	3.77	4.64	6.17	6.57	7.10	7.50	8.82	10.79	12.45						
DIV.	0.48	0.62	0.88	1.24	1.56	1.68	1.74	2.08	2.88	3.84	4.16	4.32	4.48	5.56						

CAPITALIZATION: (12/31/74)

	(000)	(%)
Debt	$ 335,796	3.2
Defer.inc.tax	36,054	0.3
Com. & Surp.	10,110,342	95.5
Total	$10,482,192	100.0%

Shs. ($5)-148,259,260

INTERIM EARNINGS:

Qu.	3/31	6/30	9/30	12/31
72	2.15	2.11	2.22	2.34
73	2.34	2.44	2.81	3.20
74	2.94	3.28	3.23	3.02
75	2.95	3.14	3.32	

DIVIDENDS:	RECORD	PAYABLE
1.50Q	8/14/74	9/10/74
1.50Q	11/13	12/10
1.50Q	2/13/75	3/10/75
1.50Q	5/13	6/10
1.75Q	8/13	9/10

BACKGROUND:

IBM is the principal manufacturer of data processing systems equipment. Computer rentals, sales and service accounted for 79% of 1973 gross income; other business equipment products totaled 18% of volume and miscellaneous; 3%. The rental system provides above-average margins and earnings stability. Foreign operations are extensive, contributing over 50% of earnings. Growth has been consistently vigorous and dividends have been paid since 1916. An antitrust suit settlement in 1955 forced IBM to offer all machines for sale and open up some of its patents free, and others on a royalty basis. Another antitrust suit was initiated by the Justice Department in 1969, relating to IBM's domination of the computer market, which may take several years to resolve.

RECENT DEVELOPMENTS:

In the third quarter of 1975, on a 15% increase in revenues to $3.6 billion, net income increased only 3% to $495.2 million. The continuing effects of worldwide inflation were blamed for the only modest earnings improvement. Outright sales of equipment showed an increase of 9% for the quarter. For the nine months, however, outright sales were down 6% from a year earlier. Total revenues for the nine months were up 10% to $10.37 billion; net income was up less than 1% to $1.4 billion.

PROSPECTS:

A pickup in outright sales should be a help to the earnings performance over the near term. The large rental base provides a solid foundation for continued good long-term growth. Office copying and power typing offer bright prospects. Progress toward resolving various antitrust suits is expected to be slow and the outcome remains uncertain. Nevertheless, IBM's strong management should continue to provide growth impetus over the longer term. Earnings should rise in 1976.

STATISTICS:

YEAR	GROSS REVS. ($ MILL.)	OPER. PROFIT MARGIN %	NET INCOME ($ 000)	WORK CAP. ($ MILL.)	SENIOR CAPITAL ($ MILL.)	NO. SHS. OUT. (000)	EARN. PER SH. $	DIV. PER SH. $	DIV. PAY. %	PRICE RANGE	PRICE X EARN.	AVG. YIELD %
65	3,573	26.4	476,902	699	398.9	135,396	3.52	1.56	44	142$^{6}_{6}$ - 105$^{1}_{7}$	35.2	1.3
66	4,248	24.5	526,130	723	458.9	139,524	3.77	1.68	45	150$_{2}$ - 112$_{3}$	35.0	1.3
67	5,345	24.3	651,500	916	521.5	140,286	4.64	1.74	38	259^{2} - 141^{3}	43.1	0.9
68	6,889	26.8	871,498	1,770	545.1	141,210	6.17	2.08	34	300 - 224$_{3}$	42.5	0.8
69	7,197	26.7	933,873	1,814	554.8	142,148	6.57	2.88	44	295$_{5}$ - 233^{3}	40.2	1.1
70	7,504	25.1	1,017,521	1,512	572.9	143,234	7.10	3.84	54	309$^{5}_{5}$ - 175$_{5}$	34.1	1.6
71	8,274	23.9	1,078,847	1,861	676.1	144,418	7.50	4.16	55	292$^{5}_{3}$ - 226$^{5}_{3}$	34.6	1.6
72	9,533	24.3	1,279,268	2,563	772.9	145,499	8.82	4.32	49	341^{3} - 265$^{3}_{1}$	34.4	1.4
73	10,993	25.2	1,575,467	3,275	652.2	146,713	10.79	4.48	42	365 - 235$^{1}_{4}$	27.8	1.5
74	12,675	25.0	1,837,639	3,800	335.8	148,259	12.47	5.56	45	254 - 150^{4}	16.2	2.8

Note: Adjusted for all stock dividends and splits thru 5-for-4 stock split 6/73.

INCORPORATED: June 16, 1911—N.Y.

PRINCIPAL OFFICE: Armonk, New York, 10504

ANNUAL MEETING: Last Monday in April

NUMBER OF STOCKHOLDERS: 589,214

TRANSFER AGENT: Company office
Wells Fargo Bank, N.A.
San Francisco, Calif.

REGISTRAR: Morgan Guaranty Trust Co., N.Y.
First National Bank, Chicago, Ill.
Crocker National Bank,
San Francisco, Calif.

INSTIT. HOLDINGS: NO.: 1,278
SHS.: 15,973,129

OFFICERS

CHAIRMAN:
F.T. Cary

PRESIDENT:
J.R. Opel

SECRETARY:
J.H. Grady

TREASURER:
B.H. Witham

INTERNATIONAL MINERALS & CHEMICAL CORPORATION

LISTED	SYMBOL	INDICATED DIV.	RECENT PRICE	PRICE RANGE (1975)	YIELD
NYSE	IGL	$2.00	37	49 - 31	5.4%

INTRINSIC INVESTMENT QUALITY: MEDIUM GRADE. RECENT OPERATING RESULTS REFLECT IMPROVED DEMAND AND HIGHER PRICES FOR FERTILIZERS.

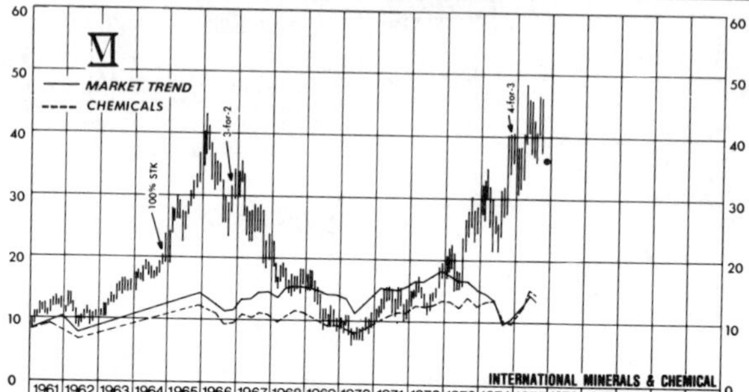

	1961	1962	1963	1964	1965	1966	1967	1968	1969	1970	1971	1972	1973	1974	1975	1976	1977	1978	1979	1980
EARN.	0.74	0.76	0.88	1.24	1.59	1.91	1.06	0.76	0.07	0.16	0.73	1.23	1.57	3.58	9.91					
DIV.	0.40	0.40	0.46	0.46	0.52	0.64	0.75	0.66	0.19	—	0.04	0.19	0.32	0.71						

CAPITALIZATION: (6/30/75)

	(000)	(%)
Debt	c$295,600	37.8
Pfd.($100)	k 29,300	3.8
Defer.inc.tax	27,900	3.6
Com. & Surp.	428,600	54.8
Total	$781,400	100.0%

Shs. ($5)-16,520,493

INTERIM EARNINGS:

Qu.	9/30	12/31	3/31	6/30
73m	0.05	0.33	0.46	0.73
74m	0.23	0.53	1.10	1.72
75m	1.85	2.48	2.97	2.61
76	1.85			

DIVIDENDS:	RECORD	PAYABLE
4-for-3 split	11/15/74	12/9/74
0.32Q	12/20	1/2/75
0.32Q	3/13/75	3/30/75
0.50Q	6/11	6/30
0.50Q	9/12	9/30

BACKGROUND:

IMC is the leading producer of phosphate and potash fertilizer. The agriculture group (57% of fiscal 1975 sales and 79% of pretax income) operates phosphate facilities in Florida with annual production capacity of over 12 million tons of rock from reserves of about 150 million tons. Potash is produced from mines in Saskatchewan, Canada, with capacity of 3.8 million tons of muriate from extensive reserves, and at Carlsbad, N.M. Additional phosphate and potash deposits are being explored. Retail fertilizer and feed ingredients are also sold. Other operations include an industry group (34% of sales, 14% of pretax net) producing carbon products, ferroalloys and metals, foundry products and steel drums, and a chemical group (9% and 7%) producing ammonia and other hydrocarbons, industrial chemicals and biochemicals. Commercial Solvents Corp. and Sobin Chemicals, Inc. were merged in 1975.

RECENT DEVELOPMENTS:

In the three months ended 9/30/75 sales rose slightly to $292.2 million and net income increased $32.1 million. Fertilizer profits rose on higher prices for export sales of phosphate rock. In 10/75, Company sold $100 million debentures due 11/1/2000; proceeds for capital spending of $180 million in 1976. Sales in the year ended 6/30/75 increased 52% and net income from operations rose 182%, principally on sharply higher prices for phosphate rock exported. Commercial Solvents Corp. was merged in 5/75 for $75.4 million.

PROSPECTS:

Export sales of the Company's highly profitable phosphate rock remain god and selling prices continue at a high level. Potash also remains in good demand. Production costs continue to rise, however, and concentrated phosphate chemical prices have softened, although a major portion of Company's domestic sales are made under long-term contracts at prices well under current market quotes. Industrial and chemical profits may be off moderately in 1976. Because of more shares outstanding, fiscal 1976 earnings could decline to about $9 a share.

STATISTICS:

YEAR	GROSS REVS. ($ MILL.)	OPER. PROFIT MARGIN %	NET INCOME ($ 000)	WORK CAP. ($ MILL.)	SENIOR CAPITAL ($ MILL.)	NO. SHS. OUT. (000)	EARN. PER SH. $	DIV. PER SH. $	DIV. PAY. %	PRICE RANGE	PRICE X EARN.	AVG. YIELD %
6/30												
66	299.3	12.6	24,627	107.1	191.7	12,646	1.91	0.64	33	43^{1} - 23^{3}	17.4	1.9
g67	329.5	9.2	b14,655	89.2	217.5	12,793	b1.06	0.75	70	35^{5} - 20^{5}	26.4	2.8
g68	497.0	5.0	b13,084	175.1	319.9	14,449	b0.76	0.66	87	22^{5} - 13^{7}	24.1	3.6
69	500.8	2.8	b3,096	143.0	270.3	14,449	b0.07	0.19	—	18^{2} - 8^{3}	—	1.4
70	505.9	3.8	4,503	138.9	268.0	14,549	0.16	Nil	—	11^{3} - 6^{1}	52.8	—
71	517.6	5.8	12,915	138.2	256.9	14,750	0.73	0.04	5	15^{4} - 10	17.3	0.3
72	491.2	6.4	20,325	124.8	211.3	14,827	1.23	0.19	16	19^{5} - 11^{2}	12.5	1.3
73	547.9	7.2	m25,487	132.2	204.5	14,831	m1.57	0.32	20	30^{1} - 15^{1}	14.4	1.4
74	858.4	11.5	m57,401	195.7	298.8	15,143	m3.58	0.71	20	40^{3} - 21^{4}	8.6	2.3
75	1,302.9	22.8	m161,800	184.9	324.9	16,520	m9.91	1.64	17	48^{4} - 30^{7}	4.0	4.2

Note: Adjusted for 50% stock dividend, 1966 and 4-for-3 stock split, 12/74. b-Before special items. c-Incl. $34.7 mill. debentures convertible into common at $37.98 a share. g-Incl. acquisitions. k-Incl. 192,743 shares each convertible at $33.24 a share. m-Before $0.7 mill. (5c a share) credit in 1973, $13.0 mill. (86c a share) credit in 1974 and $4.2 mill. (26c a share) in 1975.

INCORPORATED: June 14, 1909—N.Y.

PRINCIPAL OFFICE: IMC Plaza, Libertyville, Ill. 60048

ANNUAL MEETING: Early October

NUMBER OF STOCKHOLDERS: 29,800

TRANSFER AGENT: Bankers Trust Co., N.Y.; First National Bank, Chicago, Ill.

REGISTRAR: Chemical Bank, N.Y., N.Y.; Continental Ill. Natl. Bank & Trust Co., Chicago, Ill.

INSTIT. HOLDINGS: NO.: 77; SHS.: 2,680,288

OFFICERS

CHAIRMAN:

PRESIDENT: R.A. Lenon

SECRETARY: J.R. Taylor

TREASURER: J.T. Gibson, Jr.

INTERNATIONAL TELEPHONE & TELEGRAPH CORPORATION

LISTED	SYMBOL	INDICATED DIV.	RECENT PRICE	PRICE RANGE (1975)	YIELD
NYSE	ITT	$1.60	21	25 - 15	7.6%

INTRINSIC INVESTMENT QUALITY: INVESTMENT GRADE. GEOGRAPHIC AND PRODUCT DIVERSIFICATION ACCOUNT FOR THIS MULTI-NATIONAL COMPANY'S GOOD RECORD.

	1961	1962	1963	1964	1965	1966	1967	1968	1969	1970	1971	1972	1973	1974	1975	1976	1977	1978	1979	1980
EARN.	1.10	1.21	1.35	1.58	1.79	2.04	2.27	2.58	2.90	3.17	3.45	3.80	4.17	3.63						
DIV.	0.50	0.50	0.50	0.53	0.60	0.68	0.75	0.85	0.95	1.05	1.15	1.19	1.28	1.43						

CAPITALIZATION: (12/31/74)

	(000)	(%)
Co.& Sub Debt	$1,999,577	30.2
Minority int.	119,172	1.8
Pfds.	c 578,101	8.7
Defer.inc.tax	386,022	5.8
Com. & Surp.	3,555,908	53.5
Total	$6,638,780	100.0%

Shs. ($1)-94,393,892

INTERIM EARNINGS:

Qu.	3/31	6/30	9/30	12/31
72	0.75	0.99	0.87	1.19
73h	0.84	1.10	1.00	1.27
74	0.84	1.16	0.90	0.73
75	0.86	0.80	0.66	

DIVIDENDS:	RECORD	PAYABLE
0.38Q	11/21/74	11/1/74
0.38Q	2/21/75	4/1/75
0.38Q	5/16	7/1
0.38Q	8/22	10/1
0.40Q	11/20	1/1/76

BACKGROUND:

ITT is the world's largest manufacturer of telecommunications equipment outside the United States and operates on a worldwide basis with plants and facilities in more than 80 countries. Its products and services include telecommunication equipment, industrial and consumer products, insurance, automotive parts, natural resources, food processing and utility operations. Sales and earnings are about equally divided between domestic and overseas operations. In 1974, sales and (income) were derived: 71% and (82%), manufacturing; 25% and (26%), consumer and business services; and 4% and (-8%), divestible operations. Fully diluted earnings per share were: 1974-$3.57, 1973-$4.08, 1972-$3.71.

RECENT DEVELOPMENTS:

Third quarter 1975 net income fell 27% to $82 million, following a decline of 31% in the second quarter. Nine month net income was down 20% to $288.1 million. Nevertheless, the quarterly dividend was raised to 40c a share with the January, 1976 payment. Foreign currency translation charges cut per share earnings by about 40c. In the year-earlier period, the charge was only 5c. The Company's backlog as of 9/30/75 was up 5% over a year earlier to $4.8 billion.

PROSPECTS:

Results for the Company as a whole will be slow to recover because business outside the United States, particularly Europe, has been hurt by the worldwide recession. Inflation is also expected to continue to pressure margins. The outlook for the first half of 1976 is cloudy but comparisons should be better later in the year vs. heavily depressed 1975 results. Acquisition efforts are easing and greater effort is being placed on internal expansion.

STATISTICS:

YEAR	GROSS REVS. ($ MILL.)	OPER. PROFIT MARGIN %	NET INCOME ($ 000)	WORK CAP. ($ MILL.)	SENIOR CAPITAL ($ MILL.)	NO. SHS. OUT. (000)	EARN. PER SH. $	DIV. PER SH. $	DIV. PAY. %	PRICE RANGE	PRICE X EARN.	AVG. YIELD %
66	2,121.3	9.3	b 89,910	319	599.4	42,168	2.04	0.68	33	39^{6} - 29_{2}	16.9	2.0
g67	2,760.6	9.1	119,221	529	1,081.2	49,940	2.27	0.75	33	62 - 36^{2}	21.6	1.5
a67	3,577.8	8.5	153,767	631	1,224.5	57,579	2.19	-	-	-	-	-
a68	4,066.5	8.8	k180,162	673	1,304.4	59,059	k2.58	0.85	33	62^{4} - 44^{7}	20.8	1.6
g69	5,474.7	8.2	234,034	773	1,634.6	65,371	n2.90	0.95	33	60^{4} - 46^{2}	18.4	1.8
g70	6,364.5	8.9	353,307	729	2,026.5	67,820	n3.17	1.05	33	60^{1} - 30^{4}	14.3	2.3
g71	7,345.8	8.4	406,834	1,247	2,411.6	74,964	3.45	1.15	33	67^{3} - 45^{7}	16.4	2.0
72	8,556.8	8.2	476,626	1,324	2,502.6	95,580	3.80	1.19	31	64^{4} - 48^{2}	14.8	2.1
73	10,183.0	8.8	h521,291	1,223	2,688.6	94,537	h4.17	1.28	31	60^{3} - 25	10.2	3.0
74	11,154.4	8.4	451,070	1.195	2,577.7	94,394	3.63	1.43	39	29^{4} - 12	5.7	6.9

Note: Adjusted for 2-for-1 stock split 3/68. a-Incl. acquisitions for entire period, 1967, pro-forma. b-Before taxes on foreign subsidiaries' undistributed net. c-Incl. 20,922,448 shares each convertible into common at various prices. g-Incl. acquisitions for entire period. h-Before $6.5 mill. (5c a share) credit. k-Before special credit. n-As reported.

INCORPORATED: Jan. 31, 1968—Delaware

PRINCIPAL OFFICE: 320 Park Avenue, New York, N.Y. 10022

ANNUAL MEETING: First Wednesday in May

NUMBER OF STOCKHOLDERS: 237,000

TRANSFER AGENT: Office of the Corporation; Continental Ill. National Bank & Trust Co., Chicago, Ill.

REGISTRAR: First National City Bank, New York; Harris Trust & Savings Bank, Chicago, Ill.

INSTIT. HOLDINGS: NO.: 238; SHS.: 7,836,888

OFFICERS

CHAIRMAN: H.S. Geneen

PRESIDENT: F.J. Dunleavy

SECRETARY: J.J. Navin

TREASURER: L.C. Hamilton, Jr.

MC DONALD'S CORPORATION

LISTED	SYMBOL	INDICATED DIV.	RECENT PRICE	PRICE RANGE (1975)	YIELD
NYSE	MCD	...	55	61 - 27	...

INTRINSIC INVESTMENT QUALITY: UPPER MEDIUM GRADE. RAPID GROWTH HAS BEEN ACHIEVED IN BOTH REVENUES AND EARNINGS.

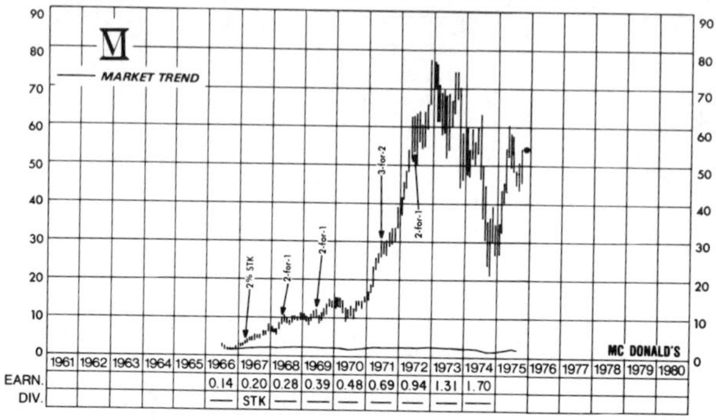

CAPITALIZATION:

	(12/31/74) (000)	(%)
Debt	$348,500	51.7
Defer. inc. tax	25,158	3.7
Com. & Surp.	330,502	44.6
Total	$674,160	100.0%

Shs. (np)-39,689,857

INTERIM EARNINGS:

Qu.	3/31	6/30	9/30	12/31
72a	0.17	0.27	0.26	0.24
73	0.27	0.37	0.35	0.32
74	0.34	0.48	0.47	0.41
75	0.44	0.59	0.61	

DIVIDENDS:	RECORD	PAYABLE
2% stk.	3/20/67	4/10/67
2-for-1 split	5/7/68	5/20/68
2-for-1 split	5/23/69	6/12/69
3-for-2 split	5/21	6/11
2-for-1 split	5/22/72	6/5/72

BACKGROUND:

McDonald's develops, licenses, leases and services a nationwide system of drive-in self-service restaurants. All units are similar in design and serve a standardized menu of low priced food. As of 9/30/75, there were about 2,343 units operated by independent licensees and about 1,073 were operated by wholly-owned licensed subsidiaries of the Company. Outside of the U.S. there are about 212 units in operation in Canada, Australia, Japan and Europe. Gross revenues in 1974 were derived from: Company owned unit sales, 78%; Rental income, 15%; Service fees, 5%; and other, 2%. Independent operators normally lease on a 20-year basis with rental derived as a percentage of sales, with a minimum fixed rent.

RECENT DEVELOPMENTS:

Revenues for the nine months ended 9/30/75 advanced 23% to $690.7 million while net income for the period advanced 32% to $65.7 million. The year-earlier results have been restated to reflect pooling of interests transactions. Increased revenues were posted in all areas of business. Restaurant businesses acquired from licensees (including related territorial rights) in pooling-of-interest transactions numbered 33 in the first half. The Company sold $80 million in notes. The proceeds will be used to reduce bank debt.

PROSPECTS:

Volume growth will continue to reflect an aggressive unit expansion program, acquisition of existing licensee units and expansion into foreign markets. Expansion into different types of locations such as shopping malls, high rise buildings and recreation parks should gain in importance. New product introductions aimed at increasing the amount spent in the average purchase, plus aggressive marketing programs should benefit same unit sales and earnings growth. Earnings in 1976 will continue to move upward.

STATISTICS:

YEAR	GROSS REVS. ($ MILL.)	OPER. PROFIT MARGIN %	NET INCOME ($ 000)	WORK CAP. ($ MILL.)	SENIOR CAPITAL ($ MILL.)	NO. SHS. OUT. (000)	EARN. PER SH. $	DIV. PER SH. $	DIV. PAY. %	PRICE RANGE	PRICE X EARN.	AVG. YIELD %
65	35.4	19.3	3,402	3.5	10.3	27,540	0.12	Nil	—	2^6 - 1^2	16.7	—
66	42.7	20.4	4,512	12.9	14.6	31,671	0.14	Nil	—	3 - 1^2	17.0	—
67	49.6	22.5	6,250	4.2	28.6	31,671	0.20	Stk	—	8^1 - 2^3	26.3	—
68	87.0	20.7	8,841	19.7	45.4	31,671	0.28	Nil	—	11^2 - 5^5	30.1	—
69	129.5	22.8	12,641	13.1	59.9	32,274	0.39	Nil	—	14^7 - 8^1	29.5	—
a70	192.4	19.9	17,691	24.4	73.2	36,987	0.48	Nil	—	15^4 - 9^2	25.8	—
71	276.3	20.3	25,798	34.4	104.7	37,526	0.69	Nil	—	39 - 14^6	38.9	—
a72	385.2	19.6	36,225	9.9	120.3	38,651	0.94	Nil	—	77^3 - 37	60.8	—
a73	592.2	18.8	51,992	22.5	230.9	39,529	1.31	Nil	—	76^7 - 44^1	46.2	—
74	729.0	22.2	67,396	11.5	348.5	39,690	1.70	Nil	—	63^2 - 21^2	—	—

Note: Adjusted for 3-for-2 stock splits 4/66 and 6/71; 2-for-1, 5/68, 6/69 and 6/72; and 2% stock dividend 4/67. a-Incl. acquisitions.

INCORPORATED: March 1, 1965—Delaware

PRINCIPAL OFFICE: McDonald's Plaza, 2111 Enco Drive, Oakbrook, Ill. 60521

ANNUAL MEETING: First Monday in May

NUMBER OF STOCKHOLDERS: 20,796

TRANSFER AGENT: American National Bank & Trust Co. Chicago, Ill.
Royal Trust Co., Toronto, Can.

REGISTRAR: Northern Trust Co., Chicago, Ill.
Montreal Trust Co., Toronto, Can.

INSTIT. HOLDINGS: NO.: 211
SHS.: 9,311,419

OFFICERS

CHAIRMAN: R.A. Kroc

PRESIDENT: F.L. Turner

SECRETARY: D.P. Horwitz

TREASURER: R.B. Ryan

NATIONAL SEMICONDUCTOR CORPORATION

LISTED	SYMBOL	INDICATED DIV.	RECENT PRICE	PRICE RANGE (1975)	YIELD
ASE	NSM	...	43	48 - 9	...

INTRINSIC INVESTMENT QUALITY: MEDIUM GRADE. GROWING MARKETS AND AN EXPANDING PRODUCT BASE ENHANCE LONG-TERM PROSPECTS.

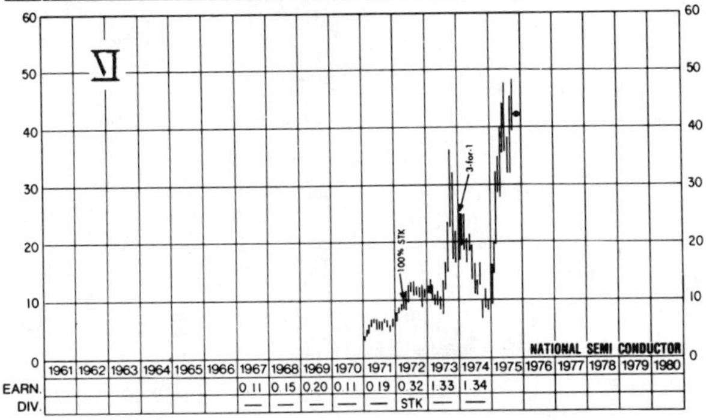

CAPITALIZATION:

	(5/31/75) (000)	(%)
Debt	$13,470	16.5
Com. & Surp.	68,272	83.5
Total	$81,742	100.0%

Shs. ($0.50)-12,268,953

INTERIM EARNINGS: a

Wks.	16	12	12	12
72	0.06	0.06	0.07	0.12
73	0.33	0.27	0.32	0.41
74	0.46	0.31	0.24	0.33
75	0.40			

DIVIDENDS:	RECORD	PAYABLE
100% stk.	3/10/72	4/7/72
3-for-1	12/19/73	1/25/74

BACKGROUND:

National Semiconductor is one of the largest U.S. manufacturers of semiconductors. National holds a major position in several growing markets, including digital integrated circuits, linear integrated circuits, MVS, microprocessors, CMOS, hybrid or special function integrated circuits, optoelectronics and discrete semiconductor devices. Some manufacturing is conducted overseas and about 25% of sales are derived from foreign markets. Operations are conducted through three divisions: semiconductors, systems and consumer products. The systems division is involved with point-of-sale (Datachecker) checkout systems. Consumer products include Novus hand-held calculators. Novus products are sold through a variety of retail outlets.

RECENT DEVELOPMENTS:

First quarter fiscal 1976 net income declined 5% to $5.2 million, despite 10% higher sales. Even though the Company's last fiscal year coincided with the severest period of the economic downturn, gains in both sales and earnings were achieved. Sales increased 10% for the year and were helped by strong demand for consumer products and point-of-sale electronic checkout systems. Although margins were under pressure for the Company as a whole, net income experienced a 2% improvement.

PROSPECTS:

The worst seems to be over in the semiconductor area which was one of the first sectors of the economy to feel the effects of the recession. A strong recovery is expected as economic activity begins to pick up. However, the characteristic volatile and cyclical nature of demand is likely to persist. National is broadening its product base by expanding into more end-use products. This should not only help reduce cyclicality but should promote a widening of operating margins.

STATISTICS:

YEAR	GROSS' REVS. ($ MILL.)	OPER. PROFIT MARGIN %	NET INCOME ($ 000)	WORK CAP. ($ MILL.)	SENIOR CAPITAL ($ MILL.)	NO. SHS. OUT. (000)	EARN. PER SH. $	DIV. PER SH. $	DIV. PAY. %	PRICE RANGE	PRICE X EARN.	AVG. YIELD %
a												
67	11.0	8.1	b 890	2.1	1.9	8,108	b0.11	Nil	—	6^1_3 - 1^1	33.0	—
68	22.9	7.1	b 1,468	1.3	1.1	9,588	b0.15	Nil	—	8_3 - 5_2	44.6	—
69	41.9	7.6	b 1,914	2.4	5.6	9,698	b0.20	Nil	—	11_7 - 7_7	46.6	—
70	38.6	6.4	1,108	6.1	5.8	9,744	0.11	Nil	—	8_7 - 1^1	48.9	—
71	60.1	6.8	2,040	7.0	5.3	10,740	0.19	Nil	—	6_2 - 3_3	26.3	—
72	99.0	6.8	3,719	14.0	3.8	11,154	0.32	Stk	—	13_2 - 4_5	27.5	—
73	213.4	13.8	16,372	27.6	9.7	11,652	1.33	Nil	—	36^2 - 7^5	16.5	—
74	235.5	12.6	16,748	45.5	13.5	12,269	1.34					

Note: Adjusted for 3-for-1 stock split 1/74 and 100% stock dividend 4/72. a-Fiscal year ends 5/31 of following year. b-After tax loss carry-forwards.

INCORPORATED: May 26, 1959—Delaware

PRINCIPAL OFFICE: 2900 Semiconductor Drive, Santa Clara, Calif. 95051

ANNUAL MEETING: Fourth Friday in Sept.

NUMBER OF STOCKHOLDERS: 2,800

TRANSFER AGENT: First National City Bank, N.Y.; Union Trust Company, Stamford, Conn.

REGISTRAR: First National City Bank, N.Y.; Hartford National Bank and Trust, Conn.

INSTIT. HOLDINGS: NO.: 68; SHS.: 4,282,500

OFFICERS

CHAIRMAN: P.J. Sprague

PRESIDENT: C.E. Sporck

SECRETARY: J.F. Hughes

TREASURER:

OCCIDENTAL PETROLEUM CORPORATION

LISTED	SYMBOL	INDICATED DIV.	RECENT PRICE	PRICE RANGE (1975)	YIELD
NYSE	OXY	$1.00	14	23 - 13	7.1%

INTRINSIC INVESTMENT QUALITY: MEDIUM GRADE. COMPANY IS CURRENTLY UPGRADING ITS COAL AND CHEMICAL OPERATIONS TO OFFSET THE DETERIORATING LIBYAN SITUATION.

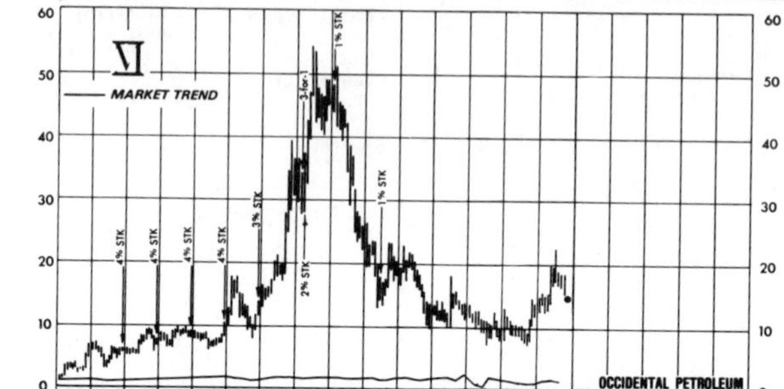

	1961	1962	1963	1964	1965	1966	1967	1968	1969	1970	1971	1972	1973	1974	1975	1976	1977	1978	1979	1980
EARN.	0.02	d	0.05	0.32	0.47	0.48	0.59	2.19	2.94	2.88	d	0.01	1.10	4.74						
DIV.			0.14	0.14	0.16	0.22	0.25	0.36	0.89	0.99	1.00	0.13	—	—						

CAPITALIZATION: (12/31/74)

	(000)	(%)
Debt	a$1,040,309	47.9
Minority int.	37,580	1.7
Pfd. ($1)	g 5,237	0.3
Com. & Surp.	1,089,207	50.1
Total	$2,172,333	100.0%

Shs. ($0.20)-55,114,454

INTERIM EARNINGS:

Qu.	3/31	6/30	9/30	12/31
72m	0.02	d0.01	d0.08	0.08
73m	0.08	0.34	0.32	0.36
74h	0.97	1.62	1.00	1.15
75	1.25	0.69	0.42	

DIVIDENDS:	RECORD	PAYABLE
0.25Q	12/10/74	1/15/75
0.25Q	3/10/75	4/15
0.25Q	6/10	7/15
0.25Q	9/10	10/15
0.25Q	12/10	1/15

BACKGROUND:

Once primarily a small oil and gas exploration and development company, Occidental has diversified its interests through several acquisitions. It acquired Best Fertilizers, a commercial fertilizer maker, and Interore, an international fertilizer sales organization in 1963. Sulphur operations were added in 1964 via acquisition of Jefferson Lake Sulphur. S.V. Hunsaker and Sons, a residential construction and development company, was purchased the same year. Deane Brothers was added in 1955, Permian Corporation was merged in 1966, McWood in 1967, and Island Creek Coal and Hooker Chemical in 1968. Proven crude oil recoverable reserves are estimated at 1.03 billion barrels.

RECENT DEVELOPMENTS:

Net income in the first nine months of 1975 decreased 30% to $146.9 million from prior year levels on 2% higher revenues of $4.24 billion. A major portion of the decline resulted from the lower profitability in Libya, where operating earnings in the nine months amounted to $18.3 million. Chemical earnings in the first nine months were $67.5 million, compared with $81.6 million in the like 1974 period. Fertilizer earnings were slightly below last year due to lower shipments and prices, especially in export markets.

PROSPECTS:

The expected strengthening of the economy in 1976 will doubtless benefit OXY's coal and chemical operations. Until deliveries of crude oil from Libya (which are suspended in the fourth quarter of 1975) are resumed, there might be an adverse impact on earnings in the oil and gas division. Production from the North Sea should start flowing later this year. Overall, we expect net income this year to compare favorably with 1975 levels.

STATISTICS:

YEAR	GROSS REVS. ($ MILL.)	OPER. PROFIT MARGIN %	NET INCOME ($ 000)	WORK CAP. ($ MILL.)	SENIOR CAPITAL ($ MILL.)	NO. SHS. OUT. (000)	EARN. PER SH. $	DIV. PER SH. $	DIV. PAY. %	PRICE RANGE	PRICE X EARN.	AVG. YIELD %
c65	606.3	2.8	18,593	54.5	103.4	34,527	0.54	—	—	.	—	—
c66	658.5	3.3	17,045	67.4	213.6	35,785	0.48	0.22	46	18 - 8	27.1	1.6
b67	825.7	4.7	k32,687	173.0	167.1	45,891	k0.59	0.25	42	39^{2} - 13	44.4	1.0
b68	1,806.8	14.5	134,138	364.2	559.9	49,021	2.19	0.36	16	54^{3} - 27^{5}	18.7	0.9
69	2,059.1	17.1	174,835	306.5	724.3	52,013	2.94	0.89	30	51 - 22	12.4	2.4
70	2,402.3	17.7	175,234	351.8	868.8	53,397	2.88	0.99	34	26^{3} - 13	6.8	5.0
71	2,635.2	15.8	md48,018	237.9	904.0	55,104	md1.22	1.00	—	22^{6} - 9^{7}	—	6.1
72	2,720.8	12.2	m19,675	253.2	1,001.0	55,103	m0.01	0.13	—	18^{2} - 10	—	0.9
73	3,455.7	9.2	79,763	313.9	969.0	55,103	1.10	Nil	—	13^{4} - 7^{6}	9.7	—
74	5,537.5	15.9	h280,677	464.6	1,045.5	55,114	h4.74	Nil	—	14^{5} - 7^{3}	2.3	—

Note: Adjusted for all stock splits and divs. thru 1%, 1970 a-Incl. $125.0 mill. debs. convertible into common at $20 a share b-Incl. acquisitions c-Consolidated; 1965 pro-forma. g-Incl. 1,249,000 shares conv. into 3.106 common shares; 3,265,000 shares conv. into 3.19 common and 548,000 shs. conv. into 3.16 common. h-Reflects LIFO inventory. k-Before special items. m-Before special items: 1971, $19.0 mill. (34c a share) charge; 1972, $11.1 mill. (17c a share) charge.

INCORPORATED: May 21, 1920—California

PRINCIPAL OFFICE: 10889 Wilshire Blvd., Los Angeles, Cal. 90024

ANNUAL MEETING: Second Tuesday in May

NUMBER OF STOCKHOLDERS: 287,000

TRANSFER AGENT: Security Pacific National Bank, Los Angeles, Calif.; Chase Manhattan Bank, N.Y.

REGISTRAR: Bank of America, Los Angeles, Calif.; First National City Bank, New York; Chase Manhattan Bank, New York

INSTIT. HOLDINGS: NO.: 51; SHS.: 1,976,765

OFFICERS

CHAIRMAN: Dr. A. Hammer

PRESIDENT: J.E. Baird

SECRETARY: P.C. Hebner

TREASURER: J.J. Dorgan

PENNZOIL CORPORATION

LISTED	SYMBOL	INDICATED DIV.	RECENT PRICE	PRICE RANGE (1975)	YIELD
NYSE	PZL	$1.20	21	24 - 17	5.7%

INTRINSIC INVESTMENT QUALITY: MEDIUM GRADE. IN RECENT YEARS, EARNINGS HAVE SHOWN A STRONG TURNAROUND, DUE IN PART TO IMPROVING OIL AND GAS OPERATIONS.

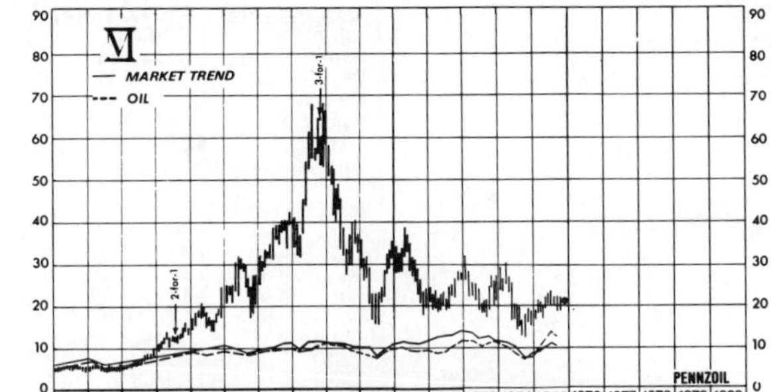

	1961	1962	1963	1964	1965	1966	1967	1968	1969	1970	1971	1972	1973	1974	1975	1976	1977	1978	1979	1980
EARN.	0.40	0.41	0.54	0.91	1.00	1.07	1.92	2.74	2.88	2.97	1.45	1.80	2.43	3.67						
DIV.	0.33	0.33	0.33	0.37	0.47	0.47	0.47	0.55	0.80	0.80	0.80	0.80	0.80	1.05						

CAPITALIZATION: (12/31/74)

		(000)	(%)
Debt	k$	649,479	48.9
Minority int.		104,406	7.9
Pref. com.	c	455	0.0
Def.inc.tax		60,215	4.5
Com. & Surp.		514,523	38.7
Total		$1,329,078	100.0%

Shs. ($0.833)-32,093,049

INTERIM EARNINGS:

Qu.	3/31	6/30	9/30	12/31
72	0.49	0.47	0.40	0.44
73	0.60	0.58	0.53	0.72
74n	1.09	0.95	0.81	0.82
75	0.77	0.76	0.77	

DIVIDENDS:	RECORD	PAYABLE
0.30Q	11/29/74	12/15/74
0.30Q	2/28/75	3/15/75
0.30Q	5/30	6/15
0.30Q	8/29	9/15
0.30Q	8/29	9/15

BACKGROUND:

Company was formed in April, 1968 by the consolidation of Pennzoil Company and United Gas Corporation. Activities encompass oil and gas exploration and production, natural gas transmission, refining and marketing of Pennzoil motor oil, and the mining and processing of copper, molybdenum, potash and sulphur. Duval Corp., a 100%-owned subsidiary, mines and processes copper and other precious metals in Ariz., Nev., N.M. & Texas. Pursuant to an SEC order, the Company was required to dispose of its retail gas distribution divisions, which was effected 6/70. In 1969, Pennzoil Offshore Gas Operators, (oil and gas exploration) was formed, and in 1971, Pennzoil Louisiana and Texas Offshore (PLATO) was formed. United Gas Pipe Line was spun-off in 1974.

RECENT DEVELOPMENTS:

In the nine months ended September 30, 1975, net income fell 18% to $81.0 million on 14% higher revenues of $774.1 million. In the third quarter, net income fell 3% to $27.1 million. During the period, margins in refining and marketing activities, including branded motor sales, began to improve in the third quarter. The decline in industrial activity here and abroad through the first half of 1975 continued to depress sales of metals and fertilizer materials, including sulphur.

PROSPECTS:

Improved margins are expected to carry over into the forepart of 1976. The Company is accelerating copper deliveries to pay off a production payment, which should expect it to participate fully in the expected recovery of the copper market. Exploration and production activities of the parent company are being expanded. Overall, we look for favorable earnings comparisons this year over 1975's estimated $3.00 a share.

STATISTICS:

YEAR	GROSS REVS. ($ MILL.)	OPER. PROFIT MARGIN %	NET INCOME ($ 000)	WORK CAP. ($ MILL.)	SENIOR CAPITAL ($ MILL.)	NO. SHS. OUT. (000)	EARN. PER SH. $	DIV. PER SH. $	DIV. PAY. %	PRICE RANGE	PRICE X EARN.	AVG. YIELD %
66	89.2	17.8	13,026	39.5	246.9	12,144	1.07	0.47	44	31^{7} - 17^{7}	23.3	1.8
g66	548.0	14.9	36,387	—	—	12,324	1.61	—	—	-	—	—
g67	576.3	15.6	b40,170	70.7	321.2	12,324	b1.92	0.47	24	42^{1} - 25^{2}	17.6	1.4
68	630.3	15.2	60,143	52.4	592.6	16,442	a2.74	0.55	20	67_{3} - 32^{5}	18.2	1.1
69	684.3	18.3	65,595	d14.4	554.6	18,137	a2.88	0.80	28	58^{2} - 28_{5}	15.0	1.9
70	739.0	16.6	70,011	168.2	801.5	19,476	a2.97	0.80	27	36 - 15^{5}	8.7	3.1
71	730.8	12.9	m47,180	37.3	651.8	20,986	m1.45	0.80	55	39_{1} - 18_{5}	19.7	2.8
72	814.8	15.1	58,655	147.8	773.4	22,095	1.80	0.80	44	28^{1} - 18^{5}	13.0	3.4
73	1,059.4	16.1	83,661	90.9	647.0	23,969	2.43	0.80	33	32_{4} - 17_{4}	10.2	3.2
74	939.6	22.7	n127,450	192.6	649.9	32,093	n3.67	1.05	29	30^{4} - 12^{6}	5.9	4.9

Note: Adjusted for stock split: 3-for-1, 10/68. a-Earnings per share as reported: 1969 $2.02; 1970, $2.16. b-Before special items. c-546,086 shares each convertible into 1.44 common shs. g-Incl. United Gas 1966 pro-forma. k-Incl. $50.0 mill. debentures convertible into common at $38.25. m-Before special items $13.9 mill. (43c a sh.) charge. n-Reflects change to LIFO accounting.

INCORPORATED: April 1, 1968—Del.

PRINCIPAL OFFICE: 900 Southwest Tower, Houston, Texas 77002

ANNUAL MEETING: First Monday in May

NUMBER OF STOCKHOLDERS: 44,364

TRANSFER AGENT: Chemical Bank, N.Y., N.Y.; Mellon Bank, N.A. Pittsburgh, Pa.

REGISTRAR: Franklin National Bank, N.Y.; Pittsburgh National Bank, Pittsburgh, Pa.

INSTIT. HOLDINGS: NO.: 112; SHS.: 4,805,559

OFFICERS

CHAIRMAN: J.H. Liedtke

PRESIDENT: W.C. Liedtke, Jr.

SECRETARY: R.B. Berryman

TREASURER: W.B. Wilkerson

PFIZER INC.

LISTED	SYMBOL	INDICATED DIV.	RECENT PRICE	PRICE RANGE (1975)	YIELD
NYSE	PFE	$0.81	30	37 - 24	2.7%

INTRINSIC INVESTMENT QUALITY: INVESTMENT GRADE. COMPANY HAS SHOWN GOOD GROWTH IN THE DRUG AND CHEMICAL INDUSTRIES. OPERATIONS ARE BEING BROADENED BY ACQUISITIONS.

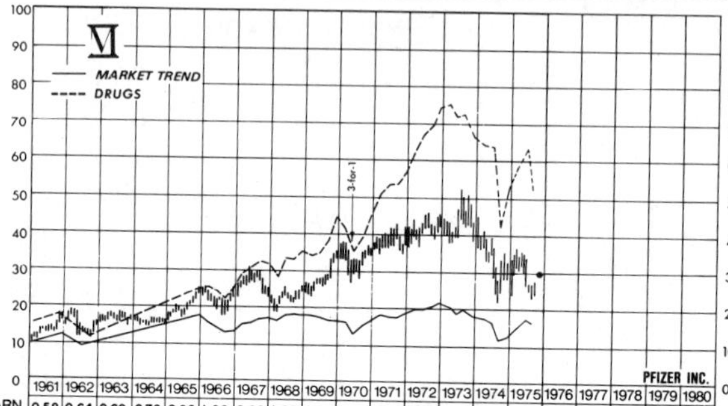

	1961	1962	1963	1964	1965	1966	1967	1968	1969	1970	1971	1972	1973	1974	1975	1976	1977	1978	1979	1980
EARN.	0.58	0.64	0.69	0.76	0.90	1.02	0.96	1.03	1.13	1.27	1.38	1.50	1.74	1.93						
DIV.	0.28	0.32	0.35	0.38	0.43	0.48	0.48	0.50	0.57	0.63	0.65	0.67	0.70	0.79						

CAPITALIZATION: ((12/31/74)

	(000)	(%)
Debt	$253,116	21.8
Defer.inc.tax	32,800	2.8
Minority int.	23,246	2.0
Com. & Surp.	850,850	73.4
Total	$1,160,012	100.0%

Shs. ($0.1111)-70,136,566

INTERIM EARNINGS:

Qu.	3/31	6/30	9/30	12/31
72	0.34	0.30	0.38	0.48
73	0.41	0.36	0.46	0.51
74b	0.51	0.41	0.50	0.51
75	0.48	0.47	0.61	

DIVIDENDS:	RECORD	PAYABLE
0.19Q	12/2/74	12/19/74
0.05E	12/2	12/19
0.19Q	3/10/75	3/28/75
0.19Q	6/2	6/27
0.19Q	9/8	9/26

BACKGROUND:

Pfizer, a leading factor in the ethical drug field, has broadened its base by acquisitions. Health care products, which accounted for 48% of sales, consist of ethical pharmaceuticals, diagnostic products and prosthetic devices. Consumer products, including cosmetics, toiletries and other personal care items account for over 14% of sales. Bulk chemicals sold by Pfizer serve food, beverage and pharmaceutical customers as well as industrial markets and account for more than 16% of sales. Another 14% of sales comes from agricultural chemicals and the remaining 8% comes from materials science products. About 53% of sales are derived from overseas. Research spending was $68 mill. in 1974.

RECENT DEVELOPMENTS:

On a 9% rise in sales in the third quarter of 1975, net income jumped 22% to a record $43.2 million. The basic trends of the first six months continued through the period. Sales of chemicals were still weak as a result of the economic slowdown around the world, but pharmaceutical and health care products posted gains in both U.S. and international markets. Gains were particularly strong overseas. For the nine months, sales increased 7%; net income rose 10%.

PROSPECTS:

Continuing growth in all major operating areas is expected. Near term benefits should be derived from the recent completion of new plants and the introduction of a number of new products. The Company should be able to achieve another good earnings gain in 1976. Over the longer term, maintenance of growth is also expected. Despite the intense competition in the drug industry (strengthened by mergers) and more intensive government regulation, Pfizer has maintained a strong position and should continue to do so.

STATISTICS:

YEAR	GROSS REVS. ($ MILL.)	OPER. PROFIT MARGIN %	NET INCOME ($ 000)	WORK CAP. ($ MILL.)	SENIOR CAPITAL ($ MILL.)	NO. SHS. OUT. (000)	EARN. PER SH. $	DIV. PER SH. $	DIV. PAY. %	PRICE RANGE	PRICE X EARN.	AVG. YIELD %
65	542.6	18.2	53,414	152.3	30.3	59,672	0.90	0.43	48	25 - 16^3	23.2	2.1
66	622.0	19.1	61,600	169.8	54.7	60,254	1.02	0.48	47	25^4 - 17^5	21.1	2.2
67	637.8	17.2	58,255	178.3	38.3	60,894	0.96	0.48	51	30 - 22^6	28.1	1.8
68	725.8	18.4	64,698	213.2	35.8	62,859	1.03	0.50	49	25^6 - 18^7	21.7	2.2
69	805.8	18.7	71,624	258.2	55.2	63,309	1.13	0.57	50	35^3 - 23^2	25.9	1.9
70	870.4	19.1	81,061	281.4	48.4	63,617	1.27	0.63	50	38^3 - 26^5	25.6	1.9
a71	951.5	15.5	90,585	273.4	45.4	65,806	1.38	0.65	47	43^1 - 34^5	27.4	1.7
72	1,093.4	17.9	103,238	453.5	191.5	69,016	1.50	0.67	45	46 - 36^5	27.5	1.6
73	1,284.4	17.4	120,700	422.0	139.7	69,618	1.74	0.70	40	52^3 - 38^4	26.1	1.5
74	1,541.7	15.6	b135,267	1,179.7	253.1	70,137	b1.93	0.79	41	45 - 21^3	17.2	2.4

Note: Adjusted for 3-for-1 stock split, 4/70. a-Incl. acquisitions. b-Reflects LIFO inventory.

INCORPORATED: 1942—Delaware

PRINCIPAL OFFICE: 235 E. 42 Street, New York, N.Y. 10017

ANNUAL MEETING: Third Monday in April

NUMBER OF STOCKHOLDERS: 70,600

TRANSFER AGENT: Chase Manhattan Bank, N.Y.

REGISTRAR: Chase Manhattan Bank, N.Y.

INSTIT. HOLDINGS: NO.: 272 SHS.: 9,705,916

OFFICERS

CHAIRMAN: E.T. Pratt, Jr.

PRESIDENT: G.D. Laubach

SECRETARY: F.A. Duckworth

TREASURER: M.P. Landers

POLAROID CORPORATION

LISTED	SYMBOL	INDICATED DIV.	RECENT PRICE	PRICE RANGE (1975)	YIELD
NYSE	PRD	$0.32	38	44 - 15	0.8%

INTRINSIC INVESTMENT QUALITY: UPPER MEDIUM GRADE. INTRODUCTION OF NEW CAMERA MODELS HAS BROADENED MARKETS BUT RELATED COSTS HAVE RESTRICTED EARNINGS.

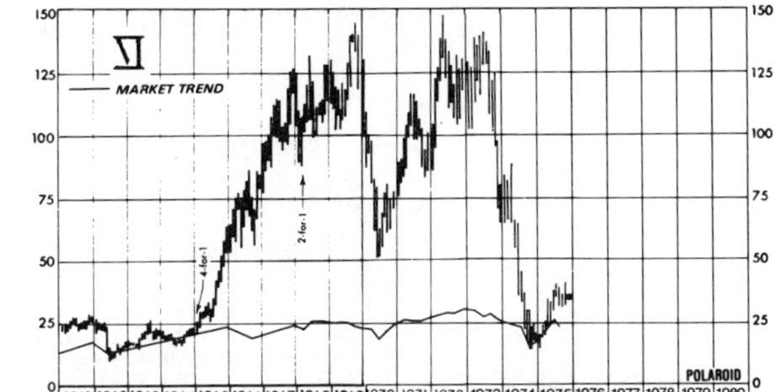

	1961	1962	1963	1964	1965	1966	1967	1968	1969	1970	1971	1972	1973	1974	1975	1976	1977	1978	1979	1980
EARN.	0.26	0.32	0.36	0.58	0.93	1.52	1.81	1.86	1.92	1.86	1.86	1.30	1.58	0.86						
DIV.	0.03	0.03	0.03	0.03	0.06	0.13	0.23	0.32	0.32	0.32	0.32	0.32	0.32	0.32						

CAPITALIZATION: (12/31/74)

Com. & Surplus $636,941,000

Shs. ($1)-32,855,475

INTERIM EARNINGS:

Qu.	3/31	6/30	9/30	12/31
72	0.27	0.22	0.27	0.54
73	0.34	0.26	0.34	0.64
74	0.30	0.07	0.21	0.28
75	0.25	0.41	0.49	

DIVIDENDS:	RECORD	PAYABLE
0.08Q	10/4/74	10/25/74
0.08Q	11/20	12/11
0.08Q	3/3/75	3/25/75
0.08Q	10/3	10/24
0.08Q	11/20	12/11

BACKGROUND:

Polaroid has achieved the second largest position in the domestic photographic industry through its quick developing films and cameras. In addition to amateur camera, film, and accessory photographic equipment, cameras and films are supplied for commercial, industrial, and scientific uses. Wholly-owned subsidiaries outside the U.S. include marketing units in 19 countries and manufacturing plants in Scotland and The Netherlands; foreign sales were $270 mill. in 1974 and are growing rapidly. The Automatic 100 Land camera was introduced in 1963, the 200 series in 1967, the 300 series in 1969, the 400 in 1971, the Square Shooter 2 and Type 88 film early in 1972, and the SX-70 camera late in 1972. Dr. Land and wife own or control 15% of the stock.

RECENT DEVELOPMENTS:

For the nine months ended 9/30/75, sales increased 7% to $543 million while net income advanced 98% to $37.9 million. In the three months ended 9/30/75, sales rose 7% and net income was up 133% to $16.2 million. The increase in third quarter earnings was attributed to continued progress in the reduction of manufacturing costs for the SX-70 camera and strong sales of color film. Profits also benefited from manufacture of color negatives for SX-70 film. These negatives had previously been purchased.

PROSPECTS:

Operating capacity rates for the SX-70 have improved, resulting in wider profit margins. Consumer demand for the Company's products is on the upswing and has resulted in increased dealer orders. International business should continue to expand in 1976, while domestic sales of the older pack cameras and film should improve as consumer spending increases in 1976. Longer-term prospects depend mainly on the development of new products.

STATISTICS:

YEAR	GROSS REVS. ($ MILL.)	OPER. PROFIT MARGIN %	NET INCOME ($ 000)	WORK CAP. ($ MILL.)	SENIOR CAPITAL ($ MILL.)	NO. SHS. OUT. (000)	EARN. PER SH. $	DIV. PER SH. $	DIV. PAY. %	PRICE RANGE	PRICE X EARN.	AVG. YIELD %
65	204.0	28.3	29,114	87.0	Nil	31,548	0.93	0.06	7	65_{4} - 21^{7}	47.0	0.1
66	322.4	29.8	47,963	102.8	Nil	31,615	1.52	0.13	8	87^{4} - 54_{3}	46.7	0.2
a67	374.4	30.6	57,377	133.4	Nil	31,660	1.81	0.23	13	127^{1} - 77^{3}	56.5	0.2
68	402.1	32.1	58,899	170.9	Nil	31,712	1.86	0.32	17	133^{5} - 87^{4}	59.5	0.3
69	465.6	27.6	b63,121	297.9	Nil	32,829	b1.92	0.32	17	145^{6} - 102^{5}	64.7	0.3
70	444.3	25.6	61,136	301.0	Nil	32,832	1.86	0.32	17	130^{6} - 51	48.9	0.4
71	525.5	19.2	61,018	330.9	Nil	32,840	1.86	0.32	17	117^{1} - 76_{1}	51.9	0.3
72	559.3	11.2	42,534	352.4	Nil	32,848	1.30	0.32	25	149^{4} - 86^{1}	90.6	0.3
73	685.5	11.0	51,818	390.7	Nil	32,855	1.58	0.32	20	143^{4} - 65^{1}	66.0	0.3
74	757.3	4.5	28,387	412.6	Nil	32,855	0.86	0.32	37	88^{4} - 14^{1}	59.7	0.6

Note: Adjusted for stock splits: 4-for-1, 1/65; 2-for-1, 3/68. a-Excl. Polaroid of Canada, previously consolidated. b-Incl. tax credit $1.3 mill. (4c a share).

INCORPORATED: Sept. 13,1937—Delaware

PRINCIPAL OFFICE: 549 Technology Square, Cambridge, Mass. 02139

ANNUAL MEETING: Fourth Tuesday in April

NUMBER OF STOCKHOLDERS: 50,730

TRANSFER AGENT: Morgan Guaranty Trust Co., N.Y. First National Bank of Boston, Mass.

REGISTRAR: Morgan Guaranty Trust Co., N.Y. First National Bank of Boston, Mass.

INSTIT. HOLDINGS: NO.: 176 SHS.: 4,273,719

OFFICERS

CHAIRMAN: E.H. Land

PRESIDENT: W.J. McCune, Jr.

SECRETARY: R.F. deLima

TREASURER: H.H. Thayer

SEARLE (G.D.) COMPANY

LISTED	SYMBOL	INDICATED DIV.	RECENT PRICE	PRICE RANGE (1975)	YIELD
NYSE	SRL	$0.88	17	26 - 13	5.2%

INTRINSIC INVESTMENT QUALITY: INVESTMENT GRADE. ALTHOUGH MARGINS HAVE NARROWED, GOOD SALES GROWTH AND A LOWER TAX RATE HAVE HELPED MAINTAIN THE PROFIT UPTREND.

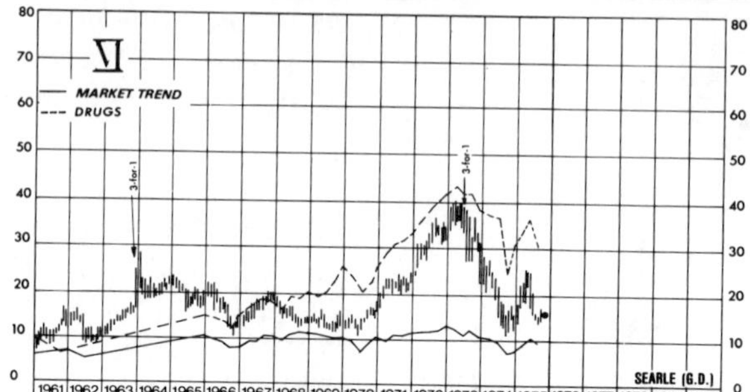

	1961	1962	1963	1964	1965	1966	1967	1968	1969	1970	1971	1972	1973	1974	1975	1976	1977	1978	1979	1980
EARN.			0.47	0.61	0.58	0.54	0.64	0.65	0.69	0.77	0.87	1.01	1.24	1.41						
DIV.			0.24	0.33	0.43	0.43	0.43	0.43	0.43	0.43	0.43	0.43	0.45	0.46						

CAPITALIZATION: (12/31/74)

	(000)	(%)
Debt	c$206,218	37.7
Com. & Surp.	340,517	62.3
Total	$546,735	100.0%

Shs. ($0.33-1/3)-51,339,021

INTERIM EARNINGS:

Qu.	3/31	6/30	9/30	12/31
72	0.22	0.24	0.26	0.29
73	0.26	0.32	0.31	0.35
74	0.33	0.36	0.34	0.38
75	0.38	0.43	0.36	

DIVIDENDS:	RECORD	PAYABLE
0.115Q	11/8/74	12/3/74
0.115Q	2/10/75	3/7/75
0.13Q	5/9	6/3
0.13Q	8/4	9/2
0.22Q	11/7	11/24

BACKGROUND:

Searle is diversified with participation in a number of health care markets. By means of acquisitions and internal expansion, dependence on the birth control market has been reduced. Oral contraceptives accounted for 18% of total pharmaceutical sales in 1974. Total pharmaceuticals contributed 42% of sales (81% of operating profits); medical instruments and optical products, 20% (7%), hospital and laboratory products, 36% (12%). The merger with Will Ross has added a broad line of non-pharmaceutical health products such as supplies, furnishings and other equipment for hospitals and other health-care institutions, plus a significant position in optical products. Research expenditures of Searle exceed 8% of sales.

RECENT DEVELOPMENTS:

In the first nine months of 1975, on an 18% increase in sales to $523.2 million, net income rose 14% to $60.4 million, net income rose 14% to $60.4 million. Third quarter sales were up 18% to $184.9 million, but net income rose only a moderate 5% to $18.4 million. This poor performance was due to a loss in the Company's medical—instrumentation and optical group. This was caused by the anticipated divestiture of Searle Medidata, an automated multiphasic health-testing operation.

PROSPECTS:

The near-term outlook is clouded by questions raised by the Food and Drug Adminstration concerning research on products developed since 1968. Longer term prospects are enhanced by reduced dependence on a single product area. The merger with Will Ross provides an enlarged base for further diversification, expansion and new product development. Net profits should benefit from tax sheltered Puerto Rican operations.

STATISTICS:

YEAR	GROSS REVS. ($ MILL.)	OPER. PROFIT MARGIN %	NET INCOME ($ 000)	WORK CAP. ($ MILL.)	SENIOR CAPITAL ($ MILL.)	NO. SHS. OUT. (000)	EARN. PER SH. $	DIV. PER SH. $	DIV. PAY. %	PRICE RANGE	PRICE X EARN.	AVG. YIELD %
b66	113.5	39.0	22,854	59.5	3.7	39,828	0.54	0.43	80	$22 - 10^{7}$	30.3	2.6
67	132.7	39.9	26,625	65.0	6.5	39,828	0.64	0.43	67	$20^{3} - 12^{4}$	25.9	2.6
b68	147.7	36.9	27,366	78.6	21.3	40,158	0.65	0.43	66	$19^{4} - 12^{6}$	24.8	2.7
69	163.9	34.6	28,491	47.8	25.6	39,393	0.69	0.43	62	$16^{7} - 11^{6}$	20.6	3.0
70	201.5	25.5	31,930	98.3	50.9	39,684	0.77	0.43	56	$18^{3} - 11^{2}$	19.2	2.9
71	226.9	22.4	36,004	124.0	53.4	40,032	0.87	0.43	50	$24^{6} - 17^{2}$	24.2	2.1
72	271.9	19.6	41,891	147.7	50.5	40,800	1.01	0.43	43	$36^{4} - 24^{1}$	30.0	1.4
a72	402.9	17.5	48,518	198.5	87.8	46,497	1.02	—	—	-	—	—
a73	471.7	16.1	59,793	287.3	198.8	48,350	1.24	0.45	36	$39^{7} - 22^{6}$	25.3	1.4
74	621.3	15.0	72,421	224.7	206.2	51,339	1.41	0.46	33	$28^{2} - 11^{3}$	14.1	2.3

Note: Adjusted for 3-for-1 stock splits 6/73. a-Incl. Will Ross for entire year; 1972 pro-forma. b-Incl. acquisitions for entire period. c-Incl. $55.1 mill. debentures convertible into common at different prices.

INCORPORATED: Nov. 2, 1955—Delaware

PRINCIPAL OFFICE: P.O. Box 1045, Skokie, Ill. 60076

ANNUAL MEETING: Fourth Saturday in April

NUMBER OF STOCKHOLDERS: 28,000

TRANSFER AGENT: Harris Trust & Savings Bank, Chicago, Ill.; Morgan Guaranty Trust Co., N.Y.

REGISTRAR: First National Bank, Chicago, Ill.; First National City Bank, N.Y.

INSTIT. HOLDINGS: NO.: 122; SHS.: 5,133,251

OFFICERS

CHAIRMAN: W.L. Searle

PRESIDENT: W.M. Dixon, Jr.

SECRETARY: H.A. Wegner

TREASURER: P.B. Higdon

SKYLINE CORPORATION

LISTED	SYMBOL	INDICATED DIV.	RECENT PRICE	PRICE RANGE (1975)	YIELD
NYSE	SKY	$0.24	16	26 - 4	1.5%

INTRINSIC INVESTMENT QUALITY: SPECULATIVE GRADE. STOCK OF THIS MAJOR PRODUCER OF MOBILE HOMES AND RECREATIONAL VEHICLES HAS BEEN VOLATILE.

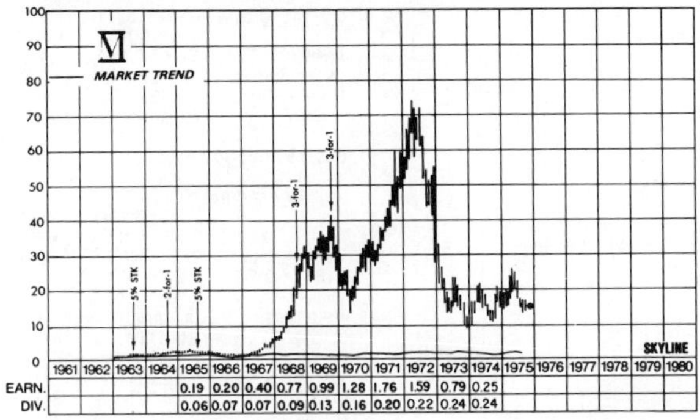

CAPITALIZATION: (5/31/75)

Cap. & Surp. $81,240,827

Shs.($2.77)-11,221,944

INTERIM EARNINGS:

Qu.	8/31	11/30	2/28	5/31
72	0.56	0.33	0.19	0.51
73	0.32	0.21	0.02	0.24
74	0.22	d0.04	d0.07	0.14
75	0.11			

DIVIDENDS:	RECORD	PAYABLE
0.06Q	9/19/74	10/1/74
0.06Q	12/18	1/2/75
0.06Q	3/20/75	4/1
0.06Q	6/20	7/1
0.06Q	9/17	10/1

BACKGROUND:

Skyline is a leading manufacturer of mobile homes and recreational vehicles. Nationwide distribution of its products through 2,800 dealers is served by the Company's manufacturing space in 32 mobile home plants and 9 recreational vehicle plants located throughout the United States. It's mobile homes usually are sold fully equipped and furnished in the factory and include a living room, dining room, kitchen, one to three bedrooms and one or more baths. The price range is from $4000 to $8500 per unit but larger units range to $16,000 each. Acquisitions include Homette Corp. and Layton Homes in 1962, Buddy Mobile Homes in 1963, Modernistic Industries in 1964 and Academy Mobile Homes in 1966.

RECENT DEVELOPMENTS:

For the quarter ended 8/31/75, sales declined 25.7% to $54.8 million and net income dropped 50.1% to $1.2 million. Sales in the fiscal year ended 5/31/75 declined 40.3% to $179.2 million while net income dropped 68.6% to $2.8 million. Weak economic conditions, inflation and high interest rates were factors which depressed consumer confidence. Price competition also contributed to declines in net income. A recreational vehicle production plant in Indiana went on stream in July 1975.

PROSPECTS:

Weak economic conditions and other consumer problems will continue to hurt demand for mobile homes and recreational vehicles and further declines in earnings appear likely. Still, a strong dealer network should enable the Company to at least maintain it's market share in the mobile home market. The higher cost of gasoline may continue to affect recreational vehicle sales, although high levels of inventory on an industry basis have been reduced considerably.

STATISTICS:

YEAR	GROSS REVS. ($ MILL.)	OPER. PROFIT MARGIN %	NET INCOME ($ 000)	WORK CAP. ($ MILL.)	SENIOR CAPITAL ($ MILL.)	NO. SHS. OUT. (000)	EARN. PER SH. $	DIV. PER SH. $	DIV. PAY. %	PRICE RANGE	PRICE X EARN.	AVG. YIELD %
a												
65	67.1	6.0	2,059	4.1	0.1	10,729	0.19	0.06	32	3^{1} - 2^{3}	14.5	2.2
66	69.7	6.1	2,184	5.4	Nil	11,181	0.20	0.07	35	2^{6} - 1^{3}	10.3	3.4
67	107.7	8.4	4,476	7.9	Nil	11,181	0.40	0.07	18	6^{4} - 1^{3}	9.8	1.8
68	181.2	10.1	8,653	12.9	Nil	11,289	0.77	0.09	12	30^{3} - 5^{7}	23.5	0.5
69	211.0	11.0	11,122	19.9	Nil	11,256	0.99	0.13	13	41^{7} - 22^{5}	32.6	0.4
70	252.4	11.0	14,409	30.3	Nil	11,250	1.28	0.16	13	34^{5} - 13^{5}	18.8	0.7
71	326.8	11.6	19,773	38.3	Nil	11,250	1.76	0.20	11	39^{7} - 27	19.0	0.6
72	357.4	10.1	17,857	45.1	Nil	11,250	1.59	0.22	14	74 - 28	32.1	0.4
73	300.5	5.4	8,851	50.5	Nil	11,250	0.79	0.24	30	33^{1} - 9^{1}	26.7	1.1
74	179.2	1.5	2,773	52.4	Nil	11,222	0.25	0.24	96	21^{5} - 10^{2}	63.7	1.5

Note: Adjusted for 3-for-1 stock splits, 9/68 and 9/69; also 5% stock dividend in 1965. a-Fiscal year ends 5/31 of following year.

INCORPORATED: May 29, 1959--Indiana

PRINCIPAL OFFICE: 2520 By Pass Road, Elkhart, Indiana 46514

ANNUAL MEETING: Fourth Monday in Sept.

NUMBER OF STOCKHOLDERS: 8,992

TRANSFER AGENT: First National Bank, Chicago, Ill. Chemical Bank, N.Y.

REGISTRAR: American National Bank & Trust Co., Chicago, Ill. Marine Midland Bank, N.Y.

INSTIT. HOLDINGS: NO.: 43 SHS.: 2,243,400

OFFICERS

CHAIRMAN: A.J. Decio

PRESIDENT: R.F. Kloska

SECRETARY: R.M. Treckelo

TREASURER: F.C. Mischke

SPERRY RAND CORPORATION

LISTED	SYMBOL	INDICATED DIV.	RECENT PRICE	PRICE RANGE (1975)	YIELD
NYSE	SY	$0.76	44	49 - 25	1.7%

INTRINSIC INVESTMENT QUALITY: MEDIUM GRADE. COMPANY IS MAINLY IDENTIFIED WITH DEFENSE AND COMPUTERS, BUT INDUSTRIAL AND AGRICULTURAL EQUIPMENT ARE IMPORTANT.

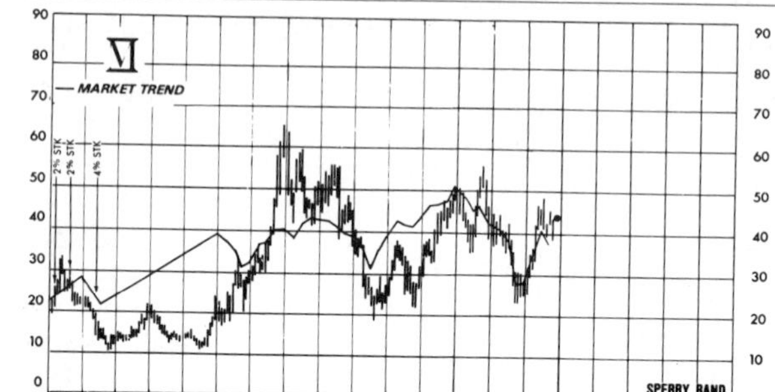

	1961	1962	1963	1964	1965	1966	1967	1968	1969	1970	1971	1972	1973	1974	1975	1976	1977	1978	1979	1980
EARN.	0.78	0.43	0.85	0.70	1.02	1.72	1.87	2.26	2.37	2.11	1.77	2.62	3.27	3.81						
DIV.	STK	STK	—	—	—	—	0.10	0.40	0.48	0.50	0.55	0.60	0.63	0.71						

CAPITALIZATION: (3/31/75)

	(000)	(%)
Debt	$ 456,153	28.4
Defer. inc. tax	89,900	5.6
Com. & Surp.	1,058,954	66.0
Total	$1,605,007	100.0%

Shs. ($0.50)-34,469,678

INTERIM EARNINGS:

Qu.	6/30	9/30	12/31	3/31
72	0.52	0.57	0.68	0.85
73	0.68	0.75	0.86	0.98
74b	0.76	0.85	1.09	p1.11
75	0.84	0.91		

DIVIDENDS:	RECORD	PAYABLE
0.19Q	10/1/74	11/15/74
0.19Q	1/2/75	2/18/75
0.19Q	4/1	5/15
0.19Q	7/1	8/15
0.19Q	10/1	11/18

BACKGROUND:

In the fiscal year ended 3/31/75, Sperry Rand's revenues were derived as follows: business equipment contributed 46%, machinery products 28%, guidance and control 22%, and all other, 4%. The business equipment category includes computers, peripheral equipment, small office machines, office systems and data processing services. Machinery products are comprised of agricultural and industrial equipment and fluid power system components. The Company also makes Remington shavers and other personal care products. In terms of markets, the Company derives 41% of sales from domestic commercial operations, 43% from overseas, and 16% from defense and aerospace business. The Univac division, with revenues of $1.3 bill., ranks third in revenues and second in profits in the computer industry.

RECENT DEVELOPMENTS:

In the first half of fiscal 1975, on a 7% increase in revenues to $1.53 billion, net income rose 10% to $60.5 million. Both revenues and earnings have risen for 14 consecutive quarters. New orders for Univac computers held up well in view of cutbacks in capital spending for many commercial customers. Commercial computer revenues rose 12%. Vickers fluid power business was hurt by low capital spending. Defense bookings increased strongly. Sperry New Holland revenues increased 21%.

PROSPECTS:

High backlogs should support further good growth over the near term. However, some areas, such as consumer products, will continue to reflect the condition of the economy. Over the longer term, the trend of earnings should be less sensitive to cyclical influences than in the past. Large computer operations now account for about half of total corporate pretax profits. Other markets, in addition to computers, should benefit from the need for greater efficiency by business and industry.

STATISTICS:

YEAR	GROSS REVS. ($ MILL.)	OPER. PROFIT MARGIN %	NET INCOME ($ 000)	WORK CAP. ($ MILL.)	SENIOR CAPITAL ($ MILL.)	NO. SHS. OUT. (000)	EARN. PER SH. $	DIV. PER SH. $	DIV. PAY. %	PRICE RANGE	PRICE X EARN.	AVG. YIELD %
a												
65	1,279.8	6.4	31,859	357.7	244.1	30,806	1.02	Nil	—	24_5 - 11^1_1	17.2	—
66	1,487.1	8.1	53,902	397.2	233.8	31,140	1.72	Nil	—	33_1 - 17_1	14.8	—
67	1,562.8	8.5	64,023	452.9	184.7	33,904	1.87	0.10	5	65_3 - 28_3	24.9	0.2
68	1,607.3	10.9	77,036	445.2	199.6	34,094	2.26	0.40	18	63_4 - 41_1	23.2	0.8
69	1,755.4	11.0	81,014	503.6	255.8	34,199	2.37	0.48	20	55_3 - 36_6	19.3	1.0
70	1,739.4	9.4	72,266	363.9	132.9	34,285	2.11	0.50	24	40_1 - 18_1	14.0	1.7
71	1,823.9	7.0	g60,780	395.6	271.1	34,326	g1.77	0.55	31	38_5 - 22_6	17.0	1.8
72	2,229.3	8.5	90,057	497.4	318.7	34,365	2.62	0.60	23	50^5 - 29_1	15.3	1.5
73	2,613.5	9.2	112,558	567.0	335.8	34,470	3.27	0.63	19	56_5 - 35_1	13.9	1.4
74	3,040.9	10.2	b131,420	617.1	456.2	34,494	b3.81	0.71	19	44^5 - 23^1	8.9	2.1

a-Fiscal years end 3/31 of following year. b-After $5.4 million gain (16c a share) on sale of land. g-Before special items: 1971, $6.8 million (20c a share) charge.

INCORPORATED: June 30, 1955—Delaware

PRINCIPAL OFFICE: 1290 Ave. of the Americas New York, N.Y. 10019

ANNUAL MEETING: Last Tuesday in July

NUMBER OF STOCKHOLDERS: 104,709

TRANSFER AGENT: First National City Bank, N.Y. Commercial Trust Co. of N.J. Jersey City, N.J.

REGISTRAR: Chase Manhattan Bank, N.Y.,

INSTIT. HOLDINGS: NO.: 204 SHS.: 8,568,360

OFFICERS

CHAIRMAN: J.P. Lyet

PRESIDENT: R.E. McDonald

SECRETARY: C.H. Schmitter

TREASURER: R.R. Brown

SYNTEX CORPORATION

LISTED	SYMBOL	INDICATED DIV.	RECENT PRICE	PRICE RANGE (1975)	YIELD
ASE*	SYN	$0.40	36	45 - 28	1.1%

INTRINSIC INVESTMENT QUALITY: SPECULATIVE GRADE. COMPANY HAS IMPOSING POTENTIALS OWING TO ITS POSITION IN SPECIALTY DRUGS AND STRONG RESEARCH CAPABILITIES.

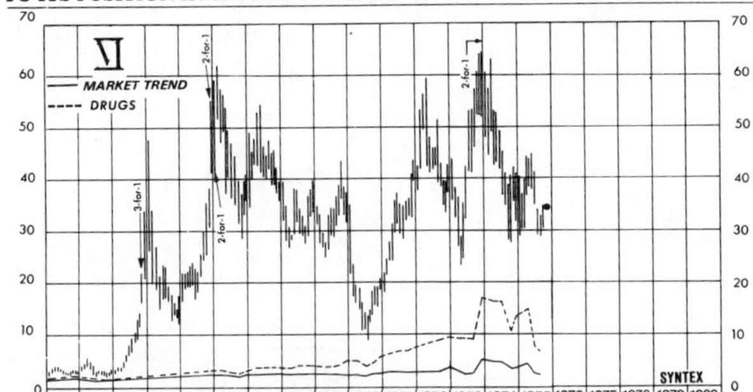

	1961	1962	1963	1964	1965	1966	1967	1968	1969	1970	1971	1972	1973	1974	1975	1976	1977	1978	1979	1980
EARN.	0.03	0.05	0.21	0.46	0.56	1.01	1.02	1.07	1.20	1.13	1.15	1.57	1.52	2.29						
DIV.	—	—	0.05	0.08	0.13	0.20	0.20	0.20	0.20	0.20	0.20	0.20	0.40	0.40						

CAPITALIZATION: (7/31/75)

	(000)	(%)
Debt	$ 42,177	12.5
Com. & Surp.	295,513	87.5
Total	$337,690	100.05

Shs. ($1)-20,600,074

INTERIM EARNINGS:

Qu.	10/31	1/31	4/30	7/31
72ab	0.41	0.40	0.40	0.30
73b	0.48	0.48	0.34	0.22
74b	0.53	0.56	0.60	0.60
75b	0.59	0.56	0.59	0.50

DIVIDENDS:	RECORD	PAYABLE
0.10Q	8/16/74	9/13/74
0.10Q	11/8	12/13
0.10Q	2/14/75	3/14/75
0.10Q	5/16	6/13
0.10Q	8/15	9/12

BACKGROUND:

Syntex and its subsidiaries are an international group engaged primarily in the manufacture and sale of pharmaceutical products, animal health products, fine chemicals and dental and scientific instruments, and in research relating thereto. Company has been responsible for major advances in the field of reproductive physiology, particularly in its development and manufacture of oral contraceptives and in the treatment of inflammatory skin diseases. Company's manufacturing facilities are located in Mexico, the U.S., Spain Bahama Islands and Brazil. Research and development operations are centered in the U.S. and Mexico. In addition, Company has a number of offices and warehouses to service its international operations.

RECENT DEVELOPMENTS:

Although sales rose 13% in fiscal 1975, net income, before tax benefit from operating loss carryovers, declined 2%. Net income was lower due to foreign exchange losses in the fourth quarter resulting from a drop of various foreign currencies relative to the U.S. dollar and because of the effects of inflation on operating costs and research programs. Fourth-quarter sales were the highest in the Company's history and reflected improvement in all lines. Growth of Naproxen contributed importantly to the performance.

PROSPECTS:

As the Company's sales base continues to broaden, the volatility of earnings, which has been characteristic of the past, should subside. As demonstrated in recent years, the Company has been able to replace lost income in one area through growth in others. Further growth should come from both new product development and acquisitions. The recent slowdown of growth is regarded as only temporary and primarily reflects substantially higher operating costs and expenses for new product introductions.

STATISTICS:

YEAR	GROSS REVS. ($ MILL.)	OPER. PROFIT MARGIN %	NET INCOME ($ 000)	WORK CAP. ($ MILL.)	SENIOR CAPITAL ($ MILL.)	NO. SHS. OUT. (000)	EARN. PER SH. $	DIV. PER SH. $	DIV. PAY. %	PRICE RANGE	PRICE X EARN.	AVG. YIELD %
7/31												
66	56.3	35.2	18,958	16.9	Nil	18,836	1.01	0.20	20	62^3 - 28^4	45.0	0.4
67	67.2	30.3	19,235	24.0	Nil	18,882	1.02	0.20	20	54^3 - 34^5	43.6	0.5
68	73.8	28.6	g20,225	37.8	Nil	18,880	g1.07	0.20	19	40 - 26^6	31.2	0.6
69	83.8	27.5	22,610	54.3	Nil	18,898	1.20	0.20	17	43^3 - 24^5	28.3	0.6
70	89.5	10.5	12,129	57.3	Nil	19,248	0.63	0.20	32	34^5 - 9^1	34.7	0.9
71	103.2	19.5	22,158	58.4	Nil	19,246	1.15	0.20	17	43^2 - 18^3	26.8	0.6
a72	140.3	21.0	b30,648	74.6	Nil	20,461	b1.51	0.20	13	59^6 - 33^2	30.9	0.4
73	160.4	20.3	b31,163	76.9	7.4	20,526	b1.52	0.40	26	64^2 - 23^1	28.7	0.9
74	217.5	23.2	b47,082	100.3	27.0	20,600	b2.29	0.40	17	63 - 27^6	19.8	0.9
75	245.9	27.2	46,817	128.1	42.2	20,632	f2.27					

Note: Adjusted for stock splits: 2-for-1, 11/66; 2-for-1, 12/73. *-Traded but not listed. a-Incl. acquisitions for entire year. b-Before $3.3 mill. ($0.17 a share) special credit in 1972 $3.7 mill. ($0.19 a share) credit in 1973; $1.5 mill. (7c a share) credit in 1974; $0.7 mill. (3c a share) credit in 1975. f-Includes tax benefit from operating loss carryforward. g-Before $0.4 mill. (2c a share) devaluation loss.

INCORPORATED: June 25, 1957—Panama

PRINCIPAL OFFICE: Edificio Omanco, Via Espana No. 200, Panama City, Panama

ANNUAL MEETING: First Friday after the first Monday in December

NUMBER OF STOCKHOLDERS: 18,530

TRANSFER AGENT: Chase Manhattan Bank, N.Y.; First Jersey National Bank, Jersey City, N.J.

REGISTRAR: Chase Manhattan Bank, N.Y.

INSTIT. HOLDINGS: NO.: 133; SHS.: 5,779,700

OFFICERS

CHAIRMAN: G. Rosenkranz

PRESIDENT: G. Rosenkranz

SECRETARY:

TREASURER:

TEXASGULF INC.

LISTED	SYMBOL	INDICATED DIV.	RECENT PRICE	PRICE RANGE (1975)	YIELD
NYSE	TG	$1.20	31	36 - 24	3.9%

INTRINSIC INVESTMENT QUALITY: MEDIUM GRADE. STRONG DEMAND FOR THE COMPANY'S FERTILIZER COMPONENTS ENHANCES EARNINGS PROSPECTS.

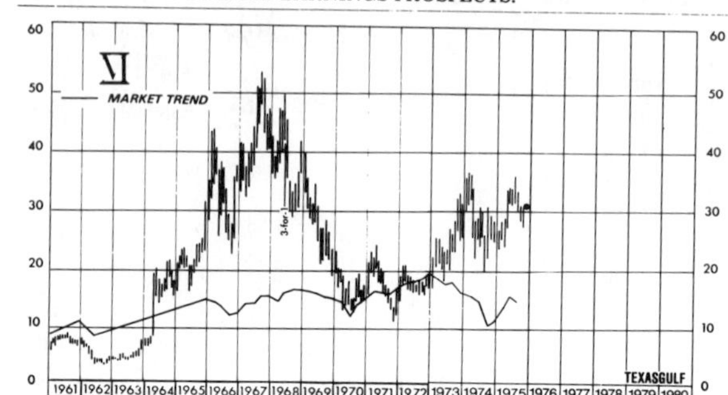

	1961	1962	1963	1964	1965	1966	1967	1968	1969	1970	1971	1972	1973	1974	1975	1976	1977	1978	1979	1980
EARN.	042	040	0.31	0.38	0.60	0.93	2.05	2.32	2.02	1.51	0.83	1.01	2.43	4.84						
DIV.	0.33	0.18	0.13	0.13	0.13	0.13	0.13	0.33	0.55	0.60	0.60	0.60	0.64	0.98						

CAPITALIZATION: (12/31/74)

	(000)	(%)
Debt	$133,265	16.1
Defer. inc. tax	132,141	16.0
Com. & Surp.	560,113	67.9
Total	$825,519	100.0%

Shs. (np)-30,548,572

INTERIM EARNINGS:

Qu.	3/31	6/30	9/30	12/31
72	0.20	0.20	0.29	0.32
73	0.29	0.46	0.80	0.88
74	0.85	1.13	1.48	1.38
75	0.98	0.82	0.82	

DIVIDENDS:	RECORD	PAYABLE
0.30Q	11/18/74	12/14/74
0.30Q	2/18/75	3/15/75
0.30Q	5/15	6/14
0.30Q	8/15	9/15
0.30Q	11/15	12/15

BACKGROUND:

Texasgulf is one of the largest producers of elemental sulphur with production of slightly above 3 mill. tons. About 85% of the sulphur is produced at the Company's 6 Frasch mines in the Gulf Coast area, namely, Gulf, Newgulf, Spindletop, Moss Bluff, Fannett and Lake Bully Camp. Potash mining and processing facilities in Utah began operations in 1964. Phosphate-fertilizer operations in North Carolina began in 1966. Canadian operations produce copper, lead and zinc concentrates and silver. Metal sales accounted for 51% of revenues in 1974, agricultural and chemical products, 46%, other, 3%. A subsidiary is exploring in Western Australia. Dividends have been paid each year since 1921. Canadian Development Corp. owns about 30% of Company's common.

RECENT DEVELOPMENTS:

For the nine months ended 9/30/75, net income fell 24% to $80.2 million on a 21% decline in sales to $327.6 million. The decline in earnings was caused mostly by reduced demand for metals and the reduction of copper prices. Lower prices for phosphate fertilizers and reduced demand for potash, phosphate and sulphur also contributed to the decline. Third quarter sales fell 30% to $109.7 million and net income dropped 45% to $24.9 million. Reduced earnings were the result of lower demand and lower prices for copper and phosphate fertilizer.

PROSPECTS:

Most of the Company's products experienced an improvement in demand in late 1975 which will probably continue in the current year. Margins will benefit from a better relationship between inventory levels and demand. Firmer metals prices are anticipated. Earnings in 1976 should be higher than a year ago. Plant expansion for sulphuric and phosphoric acid and fertilizer materials will add to the sales base and contribute to increased earnings potential. Earnings will continue to experience cyclical growth over the longer term.

STATISTICS:

YEAR	GROSS REVS. ($ MILL.)	OPER. PROFIT MARGIN %	NET INCOME ($ 000)	WORK CAP. ($ MILL.)	SENIOR CAPITAL ($ MILL.)	NO. SHS. OUT. (000)	EARN. PER SH. $	DIV. PER SH. $	DIV. PAY. %	PRICE RANGE	PRICE X EARN.	AVG. YIELD %
65	99.0	18.4	18,161	52.6	55.0	30,102	0.60	0.13	22	31^{4}_{7} - 16^{3}_{6}	39.9	0.6
66	132.7	27.6	28,096	33.5	135.0	30,145	0.93	0.13	14	43^{7} - 22^{6}_{2}	35.7	0.4
67	253.1	32.7	62,102	69.7	115.0	30,275	2.05	0.13	6	53^{3}_{7} - 32^{2}	20.9	0.3
68	309.9	31.5	70,520	153.3	125.5	30,367	2.32	0.33	14	49^{7}_{7} - 29_{1}	17.0	0.8
69	301.8	26.5	61,467	175.5	117.3	30,386	2.02	0.55	27	39^{7} - 19^{1}	14.6	1.9
70	283.0	22.9	45,823	90.2	119.9	30,386	1.51	0.60	40	23^{2} - 13_{2}	12.0	3.3
71	271.3	20.7	a25,226	87.1	168.5	30,386	a0.83	0.60	72	24^{3} - 11^{2}_{6}	21.4	3.4
72	316.0	22.9	30,562	93.7	172.1	30,408	1.01	0.60	59	20^{6}_{1} - 14^{6}_{1}	17.6	3.4
73	449.4	28.5	73,922	114.2	156.0	30,447	2.43	0.64	26	33^{1}_{5} - 17^{1}	10.3	2.6
74	568.5	47.2	147,442	185.0	133.3	30,549	4.84	0.98	20	36^{5} - 20^{1}	5.9	3.5

Note: Adjusted for 3-for-1 stock split 4/68. a-Excl. $4.7 mill. (15c a share) charge.

INCORPORATED: December 23, 1909—Texas

PRINCIPAL OFFICE: 200 Park Avenue, New York, N.Y. 10017

ANNUAL MEETING: Fourth Thursday in April

NUMBER OF STOCKHOLDERS: 66,881

TRANSFER AGENT: Morgan Guaranty Trust Co., N.Y.; Canada Trust Co., Ont. Canada

REGISTRAR: Morgan Guaranty Trust Co., N.Y.; Canada Permanent Trust Co., Canada

INSTIT. HOLDINGS: NO.: 83; SHS.: 1,986,000

OFFICERS

CHAIRMAN: C.F. Fogarty

PRESIDENT: R.D. Mollison

SECRETARY: D.M. Crawford

TREASURER: G.N. Mckee, Jr.

TEXAS INSTRUMENTS, INC.

LISTED	SYMBOL	INDICATED DIV.	RECENT PRICE	PRICE RANGE (1975)	YIELD
NYSE	TXN	$1.00	98	119 - 61	1.0%

INTRINSIC INVESTMENT QUALITY: INVESTMENT GRADE. THIS LEADING PRODUCER OF SEMICONDUCTORS HAS BEEN MOVING CLOSER TO THE CONSUMER.

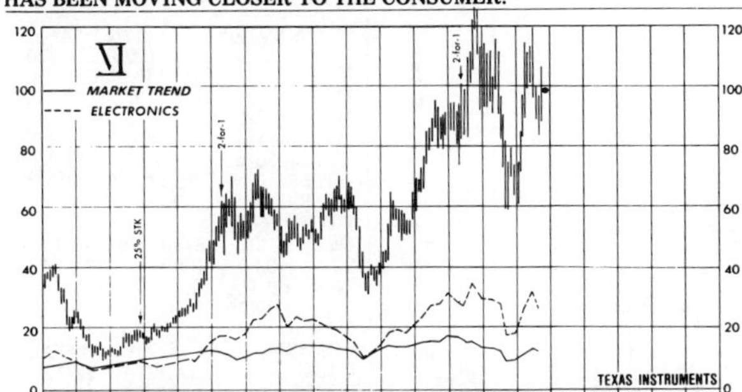

	1961	1962	1963	1964	1965	1966	1967	1968	1969	1970	1971	1972	1973	1974	1975	1976	1977	1978	1979	1980
EARN.	0.47	0.43	0.60	0.90	1.23	1.57	1.05	1.21	1.52	1.36	1.53	2.17	3.67	3.92						
DIV.	—	0.12	0.16	0.20	0.25	0.28	0.38	0.40	0.40	0.40	0.40	0.42	0.80	0.92						

CAPITALIZATION:

	(12/31/74) (000)	(%)
Debt	$ 72,755	11.8
Com. & Surp.	541,372	88.2
Total	$614,127	100.0%

Shs. ($1)-(3/31/75)-22,951,666

INTERIM EARNINGS:

Qu.	3/31	6/30	9/30	12/31
72	0.49	0.53	0.53	0.62
73	0.83	0.90	0.85	1.09
74	1.09	1.10	0.81	0.92
75	0.61	0.49	0.70	

DIVIDENDS:	RECORD	PAYABLE
0.25Q	10/7/74	10/29/74
0.25Q	1/6/75	1/27/75
0.25Q	4/7	4/28
0.25Q	7/7	7/28
0.25Q	10/9	10/28

BACKGROUND:

Texas Instruments is a technologically-based multinational company engaged in research, development, manufacture and distribution of a diversified line of products and services. Company serves governmental, industrial and consumer markets. Its broad list of products and services includes metallurgical and chemical materials, semiconductor products, electrical and thermostatic controls, electronic and electromechanical instruments and systems, and geophysical exploration and data processing services. Major industries serviced include automobiles, appliances, printing, telecommunications and electronics. Company is the largest producer of semiconductors and a major supplier to others of related chemical products for their manufacture.

RECENT DEVELOPMENTS:

Net income of $16.1 million, in the third quarter of 1975, was down 13% from the year-earlier level and 17% below the third quarter high of $19.3 million in 1973. Sales declined 16% to $313 million. There was a significant recovery from the earlier quarters of 1975. Market conditions for electrical controls for appliances and some industrial applications continued to improve. In semiconducters, demand increased in old market segments and essentially all product lines. Initial deliveries were made of a new line of digital watches.

PROSPECTS:

Growth should continue over the longer term but probably with an uneven earnings pattern as has been characteristic of the past. A broader sales base and movement closer to the consumer should help to reduce the magnitude of swings. Two important areas for further expansion are computers and electronic calculators. In the current year, earnings will be down substantially in view of poor economic conditions and selling price weakness. However, a strong profit recovery is indicated once business improves.

STATISTICS:

YEAR	GROSS REVS. ($ MILL.)	OPER. PROFIT MARGIN %	NET INCOME ($ 000)	WORK CAP. ($ MILL.)	SENIOR CAPITAL ($ MILL.)	NO. SHS. OUT. (000)	EARN. PER SH. $	DIV. PER SH. $	DIV. PAY. %	PRICE RANGE	PRICE X EARN.	AVG. YIELD %
65	436.4	10.6	24,839	97.6	48.6	20,193	1.23	0.25	20	49^{1}_{7} - 23^{3}_{7}	29.4	0.7
66	580.3	11.2	33,954	141.6	51.9	21,600	1.57	0.28	18	69_{3} - 40_{6}	35.3	0.5
67	568.5	7.2	22,855	145.4	54.3	21,754	1.05	0.38	36	72_{4} - 49_{1}	58.2	0.6
68	671.2	7.3	26,324	157.2	52.9	21,880	1.21	0.40	33	57_{1} - 43_{3}	41.7	0.8
69	831.8	7.4	33,511	189.3	94.6	22,068	1.52	0.40	26	70_{2} - 47_{6}	38.7	0.7
70	827.6	6.6	29,861	211.0	86.8	22,070	1.36	0.40	30	67_{4} - 30_{6}	36.1	0.8
71	764.3	7.7	33,723	261.4	94.8	22,102	1.53	0.40	26	64 - 39_{5}	34.2	0.8
72	943.7	8.8	48,030	282.0	71.4	22,178	2.17	0.42	19	95_{7} - 58_{3}	35.4	0.5
73	1,287.3	11.3	83,235	307.0	67.7	22,767	3.67	0.80	22	138_{6} - 74_{6}	29.1	0.8
74	1,572.5	10.8	89,621	314.3	72.8	22,870	3.92	0.92	23	115 - 58	22.3	1.1

Note: Adjusted for 2-for-1 stock splits 4/66 and 5/73.

INCORPORATED: Dec. 23, 1938—Delaware

PRINCIPAL OFFICE: P.O. Box 5474
Dallas, Texas 75222

ANNUAL MEETING: Third Wednesday in April

NUMBER OF STOCKHOLDERS: 18,977

TRANSFER AGENT: Registrar & Transfer Co., N.Y.
Republic National Bank, Dallas, Texas

REGISTRAR: Morgan Guaranty Trust Co., N.Y.
First National Bank, Dallas, Texas

INSTIT. HOLDINGS: NO.: 212
SHS.: 5,083,898

OFFICERS

CHAIRMAN:
P.E. Haggerty

PRESIDENT:
M. Shepherd, Jr.

SECRETARY:
B.F. Smith

TREASURER:
H.A. Wolf

UAL, INC.

LISTED	SYMBOL	INDICATED DIV.	RECENT PRICE	PRICE RANGE (1975)	YIELD
NYSE	UAL	$0.60	26	27 - 14	2.3%

INTRINSIC INVESTMENT QUALITY: SPECULATIVE GRADE. GROWTH HAS BEEN STRONG BUT RISING EXPENSES AND COMPETITIVE ROUTE STRUCTURE HAVE LED TO EARNINGS VOLATILITY.

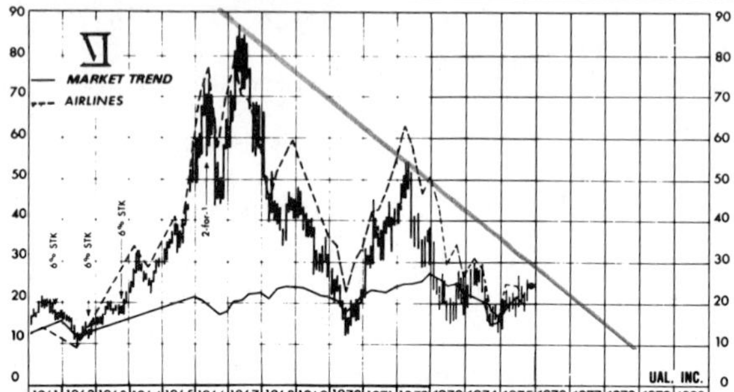

	1961	1962	1963	1964	1965	1966	1967	1968	1969	1970	1971	1972	1973	1974	1975	1976	1977	1978	1979	1980
EARN.	0.29	0.61	1.07	2.02	3.27	2.26	3.92	2.23	2.39	d	d	0.80	2.03	4.04						
DIV.	0.21	0.22	0.24	0.75	0.88	0.94	1.00	1.00	1.00	0.75	—	—	—	0.65						

CAPITALIZATION: (12/31/74)

	(000)	(%)
Debt	b$ 939,366	44.3
Pfd.	12,751	0.6
Minority Int.	1,169	0.1
Defer.inc.tax	380,960	18.0
Com. & Surp.	785,120	37.0
Total	$2,119,366	100.0%

Shs. ($5)-23,783,005

INTERIM EARNINGS:

Qu.	3/31	6/30	9/30	12/31
72	d0.60	0.09	1.27	0.04
73	d0.48	0.27	1.91	0.33
74g	0.40	1.40	1.77	0.47
75	d0.38	0.22	0.92	

DIVIDENDS:	RECORD	PAYABLE
0.15Q	11/15/74	12/15/74
0.125E	11/15	12/15
0.15Q	2/15/75	3/15/75
0.15Q	5/15	6/15
0.15Q	8/15	9/15

BACKGROUND:

United, largest of the domestic airlines, connects major eastern cities from Boston to Atlanta with major cities in the midwest and west; continuing service to Hawaii as well as routes throughout the southeastern states are also flown. The Company operates a fleet consisting of a variety of owned or leased jet aircraft, including wide-bodies and freighters, and has McDonnell Douglas DC-10's scheduled for current delivery. Commitments for property and equipment approximate $240.8 million extending to 1977. United's parent holding company, UAL, Inc., was formed in 1968 to permit diversification. Subsequently, on 7/31/70, UAL, Inc., acquired Western International Hotels for 4,249,254 shares of UAL, Inc. Series A cum. pfd.

RECENT DEVELOPMENTS:

Consolidated operating revenues during the first nine months of 1975 rose from $1.79 billion to $1.85 billion, but net income went from $89.1 million to $19.8 million. Revenues during 1974 rose to $2.4 billion, while net income advanced to $101.0 million. Both hotel and airline subsidiaries contributed to the earnings improvement during the period. Company reported a load factor of 59.6% vs. 55.8% a year ago, partly resulting from flying fewer available seat miles. Pleasure and business travel each account for roughly half of United's passenger traffic.

PROSPECTS:

Airline revenue in 1975 is expected to continue to increase, but earnings are expected to decline sharply. The traffic performance is expected to be satisfactory, but competition is pervasive and operating expenses are expected to rise. Long range profitability depends on the success of reducing excess capacity, implementing a cost control system and limiting the cost of acquisition integration. Hotel operations are expected to generate revenue growth in future years. Fare increases should help improve margins.

STATISTICS:

YEAR	GROSS REVS. ($ MILL.)	OPER. PROFIT MARGIN %	NET INCOME ($000)	WORK. CAP. ($ MILL.)	SENIOR CAPITAL ($ MILL.)	NO. SHS. OUT. (000)	EARN. PER SH. $	DIV. PER SH. $	PASS. LOAD FACT. %	PRICE RANGE	PRICE X EARN.	AVG. YIELD %
65	792.8	10.9	45,767	138.3	449.8	13,760	3.27	0.88	55.3	59^{3} - 29^{2}	13.6	2.0
66	856.9	8.3	38,308	229.3	515.7	16,587	2.26	0.94	57.6	74^{6} - 43^{6}	26.2	1.6
67	1,098.9	10.1	72,819	296.6	636.2	18,378	3.92	1.00	59.8	87^{3} - 55^{2}	18.2	1.4
68	1,261.7	7.5	41,750	45.6	845.4	18,424	2.23	1.00	54.8	66^{4} - 34	22.5	2.0
69	1,477.5	8.2	44,693	22.9	891.3	18,424	2.39	1.00	53.6	48^{4} - 26^{1}	15.6	2.7
c70	1,590.1	d	d40,877	36.6	1,075.3	18,424	d2.33	0.75	51.9	28^{3} - 12^{4}	—	3.7
71	1,617.6	2.6	d5,071	69.7	999.1	20,924	d0.36	Nil	49.9	45^{3} - 21^{3}	—	—
72	1,828.4	4.6	20,376	23.4	1,056.7	21,097	0.80	Nil	54.6	54^{2} - 28^{6}	51.9	—
73	2,060.3	7.9	51,128	166.7	998.0	21,178	2.03	Nil	55.8	34^{4} - 15^{3}	12.3	—
74	2,365.1	8.3	g101,002	369.0	952.2	23,783	g4.04	0.65	59.6	29^{7} - 13	5.3	3.0

b-Incl. $82.7 mill. debentures convertible into common at $55.32 a share, and $99.2 mill. debentures convertible into common at $77.79 a share. c-Incl. Western Int'l. Hotels. g-After $10.7 mill. (43c a share) gain.

INCORPORATED: Dec. 30, 1968—Delaware

PRINCIPAL OFFICE: 1200 Algonquin Road, Elk Grove Township, Ill.

ANNUAL MEETING: Fourth Thursday in April

NUMBER OF STOCKHOLDERS: 51,231

TRANSFER AGENT: First National City Bank, N.Y.; Continental Ill. National Bk. & Tr. Co., Chicago, Ill.

REGISTRAR: Bankers Trust Co., N.Y.; Harris Trust & Savings Bank, Chicago, Ill.

INSTIT. HOLDINGS: NO.: 122; SHS.: 7,041,699

OFFICERS

CHAIRMAN: E.E. Carlson

PRESIDENT: C.F. McErlean

SECRETARY: E.O. Fennell

TREASURER: R.H. Robertson

UNITED TECHNOLOGIES CORP.

LISTED	SYMBOL	INDICATED DIV.	RECENT PRICE	PRICE RANGE (1975)	YIELD
NYSE	UA	$2.00	50	62 - 31	4.0%

INTRINSIC INVESTMENT QUALITY: MEDIUM GRADE. THE ACQUISITION OF INDUSTRIAL PRODUCT LINES HAS PROVIDED GREATER GROWTH POTENTIAL AND STABILITY.

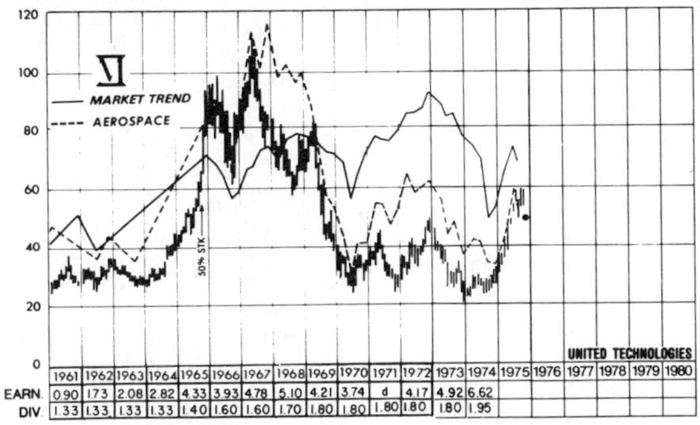

CAPITALIZATION: (12/31/74)

	(000)	(%)
Debt.	a$211,213	19.5
Defer. inc. tax	6,914	0.6
Pfd. ($2.84)	b2.433	0.2
Pfd. ($8.00)	c 254,282	23.4
Com. & Surp.	611,775	56.3
Total	$1,086,617	100.0%

Shs. ($5)-11,748,338

INTERIM EARNINGS:

Qu.	3/31	6/30	9/30	12/31
72	1.03	1.15	0.85	1.14
73	1.21	1.40	1.07	1.24
74	1.68	1.95	1.56	1.43
75	1.96	2.15	1.80	

DIVIDENDS:	RECORD	PAYABLE
0.50Q	11/22/74	12/10/74
0.50Q	2/24/75	3/10/75
0.50Q	5/23	6/10
0.50Q	8/15	9/10
0.50Q	11/14	12/10

BACKGROUND:

United Technologies operates in four major areas. The power group, which consists mainly of aircraft engines, also makes turbines for industrial and electric utility use. Such products accounted for 53% of sales (34% of operating profits) in 1974. Systems, which account for 23% of sales (31% of profits) are mainly for military applications. However, significant business is conducted in original equipment and after-market. The 1974 acquisition of Essex International (now 19% of UA's sales and 32% of profits) added a wide range of products essential to the distribution, control and application of electricity. Space and other activities provide the remaining 5% of sales and 3% of profits.

RECENT DEVELOPMENTS:

Net income in the first nine months of 1975, increased 13% to $27.8 million, on an 8% sales gain to $864.2 million. For the nine months, sales increased 3% to $2.59 billion and produced a 9% rise in net income to $88.7 million. Power related sales increased 10% to $1.48 billion; Systems, up 17% to $652 million; industrial, down 32% to $331.6 million; and space, up 42% to $65.8 million. Some signs of improvement in industrial markets were evident in the fourth quarter.

PROSPECTS:

The acquisition of Essex International has enhanced growth prospects and added stability to the Company's operations. A high degree of technological competence should enable the Company to retain its leadership position in several areas. As business in industrial and utility markets continues to grow, the proportion of Government business is expected to decline further. Developmental research in the use of the fuel cell to generate electricity is establishing the Company as a leader in this field of technology.

STATISTICS:

YEAR	GROSS REVS. ($ MILL.)	OPER. PROFIT MARGIN %	NET INCOME ($ 000)	WORK CAP. ($ MILL.)	SENIOR CAPITAL ($ MILL.)	NO. SHS. OUT. (000)	EARN. PER SH. $	DIV. PER SH. $	DIV. PAY. %	PRICE RANGE	PRICE X EARN.	AVG. YIELD %
66	1,663.2	5.2	46,515	236.5	133.9	11,824	3.93	1.60	41	99^{6} - 61^{2}	20.5	2.0
67	2,212.3	5.1	57,310	301.5	246.8	11,911	4.78	1.60	33	111^{4} - 72^{6}	19.3	1.7
68	2,408.3	5.2	61,394	303.4	242.8	12,046	5.10	1.70	33	83^{4} - 57^{5}	13.8	2.4
69	2,350.4	4.5	50,909	347.3	238.9	12,091	4.21	1.80	43	81^{1} - 38^{5}	14.2	3.0
70	2,348.9	4.2	45,280	362.1	233.8	12,106	3.74	1.80	48	40^{4} - 23^{5}	8.6	5.6
71	2,028.8	d	d43,942	326.6	29.2	12,110	d3.62	1.80	—	45^{1} - 24^{4}	—	5.2
72	2,023.8	4.6	50,600	386.0	224.4	12,122	4.17	1.80	43	49 - 28^{5}	9.3	4.6
73	2,288.9	4.6	58,136	398.7	212.7	11,748	4.92	1.80	37	46^{2} - 20^{6}	6.8	5.4
g73	3,134.1	6.0	98,720	644.9	641.6	11,748	5.52	—	—	—	—	—
g74	3,321.1	6.1	104,705	549.3	467.9	11,748	6.62	1.95	29	32^{5} - 22^{4}	4.2	7.1

a-Incl. $48.3 mill. debentures convertible into 1.55 common shares and $94.7 mill. debentures convertible into 1.35 shares. b-71,449 shares convertible into 0.4 shares of $8 pfd. c-2,987,162 shares, each convertible into 2.22 common shares. g-Incl. Essex International; 1973 pro-forma.

INCORPORATED: July 21, 1934—Delaware

PRINCIPAL OFFICE: 400 Main Street, East Hartford, Conn. 06108

ANNUAL MEETING: Second Tuesday in April

NUMBER OF STOCKHOLDERS: 43,574

TRANSFER AGENT: First National City Bank, N.Y.

REGISTRAR: Bankers Trust Co., N.Y.

INSTIT. HOLDINGS: NO.: 110; SHS.: 3,528,960

OFFICERS

CHAIRMAN: H.J. Gray

PRESIDENT: H.J. Gray

SECRETARY: G.A. Ring

TREASURER: J.A. Biernat

UPJOHN COMPANY

LISTED	SYMBOL	INDICATED DIV.	RECENT PRICE	PRICE RANGE (1975)	YIELD
NYSE	UPJ	$0.96	44	53 - 30	2.2%

INTRINSIC INVESTMENT QUALITY: HIGH GRADE. HEAVY SPENDING ON RESEARCH HAS RESTORED GROWTH FOR THIS LEADING DRUG COMPANY.

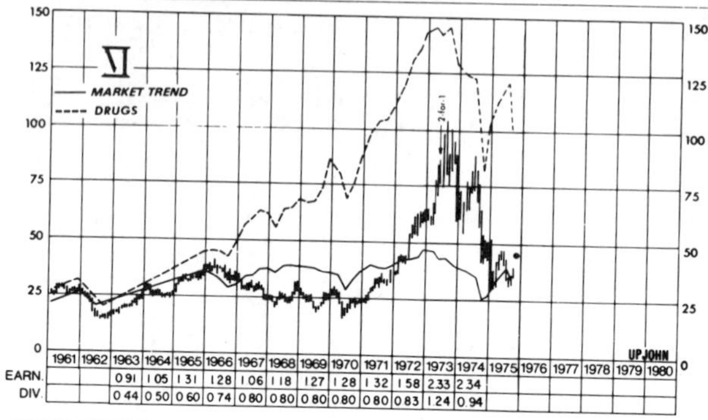

CAPITALIZATION: (12/31/74)

	(000)	(%)
Debt.	$ 57,925	11.5
Minority int.	13,442	2.7
Defer.Inc.Tax	28,039	5.5
Com. & Surp.	405,146	80.3
Total	$504,552	100.0%

Shs. ($1)-29,587,747

INTERIM EARNINGS:

Qu.	3/31	6/30	9/30	12/31
72	0.39	0.43	0.40	0.36
73	0.60	0.69	0.57	0.47
74b	0.73	0.70	0.56	0.35
75	0.64	0.66	0.51	

DIVIDENDS:	RECORD	PAYABLE
0.24Q	10/7/74	11/1/74
0.24Q	1/8/75	2/3/75
0.24Q	4/7	5/1
0.24Q	7/8	8/1
0.24Q	10/7	11/3

BACKGROUND:

Upjohn is a large international drug producer with an important stake in chemicals and agricultural products as well. Drug lines include antibiotics, steroids, antidiabetics, among the major ethical products, plus over-the-counter pharmaceuticals. The Company has been a pioneer in the study and application of prostaglandines (hormone-like substances). Through its chemical division, Company is a major producer of urethane. In 1974, antibiotics accounted for 25% of sales; steroids, 18%; antidiabetes drugs, 6%; other drugs, 9%; medical services, 6%; pharmaceutical chemicals, 4%; chemicals, 17%; and agricultural products, 14%. Overseas sales represent about 38% of the total. Almost 9% of sales goes for research.

RECENT DEVELOPMENTS:

In the first nine months of 1975, despite a 12% sales gain to $664.3 million, net income declined 9% to $53.4 million. Several factors contributed to the pressure on profits. They included an unfavorable sales mix, higher non-operating costs, currency losses and a higher tax rate. Profits also were hurt by lower technology income and lower interest income. Worldwide human health care volume increased 18%, agricultural specialties increased 15%, but chemical volume declined 7%.

PROSPECTS:

Foreign activities and non-drug lines should provide above-average contributions to consolidated results in the years ahead. The decline in sales of antidiabetic drugs may have run its course. Sales of chemicals, plastics and other non-pharmaceuticals are being expanded. Longer-term prospects are enhanced by the potential contributions from prostaglandins. As for the near term, net profits should benefit from the start-up of tax sheltered antibiotic production in Puerto Rico. Good earnings growth is expected to continue.

STATISTICS:

YEAR	GROSS REVS. ($ MILL.)	OPER. PROFIT MARGIN %	NET INCOME ($ 000)	WORK CAP. ($ MILL.)	SENIOR CAPITAL ($ MILL.)	NO. SHS. OUT. (000)	EARN. PER SH. $	DIV. PER SH. $	DIV. PAY. %	PRICE RANGE	PRICE X EARN.	AVG YIELD %
65	242.4	26.6	37,203	101.7	Nil	28,362	1.31	0.60	46	38^{4} - 26^{1}	24.7	1.9
66	257.6	24.7	36,348	94.0	Nil	28,378	1.28	0.74	58	41^{5} - 30^{4}	28.2	2.1
67	273.0	20.1	30,057	90.1	Nil	28,470	1.06	0.80	76	34^{6} - 23^{5}	27.6	2.7
68	333.2	21.6	34,441	113.1	Nil	29,332	1.18	0.80	68	32 - 20^{7}	22.5	3.0
69	371.0	21.0	37,362	121.0	Nil	29,362	1.27	0.80	63	29^{1} - 18^{6}	18.8	3.4
70	397.7	20.3	37,674	146.2	Nil	29,432	1.28	0.80	63	29^{6} - 16^{3}	18.0	3.5
71	438.4	17.9	a38,757	137.8	Nil	29,438	a1.32	0.80	59	37^{6} - 23^{1}	23.1	2.6
72	511.3	18.9	46,536	185.1	42.9	29,438	1.58	0.83	52	64^{3} - 35^{2}	31.5	1.7
73	647.5	20.8	68,555	217.3	61.1	29,457	2.33	1.24	53	104^{6} - 58^{4}	35.0	1.5
c74	794.6	17.4	b69,105	188.7	57.9	29,588	b2.34	0.94	40	88^{2} - 41^{5}	27.8	1.5

Note: Adjusted for 2-for-1 stock split 6/73. a-Before special items; $1.0 mill. (4c a share) credit. b-Reflects change to LIFO accounting. c-Incl. acqusitions for entire year.

INCORPORATED: Nov. 26, 1958—Delaware

PRINCIPAL OFFICE: 7000 Portage Road, Kalamazoo, Mich. 49001

ANNUAL MEETING: Third Tuesday in May

NUMBER OF STOCKHOLDERS: 18,500

TRANSFER AGENT: First National City Bank, N.Y.; American National Bank & Trust Co., Kalamazoo, Mich.

REGISTRAR: Morgan Guaranty Trust Co., New York; First National Bank & Trust Co., Kalamazoo, Mich.

INSTIT. HOLDINGS: NO.: 148; SHS.: 4,915,480

OFFICERS

CHAIRMAN: R.T. Parfet, Jr.

PRESIDENT: Dr. W.N. Hubbard, Jr.

SECRETARY: G. Thomas

TREASURER: C.H. Ludlow

UTAH INTERNATIONAL, INC.

LISTED	SYMBOL	INDICATED DIV.	RECENT PRICE	PRICE RANGE (1975)	YIELD
NYSE	UC	$1.05	49	75 - 39	2.1%

INTRINSIC INVESTMENT QUALITY: MEDIUM GRADE. PRINCIPAL BUSINESS OF MINING OF COAL, URANIUM, IRON ORE AND COPPER HAS PROVIDED CONSISTENT GAINS.

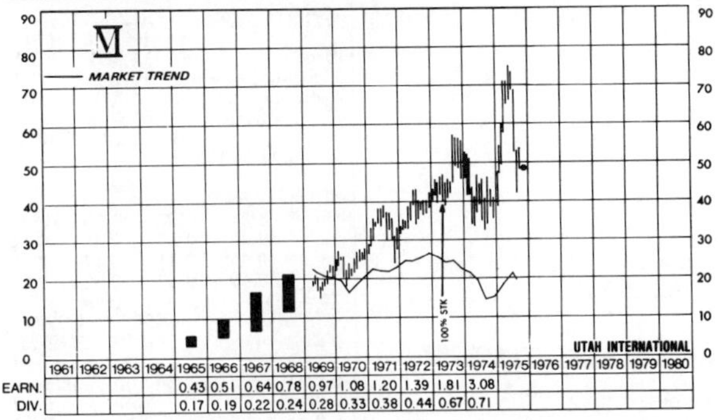

CAPITALIZATION:

	(10/31/74) (000)	(%)
Debt	$233,688	33.6
Minority int.	12,798	1.9
Com. & Surpl.	448,256	64.5
Total	$694,742	100.0%

Shs. ($2)-31,532,997

INTERIM EARNINGS:

Qu.	1/31	4/30	7/31	10/31
72	0.28	0.33	0.33	0.45
73	0.32	0.43	0.51	0.55
74	0.68	0.50	0.96	0.94
75	0.86	0.91	g1.61	

DIVIDENDS:	RECORD	PAYABLE
0.20Q	12/31/74	1/15/75
0.25Q	3/31/75	4/15
0.25Q	6/30	7/15
0.25Q	9/30	10/15
0.05E	9/30	10/15

BACKGROUND:

Utah International is engaged in the exploration and development of natural resources. International activities are comprised of operations in coal, iron ore, copper and uranium as well as oil and gas. Other activity includes land development in California. Utah Development Co., the 90% owned subsidiary with coking coal operations in Queensland, Australia and one-third interest in Mount Goldsworthy iron operations in Western Australia, is a major source of the Company's revenues and earnings. 46%-owned affiliate Marcona Corporation's operations include iron ore in Peru and New Zealand and an extensive ocean shipping business. 25%-owned Cyprus Pima operates a copper mine near Tucson, Arizona. Ladd Petroleum was acquired in 1973. Clarcan Petroleum, and LVO Corp. were acquired in 1974.

RECENT DEVELOPMENTS:

In the first nine months of fiscal 1975, revenues were $506.5 million, up from $351.9 (restated) in the year-earlier period. Results for 1974 have been restated to reflect the merger of LVO Corporation in to Utah International in October of that year. On the same basis, net income was $106.6 million vs. $67.3 million. In the third quarter, there was an extraordinary charge of $19.1 million (60c a share) relating to the Peruvian expropriation loss of Marcona Mining, the subsidiary of an affiliate.

PROSPECTS:

Company is expected to achieve higher profit levels in fiscal 1976. The earnings improvement as a result of higher price realizations for coking coal and iron ore and by production from the new Saraji coal mine in Queensland, Australia, is expected to more than offset a reduction from last year's record contribution from copper. The long-term outlook for UC is enhanced by a high mineral sales backlog, over 90% of which is represented by contracts containing cost escalation provisions, and last year's acquisitions of oil and gas producing companies.

STATISTICS:

YEAR	GROSS REVS. ($ MILL.)	OPER. PROFIT MARGIN %	NET INCOME ($ 000)	WORK CAP. ($ MILL.)	SENIOR CAPITAL ($ MILL.)	NO. SHS. OUT. (000)	EARN. PER SH. $	DIV. PER SH. $	DIV. PAY. %	PRICE RANGE	PRICE X EARN.	AVG. YIELD %
10/31	c											
65	89.3	14.5	11,016	7.2	29.3	25,801	0.43	0.17	40	5^{4}_{1} - 3^{3}_{1}	10.4	3.7
66	98.5	11.8	13,175	10.8	41.7	25,801	0.51	0.19	37	7^{1} - 5^{1}_{1}	11.9	3.0
67	113.3	11.7	16,543	9.8	52.9	25,801	0.64	0.22	34	16 - 7_{6}	18.1	1.9
68	118.3	14.4	19,944	55.0	114.6	25,812	0.78	0.24	31	21_{4} - 11_{7}	21.1	1.5
69	68.9	22.3	24,878	42.2	116.5	25,834	0.97	0.28	29	23^{4}_{7} - 14^{7}_{2}	19.9	1.5
70	91.0	27.9	30,273	13.8	96.1	28,200	1.08	0.33	31	27^{7} - 18^{2}_{7}	21.5	1.4
71	104.4	27.1	b34,146	7.1	206.5	28,643	1.20	0.38	32	39_{1} - 23^{7}_{5}	26.2	1.2
72	209.8	27.0	39,842	21.7	218.7	28,752	1.39	0.44	32	43^{1} - 31^{5}_{7}	26.9	1.2
73	315.6	28.2	52,050	12.4	229.8	28,817	1.81	0.67	37	57_{7} - 39^{7}	26.8	1.4
74	501.2	34.1	96,841	14.3	233.7	31,533	3.08	0.71	23	52^{7} - 32^{5}	13.9	1.7

Note: Adjusted for stock dividends: 200%, 2/69 and 100%, 5/73. b-Before $1.4 mill. (5c a share) credit. c-Includes revenues from discontinued operations through 1971. g-Before extraordinary charge of $19.1 million (60c a share).

INCORPORATED: December, 1956—Delaware

PRINCIPAL OFFICE: 550 California St. San Francisco, Calif. 94104

ANNUAL MEETING: Second Friday in February

NUMBER OF STOCKHOLDERS: 31,311

TRANSFER AGENT: Bankers Trust Co., New York, N.Y.
Crocker National Bank, S.F., Calif.
First Security Bk. of Utah, N.A.
Salt Lake City

REGISTRAR: Bankers Trust Co., New York
Crocker National Bank,
San Francisco, Calif.

INSTIT. HOLDINGS: NO.: 119
SHS.: 4,675,340

OFFICERS

CHAIRMAN:
E.W. Littlefield

PRESIDENT:
A.M. Wilson

SECRETARY:
B.T. Mitchell

TREASURER:
J.T. Curry

WARNER-LAMBERT COMPANY

LISTED	SYMBOL	INDICATED DIV.	RECENT PRICE	PRICE RANGE (1975)	YIELD
NYSE	WLA	$0.92	36	39 - 25	2.6%

INTRINSIC INVESTMENT QUALITY: HIGH GRADE. COMPANY HAS ABILITY NOT ONLY TO GENERATE INTERNAL GROWTH BUT TO INTEGRATE ACQUISITIONS EFFECTIVELY.

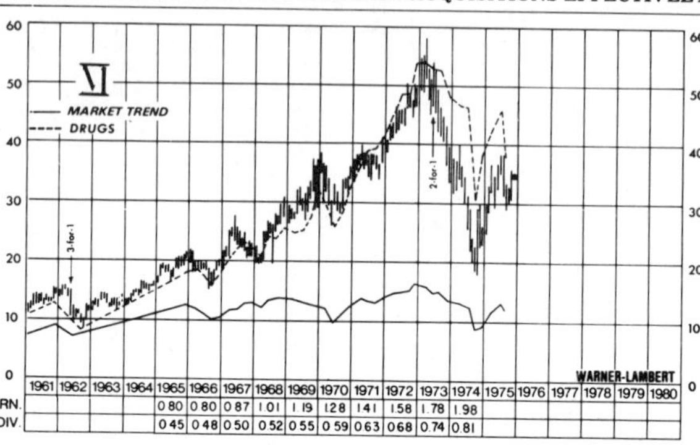

CAPITALIZATION: (12/31/74)

	(000)	(%)
Debt	b$ 113,586	9.7
Minority int.	10,135	0.9
Defer.inc.tax	44,547	3.8
Com. & Surp.	1,001,016	85.6
Total	$1,169,284	100.0%

Shs. ($1)-78,473,552

INTERIM EARNINGS:

Qu.	3/31	6/30	9/30	12/31
72	0.39	0.37	0.41	0.41
73	0.44	0.41	0.47	0.46
74	0.49	0.47	0.52	0.50
75	-------1.10-----		0.59	

DIVIDENDS:	RECORD	PAYABLE
0.21Q	8/9/74	9/10/74
0.21Q	11/8	12/10
0.21Q	2/6/75	3/10/75
0.23Q	5/9	6/10
0.23Q	8/8	9/10

BACKGROUND:

Warner-Lambert is a broadly based producer and marketer of consumer and professional health care products. Large overseas operations (spanning more than 100 countries) accounted for 43% of sales (42% of pretax profits) in 1974. Domestic professional health care products, 33% of sales (29%) include ethical pharmaceuticals, diagnostic products, dental specialties, optical products, hospital and surgical supplies and scientific and medical instruments. Consumer products, which accounted 24% of sales (29%), include proprietary drugs, toiletries, cosmetics, chewing gum, breath products, razors, blades and sunglasses. Among the well known brand names are Listerine, Efferdent, Certs, Dentyne, Rolaids, Trident, Chiclets, American Optical, Schick and Parke-Davis.

RECENT DEVELOPMENTS:

Sales in the first nine months of 1975 increased 15% to $1.6 billion and produced a 16% rise in net income to $133.2 million. Comparisons now include the effects of foreign currency exchange fluctuations for both periods. For comparison, third quarter earnings were 59c vs. 57c (restated) in the 1974 period; nine month earnings were $1.69 vs. $1.46 (restated). Excluding the effect of foreign exchange on both periods, earnings from operations were up 12% for the first nine months of 1975.

PROSPECTS:

Over the long-term, sales and earnings should continue to benefit from the Company's ability to expand operations through new product development and aggressive merchandising and to integrate and raise the profitability of acquisitions. A major impetus will come from international operations which will continue to generate above average growth. As for the near-term, prospects are enhanced by the large list of new products recently introduced or scheduled to be introduced shortly. Another good earnings gain is indicated for 1976.

STATISTICS:

YEAR	GROSS REVS. ($ MILL.)	OPER. PROFIT MARGIN %	NET INCOME ($ 000)	WORK CAP. ($ MILL.)	SENIOR CAPITAL ($ MILL.)	NO. SHS. OUT. (000)	EARN. PER SH. $	DIV. PER SH. $	DIV. PAY. %	PRICE RANGE	PRICE X EARN.	AVG. YIELD %
g66	601.3	15.7	53,318	169.4	63.5	57,156	0.91	—	—		—	—
g67	656.8	13.8	51,552	156.9	57.1	57,874	0.87	0.50	57	27^{5}_{6} - 18^{5}_{5}	26.7	2.2
68	717.8	15.5	60,455	213.0	49.4	59,886	1.01	0.52	51	30_{3} - 19_{2}	24.9	2.0
a69	807.5	16.5	71,855	248.8	43.2	60,390	1.19	0.55	46	37^{3} - 26^{2}	26.7	1.7
a69	1,150.4	14.5	94,100	373.6	57.2	75,718	1.25	—	—		—	—
70	1,256.6	13.8	98,335	405.2	50.8	76,682	1.28	0.59	46	38^{2} - 26_{5}	25.1	1.8
71	1,346.1	13.3	108,095	447.9	45.5	77,054	1.41	0.63	44	41_{4} - 33_{5}	26.5	1.7
72	1,487.5	12.5	122,657	538.2	83.3	77,750	1.58	0.68	43	50^{4} - 38_{5}	28.2	1.5
73	1,670.4	13.6	138,638	630.0	109.5	78,003	1.78	0.74	42	58_{7} - 33_{1}	25.7	1.6
74	1,911.0	13.2	155,323	664.8	113.6	78,958	1.98	0.81	41	39^{7} - 18^{1}	14.6	2.8

Note: Adjusted for 2-for-1 split 6/73. a-Pro forma to reflect Parke-Davis and Eversharp mergers. b-Incl. $1.8 mill. debentures convertible into common at $23 a share $40.0 mill. at $48 a share and $8.9 mill. at $29 a share, and $30.0 mill. at $61.50 a share. g-Incl. Amer. Optical; 1966 pro-forma.

INCORPORATED: Nov. 8, 1920—Delaware

PRINCIPAL OFFICE: 201 Tabor Road, Morris Plains, N.J. 07950

ANNUAL MEETING: Last Tuesday in April

NUMBER OF STOCKHOLDERS: 87,712

TRANSFER AGENT: Irving Trust Co., N.Y.
Northern Trust Co., Chicago, Ill.
Crocker National Bank, Los Angeles, Cal.

REGISTRAR: Chemical Bank, N.Y., N.Y.
First National Bank, Chicago, Ill.
Bank of America, Los Angeles, Calif.

INSTIT. HOLDINGS: NO.: 264
SHS: 11,322,324

OFFICERS

CHAIRMAN: E.B. Giblin

PRESIDENT: R.T. Wieringa

SECRETARY: J.B. Cain

TREASURER: G. Hromadko

XEROX CORPORATION

LISTED	SYMBOL	INDICATED DIV.	RECENT PRICE	PRICE RANGE (1975)	YIELD
NYSE	XRX	$1.00	55	88 - 51	1.8%

INTRINSIC INVESTMENT QUALITY: INVESTMENT GRADE. THIS DOMINANT COPIER MAKER IS FINDING IT INCREASINGLY DIFFICULT TO GENERATE STRONG GROWTH.

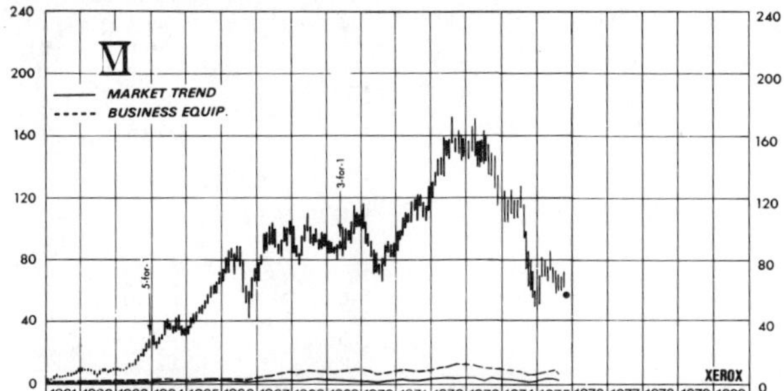

	1961	1962	1963	1964	1965	1966	1967	1968	1969	1970	1971	1972	1973	1974	1975	1976	1977	1978	1979	1980
EARN.	0.09	0.24	0.38	0.63	0.93	1.24	1.48	1.73	2.07	2.39	2.71	3.16	3.80	4.18						
DIV.	0.02	0.04	0.07	0.13	0.18	0.28	0.37	0.48	0.57	0.60	0.80	0.83	0.86	1.00						

CAPITALIZATION: (12/31/74)

	(000)	(%)
Debt	b$1,031,252	33.7
Minority int.	230,787	7.6
Defer.inc.tax	40,277	1.3
Com. & Surp.	1,754,026	57.4
Total	$3,056,342	100.0%

Shs. ($1)-(Com. & C1.B)-79,241,907

INTERIM EARNINGS:

Qu.	3/31	6/30	9/30	12/31
72	0.73	0.80	0.80	0.83
73	0.88	0.97	0.97	0.98
74	1.00	1.11	1.04	1.03
75g	1.04	0.05	1.01	

DIVIDENDS:	RECORD	PAYABLE
0.25Q	12/6/74	1/2/75
0.25Q	3/7/75	4/1
0.25Q	6/6	7/1
0.25Q	9/5	10/1
0.25Q	12/5	1/2/76

BACKGROUND:

Xerox Corp. produces a wide variety of equipment for the reproduction, reduction and transmission of printed information. Although office copiers and duplicators are the primary source of revenue, the Company is also engaged in the publication of education material and the manufacture and marketing of computers. In 1974, the Company derived 79% of revenues from rentals and 21% from outright sales. Overall revenues from international operations accounted for 42% of total operating revenues and 52% of net income. Such operations include 51%-owned Rank Xerox Ltd. and Fuji Xerox Co. Ltd. of Japan, equally owned by Fuji Photo and Rank Xerox.

RECENT DEVELOPMENTS:

Revenues from continuing operations increased 18%, in the first nine months of 1975, to almost $3 billion. Net income, however, before losses on discontinued operations, rose less than 1%. Comparisons exclude the mainframe computer business for which Xerox took a write-off of $84.4 million in the second quarter of 1975. In order to stimulate greater usage per installed copying machine, Xerox has restructured its price schedules. Customers will have a wide choice of pricing arrangements, based on volume.

PROSPECTS:

The Company's decision to withdraw from the computer business further complicates an already cloudy outlook for copiers. The absence of computer losses will, of course, be beneficial to near term earnings performance. However, the big question is where the Company will seek out new growth opportunities not only to replace computers, but also to help offset competitive pressures in copiers. Earnings comparisons of operations restated to exclude computer losses may be disappointing in the short run.

STATISTICS:

YEAR	GROSS REVS. ($ MILL.)	OPER. PROFIT MARGIN %	NET INCOME ($ 000)	WORK CAP. ($ MILL.)	SENIOR CAPITAL ($ MILL.)	NO. SHS. OUT. (000)	EARN. PER SH. $	DIV. PER SH. $	DIV. PAY. %	PRICE RANGE	PRICE X EARN.	AVG. YIELD %
66	528.3	26.3	79,821	122.2	261.8	64,122	1.24	0.28	23	89^{2} - 41^{6}	52.7	0.4
67	701.4	24.4	97,281	132.5	224.2	65,907	1.48	0.37	25	104^{6} - 65^{6}	57.7	0.4
68	896.4	24.7	116,194	138.5	140.1	67,306	1.73	0.48	28	109^{4} - 76^{3}	53.8	0.5
a68	1,224.4	26.5	128,950	181.6	194.8	76,772	1.68	—	—	-	—	—
a69	1,482.9	27.5	161,368	257.8	265.8	77,901	2.07	0.57	28	115 - 80^{3}	47.2	0.6
70	1,718.6	26.4	187,691	367.8	361.7	78,429	2.39	0.60	25	115^{6} - 65^{2}	37.9	0.7
71	1,961.4	25.1	212,610	383.9	424.8	78,612	2.71	0.80	30	126^{6} - 84^{6}	39.2	0.8
72	2,419.1	24.4	249,507	407.5	446.8	79,014	3.16	0.83	26	171^{7} - 120^{4}	46.3	0.6
73	2,990.0	23.7	300,484	437.0	569.2	79,174	3.80	0.86	23	170 - 114^{6}	37.5	0.6
74	3,576.4	23.4	331,083	592.9	1,031.3	79,242	4.18	1.00	24	127^{1} - 49	21.1	1.1

Note: Adjusted for stock split: 3-for-1, 5/69. a-Incl. Scientific Data Systems and reflects consolidation of Rank Xerox Ltd., 1968 pro-forma. b-Incl. $155.5 mill. debentures convertible into common at $92 a share and $75.0 mill. debentures convertible into common at $148.00 a share. g-After $97.3 loss ($1.23 a share) from discontinued operations.

INCORPORATED: April 18, 1906—New York

PRINCIPAL OFFICE: Stamford, Conn. 06904

ANNUAL MEETING: In May

NUMBER OF STOCKHOLDERS: 137,351

TRANSFER AGENT: Lincoln First Bank of Rochester, N.Y.
First National City Bank, N.Y.
Northern Trust Co., Chicago, Ill.
Wells Fargo Bank, San. Fran., Cal.

REGISTRAR: Security Trust Co., Rochester, N.Y.
Morgan Guaranty Trust Company, N.Y.
First National Bank of Chicago
Bank of America, San Fran., Cal.

INSTIT. HOLDINGS: NO.: 614
SHS.: 10,182,653

OFFICERS

CHAIRMAN:
C.P. McColough

PRESIDENT:
A.R. McCardell

SECRETARY:
E.K. Damon

TREASURER:
E.K. Damon

ZENITH RADIO CORPORATION

LISTED	SYMBOL	INDICATED DIV.	RECENT PRICE	PRICE RANGE (1975)	YIELD
NYSE	ZE	$1.00	26	29 - 10	3.8%

INTRINSIC INVESTMENT QUALITY: MEDIUM GRADE. EARNINGS TREND HAS BECOME CYCLICAL AS TELEVISION MARKET APPROACHES SATURATION.

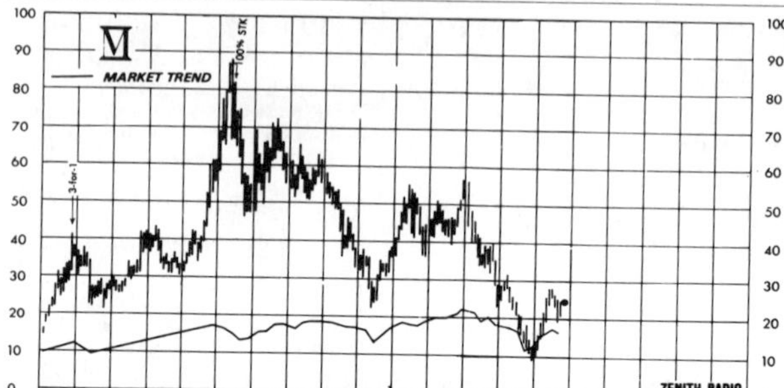

	1961	1962	1963	1964	1965	1966	1967	1968	1969	1970	1971	1972	1973	1974	1975	1976	1977	1978	1979	1980
EARN.	1.00	1.08	1.14	1.31	1.80	2.31	2.18	2.50	2.08	1.30	1.65	2.55	2.90	0.70						
DIV.	0.59	0.60	0.68	0.70	1.00	1.35	1.35	1.40	1.40	1.40	1.40	1.40	1.49	1.39						

CAPITALIZATION: (12/31/74)

	(000)	(%)
Debt	$ 9,825	3.5
Defer.Inc.Tax	7,852	2.8
Com. & Surp.	261,412	93.7
Total	$279,089	100.0%

Shs. ($1)-18,796,870

INTERIM EARNINGS:

Qu.	3/31	6/30	9/30	12/31
72	0.53	0.20	0.70	1.12
73	0.84	0.35	0.79	0.92
74b	0.48	0.06	d0.30	0.46
75	0.18	0.12	0.46	

DIVIDENDS:	RECORD	PAYABLE
0.25Q	12/6/74	12/28/74
0.25Q	3/10/75	3/31/75
0.25Q	6/9	6/30
0.25Q	9/9	9/30
0.25Q	12/5	12/29

BACKGROUND:

Zenith is engaged in the design, development, manufacture and sale of home entertainment products, hearing aid instruments and timepieces. Television sets represent about 80% of sales; sales of all home entertainment products represent 90% of the total. Home entertainment products include black-and-white and color TV sets, radio receivers and stereo and phonograph sets. These products are sold primarily through independently-owned distributors. Zenith ranks first in the production of color and black-and-white television sets. Sales are worldwide. Hearing aids are sold primarily to retail dealers in the U.S. Timepieces are sold in major international markets under the brand names Movado and Zenith.

RECENT DEVELOPMENTS:

Net income was $8.6 million in the third quarter of 1975 vs. a year-earlier loss of $5.6 million. The 1974 third-quarter loss was due largely to a 10-week strike at one of the Company's large color TV plants. Sales for the third quarter registered a 30% increase to $248.1 million. Net income for the nine months, including the effect of a number of accounting changes, was $14.3 million, up sharply from $4.5 million in the comparable year-earlier period.

PROSPECTS:

After a strong period of industry growth in color TV sales, a substantial slowdown has occurred. A partially offsetting factor is the growing replacement market for color TV's. Zenith should continue to hold its top position in the color TV industry. The Company can be expected to act aggressively to retain its market share and protect its manufacturing operations in the U.S., even when such actions require the acceptance of lower profit margins. A recovery from depressed earnings levels is expected in 1976.

STATISTICS:

YEAR	GROSS REVS. ($ MILL.)	OPER. PROFIT MARGIN %	NET INCOME ($ 000)	WORK CAP. ($ MILL.)	SENIOR CAPITAL ($ MILL.)	NO. SHS. OUT. (000)	EARN. PER SH. $	DIV. PER SH. $	DIV. PAY. %	PRICE RANGE	PRICE X EARN.	AVG. YIELD %
65	470.5	13.7	33,553	110.5	Nil	18,709	1.80	1.00	56	61^{1}_{6} - 31^{3}_{1}	25.8	2.2
66	625.0	13.3	43,475	114.5	Nil	18,783	2.31	1.35	58	88_{2} - 46_{6}	29.2	2.0
67	653.9	12.0	41,022	120.7	Nil	18,849	2.18	1.35	62	72_{4} - 47_{5}	27.5	2.3
68	705.4	14.1	47,315	147.0	Nil	18,924	2.50	1.40	56	65 - 50_{7}	23.2	2.4
69	676.6	12.6	39,621	153.4	Nil	19,020	2.08	1.40	67	58_{4} - 32_{2}	21.8	3.1
70	573.1	7.4	24,702	152.9	Nil	19,020	1.30	1.40	—	38_{7} - 22	23.4	4.6
71	613.1	9.7	a31,311	153.5	7.8	19,028	a1.65	1.40	85	54_{5} - 36_{6}	27.5	3.1
72	795.9	11.5	48,579	180.5	6.6	19,043	2.55	1.40	55	56 - 39	18.9	2.9
73	1,007.2	11.2	52,950	175.0	7.7	18,797	2.90	1.49	51	56_{5} - 23_{3}	13.6	3.8
74	910.5	2.7	b13,195	147.1	9.8	18,797	b0.70	1.39	—	31 - 9	29.3	6.8

Note: Adjusted for 2-for-1 stock split, 6/66. a-Before special credit $6.1 mill. (32c a share). b-Reflects change to LIFO accounting.

INCORPORATED: March 31, 1958—Delaware

PRINCIPAL OFFICE: 1900 N. Austin Ave. Chicago, Ill. 60639

ANNUAL MEETING: Fourth Tuesday in April

NUMBER OF STOCKHOLDERS: 47,400

TRANSFER AGENT: First National Bank, Chicago, Ill. Chemical Bank, N.Y.

REGISTRAR: Continental Illinois National Bank & Trust Co., Chicago, Ill. Chase Manhattan Bank, N.Y.

INSTIT. HOLDINGS: NO.: 96 SHS.: 3,113,610

OFFICERS

CHAIRMAN: J.S. Wright

PRESIDENT: J.J. Nevin

SECRETARY: E.M. Schroeder

TREASURER: P.A. Dwyer

Index